Disability Studies

SAGE has been part of the global academic community since 1965, supporting high quality research and learning that transforms society and our understanding of individuals, groups, and cultures. SAGE is the independent, innovative, natural home for authors, editors and societies who share our commitment and passion for the social sciences.

Find out more at: **www.sagepublications.com**

Disability
Studies
a student's guide

edited by

Colin Cameron

Los Angeles | London | New Delhi
Singapore | Washington DC

Los Angeles | London | New Delhi
Singapore | Washington DC

SAGE Publications Ltd
1 Oliver's Yard
55 City Road
London EC1Y 1SP

SAGE Publications Inc.
2455 Teller Road
Thousand Oaks, California 91320

SAGE Publications India Pvt Ltd
B 1/I 1 Mohan Cooperative Industrial Area
Mathura Road
New Delhi 110 044

SAGE Publications Asia-Pacific Pte Ltd
3 Church Street
#10-04 Samsung Hub
Singapore 049483

Editor: Kate Wharton
Assistant editor: Emma Milman
Production editor: Katie Forsythe
Copyeditor: Rose James
Proofreader: Thea Watson
Indexer: Silvia Benvenuto
Marketing manager: Tamara Navaratnam
Cover design: Lisa Harper
Typeset by: C&M Digitals (P) Ltd, Chennai, India
Printed in Great Britain by Henry Ling Limited at
The Dorset Press, Dorchester, DT1 1HD

Editorial arrangement, Introduction, Chapters 2, 4, 6, 7, 8, 11,
13, 14, 20, 21, 22, 23, 24, 25, 30, 31, 34, 35, 37, 44, 45, 46, 47,
49 © Colin Cameron 2014
Chapter 1 © Tony Heaton 2014
Chapter 3 © Sarah Keyes 2014
Chapter 5 © Laurence Clark 2014
Chapter 9 © WaiYeen Peng 2014
Chapter 10 © Colin Hambrook 2014
Chapter 12 © Colin Cameron and Michele Moore 2014
Chapter 15 © Nicola Martin 2014
Chapter 16 © Dawn Benson 2014
Chapter 17 © Emmeline Burdett 2014
Chapter 18 © Alison Wilde and Adele Hoskison-Clark 2014
Chapter 19 © Ana Bê 2014
Chapter 26 © Florence Garabedian 2014
Chapter 27 © Michele Moore 2014
Chapter 28 © Sarah Woodin 2014
Chapter 29 © Rebecca Mallett and Jenny Slater 2014
Chapter 32 © Tanya Titchkosky and Rod Michalko 2014
Chapter 33 © Larry Arnold 2014
Chapter 36 © Alan Roulstone 2014
Chapter 38 © Toby Brandon 2014
Chapter 39 © Donna Reeve 2014
Chapter 40 © Katherine Runswick-Cole and Dan Goodley 2014
Chapter 41 © Joanne Brown 2014
Chapter 42 © Peter Beresford 2014
Chapter 43 © Margrit Shildrick 2014
Chapter 48 © Rosaleen McDonagh 2014
Chapter 50 © Bill Scott 2014

First published 2014

Library of Congress Control Number: 2013940426

British Library Cataloguing in Publication data

A catalogue record for this book is available from
the British Library

ISBN 978-1-4462-6766-0
ISBN 978-1-4462-6767-7 (pbk)

To Maggie

Oh I love to be a cripple

Not a Raspberry or Ripple

But a downright dirty cripple

(Garry Robson, 'Raspberry', 2010)

Contents

About the Editor and Contributors

Larry Arnold is an autistic activist and academic who has been involved in the disability movement since the early 1980s. He seeks to redefine normalcy as only one of the many ways of being human. He is what he is, not what he could never be, and never what he isn't.

Ana Bê is currently a doctoral candidate at Lancaster University. Her research is located primarily in Disability Studies and feminist theory. More about her can be found at www.AnaBeOnline.com.

Dawn Benson is a senior lecturer in Disability Studies and inclusive education at Northumbria University, Newcastle upon Tyne. She is a parent of disabled teenagers.

Peter Beresford OBE is professor of social policy and director of the Centre for Citizen Participation at Brunel University. He is a long-term user of mental health services and Chair of Shaping Our Lives, the national independent user-controlled organisation and network.

Toby Brandon is a reader in disability and mental health at Northumbria University, Newcastle upon Tyne. He has published around disablist hate crime, advocacy and disability theory, and is a review editor for the international journal *Disability & Society*. He is also Chair of the charity Disability North.

In 2012 **Joanne Brown** graduated with first class honours in BA Joint Honours Disability Studies at Northumbria University, Newcastle upon Tyne, in 2012. She completed her MRes in Social Sciences at Northumbria in 2013, and has recently been accepted to commence doctoral study at the University of Glasgow.

Emmeline Burdett gained her PhD from University College London in 2011. Her research interests include disability and bioethics, and representations of disability in history and literature. She is a book reviewer for H-Disability.

Colin Cameron is a senior lecturer in Disability Studies and social work at Northumbria University, Newcastle upon Tyne. He is a member of the boards of directors of Disability Arts Online, Lothian Centre for Inclusive Living and Shaping Our Lives, and of the editorial board of *Disability & Society*.

Laurence Clark divides his time between research and consultancy through his company Difference Matters and performing stand-up comedy. Research interests include personalisation, access to information and media representations of disabled people. He lives in Liverpool.

Florence Garabedian is chief executive of Lothian Centre for Inclusive Living. She is also Chair of Self-directed Support Scotland and works closely with Inclusion Scotland and Independent Living in Scotland.

Dan Goodley is professor of Disability Studies and education at the University of Sheffield, a proud dad to two girls and a fan of Nottingham Forest. Recent writing includes *Disability Studies: An Interdisciplinary Introduction* (2011).

Colin Hambrook is a disabled artist and founder/editor of disabilityartsonline.org.uk – a unique journal dedicated to showcasing the artistic practice of disabled artists, writers and performers through blogs, reviews and discussion. He lives in Hove, East Sussex.

Tony Heaton OBE is the chief executive officer of the disability arts organisation Shape and is a practising sculptor with a long involvement in the creative, social and political aspects of disability. He lives and works in London.

Adele Hoskison-Clark is a disabled parent, the mother of two boys, Tom and Jamie. She is currently undertaking an MA in Social Work at Lancaster University. Her dissertation focused on self-directed support and disabled parents. She lives in Liverpool.

Sarah Keyes is currently a researcher in ageing and dementia in the School of Health and Social Science at the University of Edinburgh. Her work focuses on meaningful involvement of people with dementia within research processes that impact on the development of inclusive policy and practice.

Dr Rebecca Mallett (Senior Lecturer in Education and Disability Studies, Sheffield Hallam University: r.mallett@shu.ac.uk). Rebecca's main research areas include 'disability' in popular culture, methods of interpretation within Cultural Disability Studies and, more recently, the commodification of impairment categories, such as 'autism'.

Nicola Martin is Principal Lecturer at London South Bank University. She is an Honorary Visiting Fellow at Cambridge University and editor of *The Journal of Inclusive Practice in Further and Higher Education*. Her research interests include critical Disability Studies, identity, autism and post-school inclusion.

Rosaleen McDonagh is a feminist disabled Traveller living in Dublin. Active in disability and Traveller politics for many years, she has written for theatre and TV, and has had several of her plays performed in Ireland.

Rod Michalko taught Disability Studies at the University of Toronto and is now retired. He has written three books and numerous articles. Rod is currently writing fiction with the theme of blindness.

Michele Moore is professor of inclusive education at Northumbria University, Newcastle upon Tyne, and editor of the leading international journal *Disability & Society*. Her current research is concerned with understanding international perspectives on disability to advance the global agenda for inclusion.

WaiYeen Peng graduated with first class honours in BA Joint Honours Disability Studies at Northumbria University, Newcastle upon Tyne, in 2012. She is currently engaged in postgraduate study at Northumbria to gain Early Years Professional Status.

Donna Reeve is an honorary teaching fellow at Lancaster University with research interests in psycho-emotional disablism, identity, the body, social theory and disability.

Alan Roulstone is professor of disability and inclusion at Northumbria University, Newcastle upon Tyne. He has researched, taught and written on disability issues for over twenty years, and aims to produce research with disabled people which furthers the struggle towards a more enabling society.

Katherine Runswick-Cole is Senior Research Fellow in Disability Studies and Psychology at Manchester Metropolitan University, Manchester. Much of her research focuses on the lives of disabled children, young people and their families. She has published extensively in the area and is co-editor of *Disabled Children's Childhood Studies: Critical Perspectives in a Global Context* (2013, Palgrave).

Margrit Shildrick is professor of gender and knowledge production at Linköping University, Sweden, and adjunct professor of critical Disability Studies at York University, Toronto. Her publications include *Dangerous Discourses of Disability, Sexuality and Subjectivity* (2009), as well as several other books and edited collections and many journal articles.

Bill Scott is the manager of Inclusion Scotland, a national network of disabled people's organisations funded by the Scottish Government. He lives in Edinburgh.

Jenny Slater is a lecturer in education and Disability Studies at Sheffield Hallam University. Her research interests include the intersections of disability, youth, gender and sexuality.

Tanya Titchkosky teaches Disability Studies in the Department of Humanities, Social Science and Social Justice Education at the University of Toronto, Canada. Her writing includes *The Question of Access: Disability, Space, Meaning* (2011); *Reading and Writing Disability Differently* (2007); and *Disability, Self and Society* (2003).

Alison Wilde is currently lecturer in special educational needs (SEN) and inclusion in the School of Education, Bangor University, Wales. Her teaching and research is primarily in the areas of SEN and inclusion, Disability Studies and cultural/media representation.

Sarah Woodin is a research fellow in sociology and social policy at the University of Leeds. Her research interests focus on disability and independent living in its broadest sense.

Acknowledgements

There are a number of people I would like to thank for their involvement in the emergence of this book. Nigel Stinton, for the conversation on the train from Alnmouth during which I first thought of it. Sarah Gibson, Emma Milman and Katie Forsythe at Sage, for their support during the production process. The Joint Hons. Disability Studies students at Northumbria, for the opportunity to develop and rehearse my ideas. Professor Kath McCourt and Gerry Rice, for the sabbatical leave without which I couldn't have managed to get so much of it organised and written. Everyone else in the contributors list, for agreeing to write the other chapters and then doing so. Gordon Cameron, Maggie Cameron, Andie Reynolds, Esther Woodbury, Martin Sarosi and Dr Donald Cameron, for reading various chapters at various stages and giving generally very helpful advice. Paula Curtis, for coming up with just the right quote at just the right time. Dr Emmeline Burdett and Professor Michele Moore, for their assistance with editing. Finally, David Feingold, for the permission to use his artwork on the front cover. To all of you, again, many, many thanks.

Introduction

An editorial in *The Guardian* newspaper in January 2013, reflecting on the achievements of the 2012 London Paralympic Games, contained the following statement: 'A nation learned to see through disability – to the person inside' (*The Guardian* 2013). An article in *The Observer* newspaper a couple of months later stated that 'We extend greater understanding to people with disabilities, especially those who overcome their disadvantages in competition' (Porter 2013). Reading both of these made me groan and wonder how supposedly high-quality, well-informed broadsheets can still – after more than four decades of campaigning by disabled people – get it so fundamentally wrong. To start with, apart from making a dodgy Cartesian body/person distinction, the first statement suggests that a view which overlooks impairment is in some way progressive. This is quite contrary to the thinking developed by the disabled people's movement, which argues that our impairments are a core part of who we are and are important in having shaped the experiences that have made us who we are. To suggest that it is a kindness to overlook a disabled person's impairment is as absurd and insulting as to suggest it is a kindness to overlook a woman's gender or a black person's skin colour – both ways of thinking which have long been consigned to the dustbin of ludicrous historical ideas. The second statement suggests that greater understanding is a favour to be bestowed by the non-disabled on disabled people, on condition that disabled people acquiesce with a view that identifies disadvantage as caused by impaired physicality and take responsibility for overcoming disadvantage through individual effort. This is not understanding, it is tolerance. It suggests that disabled people will be tolerated so long as they acknowledge their own deficit and their need to change. It is paternalistic and carries what Read (2000: 33) has described as 'a strong whiff of charity'. The disabled people's movement argues that disabled people's disadvantage is structural and is caused by physical and social barriers – such as the attitudes revealed in these two statements. We really don't seem to have come far since Miller and Gwynne (1972: 44) wrote over forty years ago:

> In many respects the cripple has 'never had it so good'. Public attitudes are less prejudiced, more enlightened. Children are taught not to laugh at cripples but instead to sympathise with them as unfortunate fellow-beings.

The self-congratulatory tone persists. While it is still being announced that society's views towards disabled people are becoming less prejudiced and more enlightened there remains an attachment to a way of thinking unable to regard impairment other than as misfortune. Whether impairment is to be sympathised with, 'looked through' or transcended, it is consistently looked upon as a regrettable attribute with the potential to reduce its bearer in the eyes of others. This is a hegemonic view, an ideological position regarded as obvious and uncontroversial, and is considered part of common sense.

While attitudes towards disabled people seem always to be represented as 'improving' it is possible, however, to look at things differently. As Barton (2001: 169) observes:

> disability also must be defined as a more complex social construct, one which reflects not a benign evolution of acceptance but a dynamic set of representations that are deeply embedded in historical and cultural contexts.

Disability is not a fixed characteristic belonging to individuals, but an oppressive social relationship 'imposed on top of our impairments' (Union of the Physically Impaired Against Segregation 1976: 14). Ideology involves the power of ideas to maintain existing structures and social relations (Thompson 2001: 27), and disability is an ideological construct that has been used to strengthen perceptions of the value of conformity. For as long as impairment is understood as a sign of suffering or tragedy, as something 'wrong' with people rather than as part of human diversity, it doesn't really matter how much else changes. Disabled people will never be 'really' equal, for power relations will continue to mark them as deficient and this will have real, material consequences.

This is where Disability Studies comes in. Grounded in the thinking of the disabled people's movement, Disability Studies offers a critical perspective with which to think differently about the way disability is constructed, created, and related to in everyday life. Still a young academic discipline, Disability Studies is part of a movement for change which looks for new answers to old questions, in insights developed by disabled people themselves. It is not about the study of physical conditions, but about the study of the social relations which exclude people with impairments from full participation as equals in ordinary community life. It is not about bodies as objects for study, but about the way society structures the way bodies are experienced. It is not just about the study of disabled people in society, but about the way difference is used to define the boundaries of what is considered normal.

Disability Studies: A Student's Guide is intended as an introduction to many of the themes and issues explored within the discipline. It is a reference book not just for Disability Studies students, but for students on a range of courses – social work, nursing and other health professions, education, community studies, for example – in which disability is considered as an issue but where perhaps there is not the time to peruse lengthy tomes on the subject. I hope, though, that it will also be regarded as a starting point from which to begin to explore Disability Studies in greater depth. One of the book's distinguishing characteristics is the brevity of its chapters, but it needs to be emphasised that these are tasters. There are questions to encourage discussion and recommendations for further reading at the end of each chapter. Many of these recommendations are for journal articles which, if you are a student, you will be able to access through your university e-library. Chapters have been organised alphabetically, though they do not need to be read in this way. If this is an area completely new to you, you might want to start by reading the chapters on models of disability, particularly the medical and social models, as the distinction between these provides the foundation for most of what is written in the rest of the book.

This book has been written by a lot of people, most of whom are disabled and some of whom aren't, but who all have a background either in Disability Studies or in the disabled people's movement. When inviting people to contribute to the book I felt that to involve academics, activists and students would give it strength. As well as chapters written by people involved in developing Disability Studies theory, teaching and research, there are others by people daily involved at the cutting edge of disability politics and culture, and two by recent Disability Studies graduates at Northumbria University. This means, among other things, that many of the chapters have been written in different styles. It also means that some points are made more than once, by different people coming from different angles. I don't see this as a problem though.

Isaiah Berlin (2008: 22) distinguished between writers he characterised as 'hedgehogs' and 'foxes'. While foxes are 'those who pursue many ends, often unrelated and even contradictory', hedgehogs are those 'who relate everything to a single central vision, one system more or less coherent or articulate, in terms of which they understand, think and feel'. I think that I would describe most of the contributors to this book, myself included, with only one or two exceptions, as hedgehogs (I hope they don't mind being called that). Our thinking is underpinned by the social model which identifies disability as a social structural issue rather than as a problem to do with some people's bodies. In other words, people with impairments do not 'have' disabilities, but are disabled by the physical and social barriers they encounter in everyday life. Given this shared understanding, it was almost inevitable that there should be some repetition of ideas, but in terms of the scope of the book I think that what is revealed by this is consistency.

Dr Colin Cameron,
Whitley Bay, 2013

References

Barton, E.L. (2001) 'Textual practices of erasure: representations of disability and the founding of the United Way', in J.C. Wilson and C. Lewiecki-Wilson (eds), *Embodied Rhetorics: Disability in Language and Culture*. Carbondale, IL: Southern Illinois University Press, pp. 169–99.

Berlin, I. (2008) 'The hedgehog and the fox', in *Russian Thinkers*. London: Penguin, pp. 22–81.

Guardian, The (2013) 'Across the disabling divide', *The Guardian*, 12 January 2013.

Miller, E.J. and Gwynne, G.V. (1972) *A Life Apart: A Pilot Study of Residential Institutions for the Physically Handicapped and the Young Chronic Sick*. London: Tavistock.

Porter, H. (2013) 'Britain is signing away the right to call itself a liberal democracy', *The Observer*, 31 March 2013.

Read, J. (2000) *Disability, the Family and Society: Listening to Mothers*. Buckingham: Open University Press.

Thompson, N. (2001) *Anti-Discriminatory Practice*. Basingstoke: Macmillan.

Union of the Physically Impaired Against Segregation (1976) *Fundamental Principles of Disability*. London: UPIAS.

1 Access

Tony Heaton

Access, or lack of it, is still the fundamental issue preventing disabled people from fully taking part in society in the UK, yet we are still – over forty years after legislation began to be introduced to begin to address this – creating buildings and transport systems that perpetuate discrimination. We have moved slowly since the late Alf Morris managed to get the Chronically Sick and Disabled Persons Act 1970 passed by Parliament. This was the first legislation in the world to make it unlawful to discriminate on the grounds of disability; it was a landmark victory and a paradigm shift for many (Campbell and Oliver 1996).

'Can disabled people go where you go?' was the slogan of the Silver Jubilee Committee on access for disabled people back in 1977. It could just as easily have been the slogan for the recent Diamond Jubilee in 2012, because there are still many subtle 'no go' areas. Back then, local authorities started to look at the services they provided, realising that in many cases their approach to disabled people would need to move from 'care and control' to 'choices and rights'. This was becoming evident from the burgeoning disability rights movement, ignited by the social model of disability (Oliver and Barnes 2012).

More enlightened local authorities introduced codes of good practice building on the requirements of the Act. Access Groups were set up, driven by disabled people who challenged local authorities about lack of access provision and who, as a result, began working with planning departments to fight for local solutions. This direct action resulted in positive changes as politicised disabled people 'policed' local developments.

Living as a disabled person throughout this time and being active in the war of attrition that has taken place between disabled people, governments, local authorities and institutions has given me certain insights. We have had allies in both government and some authorities, but our battles have been hard won against the many who simply do not care enough about access to simply think about how they, as people with power, might facilitate change.

Architecture and design are two great unseen social drivers that have a profound effect on access for disabled people, but there is very little time spent in considering this within the teaching institutions – it is simply not on the curriculum (Hemingway 2011; Morris 1993). The building regulations demand minimum requirements to be in place, but many think these requirements are best practice when actually they are a bare minimum. Part M of the Building Regulations 1985, updated in 2004, now states that the requirements of the new part M no longer refer to 'Disabled People' – the aim of the new part M being to foster a more inclusive approach to design to accommodate the needs of *all* people. Similarly, the explanation of the relationship between part M and the Disability

Discrimination Act 1995 has been amended in 'use of guidance' to reflect regulations made or revoked. Interestingly, the guidance states that:

> There may be alternative ways of achieving compliance within the requirements. Thus there is no obligation to adopt any particular solution contained in an approved document if you prefer to meet the relevant requirement in some other way.

(Planningportal.govuk 2008)

This unlocked architects and designers from the rigid and often lazy way access solutions were imposed, frequently reflecting a medicalised approach – for example, the ludicrous situation of sumptuously designed toilet facilities in keeping with the general design ethic of a building but with the accessible toilet looking like something out of a hospital. Nevertheless it seems that few architects or designers exercise this freedom to seek more aesthetic solutions. It could be argued this is because they never even think to consult disabled people as potential users of the public spaces they are creating. This is another example of the professional assuming they have all the answers or relying on theoretical solutions rather than lived experience.

In the 1980s, when local authorities were developing their codes of good practice, the Disabled Persons (Services, Consultation and Representation) Act 1986 required them to start seeking input from disabled people (Barnes 1996). I recall developing a county-wide mobility handbook under the leadership of the county surveyor and being told that I was considered to be an idealist and dreamer to imagine that wheelchair users in the future would be able to travel by bus. This was considered unthinkable and unachievable, yet twenty-five years later, that is exactly what I am doing – all it took was a change in design, a simple requirement. It is both shocking and amazing that it took so long. Ironically, however, as I sit in my space on the bus, as decreed by law, should another wheelchair user at the next stop want to get on they will be denied because there is usually only space for one wheelchair user, even if the rest of the bus is empty. So both a partial victory and a validation on dreaming.

My earliest journeys on the train were taken in the goods van, locked in without access to any facilities and paying for the privilege. This has slowly changed, but again space is limited and it is unlikely that two wheelchair users could travel together. Having to request that passengers remove their luggage from the wheelchair space and waiting in hope that a staff member with a portable ramp will appear to get a wheelchair user off a train once all the ambulant travellers have alighted is partial, rather than full access.

Theatres and cinemas provide limited access. Wheelchair users are segregated into specific areas while British Sign Language (BSL), subtitled and 'relaxed' performances are few and far between. Booking concert and travel tickets may have been revolutionised via online booking systems, but if you want the accessible seats or spaces then you are forced to go through to an access phone line which will almost inevitably have limited opening hours and have the cost of the call attached: again, partial access. Or, you are provided with a wheelchair space but your non-disabled companion cannot sit with you due to spurious health and safety rules consigning all the 'wheelchairs' to sit in a ghetto with companions in a seated area elsewhere.

Recently when talking to architectural students I asked where they would go to seek access advice. They suggested doctors, physiotherapists, social workers. No one proposed consulting with disabled people, even though one was leading the discussion and seminar!

In conclusion it could be argued that we are achieving partial access, but is this potentially more disempowering? As it hints at the possibility of inclusion but the frustrating reality for many still remains tantalisingly out of reach and an unsatisfactory concession, it seems that, as a nation, we are prepared to accept a tokenistic solution. It may be thought that due to legislation the job is done, but it isn't, and we are in a dangerous position in thinking everything is in place to ensure disabled people have an equal opportunity to take part in society. This simply is not the case. These partial victories need consolidating before they become lost.

For Discussion

- Can disabled people go where you go?
- What examples of partial access can you think of?
- What constitutes an inclusive environment and what are the imperatives for creating and developing inclusive design solutions?

Further Reading

Brown, D., Gertig, P. and Gilman, M. with Anderson, J., Clarke, C. and Powell, S. (2014) 'Accessing social and leisure activities – barriers to inclusion experienced by visually impaired people', in J. Swain, S. French, C. Barnes and C. Thomas (eds), *Disabling Barriers – Enabling Environments*, 3rd edn. London: Sage, pp. 214–21.

HMSO (2003) *Planning and Access for Disabled People: A Good Practice Guide*, www.gov.uk/government/uploads/system/uploads/attachment_data/file/7776/156681.pdf, accessed 19 November 2012.

Titchkosky, T. (2011) *The Question of Access: Disability, Space, Meaning*. Toronto: University of Toronto Press.

References

Barnes, C. (1996) *Social Models as a Basis for Commissioning: The Social Model, User Involvement and Services*, www.leeds.ac.uk/disability-studies/archiveuk/Barnes/social%20models.pdf, accessed 19 November 2012.

Campbell, J. and Oliver, M. (1996) *Disability Politics: Understanding Our Past, Changing Our Future*. London: Routledge.

Hemingway, L. (2011) *Disabled People and Housing: Choices, Opportunities and Barriers*. Bristol: Policy Press.

Morris, J. (1993) 'Housing, independent living and physically disabled people', in J. Swain, S. French, C. Barnes and C. Thomas (eds), *Disabling Barriers – Enabling Environments*. London: Sage, pp. 136–44.

Oliver, M. and Barnes, C. (2012) *The New Politics of Disablement*. Basingstoke: Palgrave Macmillan.

Planningportal.gov.uk (2008) *Frequently Asked Questions*, www.planningportal.gov.uk/building regulations/approveddocuments/partm/faqs, accessed 19 November 2012.

2   The Affirmation Model

Colin Cameron

The affirmation model was first named and suggested by Swain and French (2000) as an intervention in the ongoing debate around the social model (see Chapter 44). Disabled feminists (e.g. Crow 1996; Morris 1991; Thomas 1999) had argued that the social model over-emphasises social structural barriers and ignores personal and experiential aspects of disability, and the affirmation model was proposed to address these criticisms. Rooting their idea in the values of Disability Pride and perspectives emerging from the disability arts movement, Swain and French identified the affirmation model as a critique of the personal tragedy model corresponding to the social model as a critique of the medical model.

The affirmation model was, they stated:

> essentially a non-tragic view of disability and impairment which encompasses positive social identities, both individual and collective, for disabled people, grounded in the benefits of a lifestyle of being impaired and disabled.

> (Swain and French 2000: 569)

In proposing an affirmation model, Swain and French set out a position from which it could be asserted that, far from being necessarily tragic, living with impairment can be experienced as valuable, interesting and intrinsically satisfying. This is not to deny there can be negative experiences resulting from impairment, but to make the point that this is not all that impairment is about. While Swain and French made it very clear that the affirmation model builds upon the social model (rather than being proposed as an alternative) they suggested that the need for an affirmation model is established, in that it is not a purpose of the social model to reject a tragic view of impairment: 'even in an ideal world of full civil rights and participative citizenship for disabled people, an impairment could be seen to be a personal tragedy' (Swain and French 2000: 571).

In Cameron (2010) I aimed to give structure to the affirmation model. While Swain and French had described what the affirmation model is *about* and what it is *like* (Swain and French 2000: 580) they had stopped short of specifying what it *is* (Cameron 2008). One of my research aims was to enquire whether useful affirmation model definitions of impairment and disability might be fashioned so that it could be used as a practical tool rather than remaining just a good idea. My research involved gathering and interpreting qualitative data gained through a series of interviews and observations of everyday life experiences with sixteen disabled people from around Scotland and England.

Swain and French had identified a number of features by which the affirmation model is, and is not, characterised. The affirmation model is, they stated, about:

- being different and thinking differently about being different, both individually and collectively;
- the affirmation of unique ways of being situated in society;
- disabled people challenging presumptions about themselves and their lives in terms of not only how they differ from what is average or normal, but also about the assertion, on their own terms, of human embodiment, lifestyles, quality of life and identity;
- ways of being that embrace difference (Swain and French 2008: 185).

These descriptions are reflected in remarks by Lola, a wheelchair-user from London:

> I haven't been terribly well but ... I'd rather be me than not be the whole mix ... positive, negative, flawed, happy, sad mixture that I am ... that makes me *me* ... and, you know, you can play the sort of games with yourself, thinking ... if you had that or you didn't have that would it still make you who you were ... and I don't believe I would be the same person.

(Cameron 2010: 237)

For Lola, being a disabled woman is an experience she would not want to be without. While she acknowledges the sometimes uncomfortable reality of her impairment, she rejects the futile seductions of the ideology of normality (Oliver 1996). She regards her impairment as a core part of her person, something without which she would not be who she is.

Swain and French (2008) emphasised that the affirmation model is *not* about:

- all people with impairments celebrating difference
- disabled people 'coming to terms' with disability and impairment
- disabled people being 'can-do' or 'lovely' people
- the benefits of living and being marginalised and oppressed in a disabling society.

Roshni, a blind woman from Glasgow, remarked:

> I've yet to meet anybody who is a hundred per cent happy with who they are ... I don't necessarily think that because you're disabled you are extra unhappy with who you are ... but equally I've yet to meet the person who's jumping up and down, celebrating that they've got dodgy eyesight ... but, having said that, it's certainly not a cause for me to cry and weep and wring my hands and give up on the world ... there are lots of things I'm not happy about ... I'm not happy about the fact that I've got dry rot in the next room and the ceiling needs replacing ... I think my visual impairment is on the same scale as that ... life happens.

(Cameron 2011: 19)

Roshni suggests that impairment is something to live with rather than a source of perpetual distress. Her blindness is something ordinary for her, part of her everyday experience of life. She is realistic about her situation, recognising that to be blind does not make life any easier, but at the same time, she does not regard her life as a blind person as being one long worthless experience. She leads a busy and interesting life which she enjoys.

In that it involves a rejection of assumptions of tragedy, yet seeks to build on the social model, the affirmation model requires recognition of the oppressive contexts within which everyday life is experienced by disabled people. This was brought into focus by Charles, a wheelchair-user from Liverpool, who said:

> when I was talking in the pub with Erin and yourself tonight ... with every sentence I wasn't thinking oh, I'm going to say this sentence with a speech impairment ... blah blah blah ... now I'm going to say this with a speech impairment ... blah blah blah ... I'm going to move back, but I'm moving back in my wheelchair ... you know ... you don't think ... but ... when you catch somebody looking at you ... and looking at the effects of your impairment ... concentrating on your impairment ... then you're suddenly aware that you're speaking differently.

(Cameron 2010: 250)

Charles' point is that while impairment is not necessarily experienced as a problem for the person concerned, he finds it is often made into a problem by other people. It is not the experience of impairment which is negative, but other people's response to impairment. The problematising of impairment by those identifying as normal involves a transactional exchange which validates their own sense of self.

At its simplest, the affirmation model makes the point that impairment is not an unfortunate aberration or an undesirable deviation from a norm, but is a relatively common and ordinary part of human life. My data led me to propose the following affirmation model definitions:

Impairment: physical, sensory, emotional and cognitive difference, divergent from culturally valued norms of embodiment, to be expected and respected on its own terms in a diverse society.

Disability: a personal and social role which simultaneously invalidates the subject position of people with impairments and validates the subject position of those considered normal.

In naming impairment as difference to be expected and respected on its own terms, the affirmation model allows for a respectful stance to be taken towards disabled people's physicality. In naming disability as role, it identifies disability as a productive as well as a restrictive relationship. Disability is not just about what people with impairments are excluded from and prevented from being, but about the kind of social actors they are required to become instead. This may involve the performance of disability as passive dependency or in terms of denial of the significance of impairment. Either part negates the lived experience of impairment and signifies the desirability of normality. Identifying disability this way, the affirmation model can be used as a tool for making sense of what is going on in disabling encounters and interactions, and as a resource to be used by disabled people in refusing to be what we are expected to become.

For Discussion

- In your own words, what does the word 'affirmation' mean in this chapter?
- How does the affirmation model build on the social model?
- Why does being okay about being impaired involve audacity in the face of other people's expectations?

Further Reading

Cameron, C. and Tossell, D. (2012) 'Another way of looking', *Social Work Education*, 31 (2): 241–45.
Cameron, C. (2014) 'Developing an affirmative model of disability and impairment', in J. Swain, S. French, C. Barnes and S. Thomas (eds), *Disabling Barriers – Enabling Environments*, 3rd edn. London: Sage, pp. 24–30.
Swain, J. and French, S. (2008) *Disability On Equal Terms*. London: Sage.

References

Cameron, C. (2008) 'Further towards an affirmation model', in T. Campbell, F. Fontes, L. Hemingway, A. Soorenian and C. Till (eds), *Disability Studies: Emerging Insights and Perspectives*. Leeds: The Disability Press, pp. 14–30.
Cameron, C. (2010) 'Does anybody like being disabled? A critical exploration of impairment, identity, media and everyday life in a disabling society'. PhD thesis, Queen Margaret University, http://etheses.qmu.ac.uk/258/1/258.pdf.
Cameron, C. (2011) 'Not our problem: impairment as difference, disability as role', *The Journal of Inclusive Practice in Further and Higher Education*, 3 (2): 10–25.
Crow, L. (1996) 'Including all our lives: renewing the social model of disability', in J. Morris (ed.), *Encounters With Strangers: Feminism and Disability*. London: Women's Press, pp. 206–26.
Morris, J. (1991) *Pride Against Prejudice: Transforming Attitudes to Disability*. London: Women's Press.
Oliver, M. (1996) *Understanding Disability: From Theory to Practice*. Basingstoke: Macmillan.
Swain, J. and French, S. (2000) 'Towards an affirmation model', *Disability & Society*, 15 (4): 569–82.
Swain, J. and French, S. (2008) *Disability On Equal Terms*. London: Sage.
Thomas, C. (1999) *Female Forms: Experiencing and Understanding Disability*. Buckingham: Open University Press.

3   Ageing

Sarah Keyes

It is nigh on impossible to escape the fact that advances in healthcare, in particular in the West, have resulted in increased life expectancy. Yet many older people face physical, environmental, psycho-emotional and attitudinal barriers to meaningful inclusion. Recent high-profile cases have highlighted older people facing a lack of access to even the most basic of provision and support which most non-disabled people in Western society take for granted.

This chapter uses the social model of disability, described by Oliver (2004), as a tool to explore ageing and the experiences of older people. It introduces key concepts in the commonalities and differences between ageing and disability, and asks what can be learnt from dialogue between them. Significant aspects of that dialogue include: the experiences of groups of older people and disabled people; commonalities and differences between the two groups; and empowerment through collective action.

The individual, medical model approach to understanding the experiences of disabled people asks 'What is wrong with the individual?' and 'What can be done to cure them?' The social model, conversely, involves asking 'What is wrong with society?' and 'What can be done to challenge the barriers that prevent inclusivity within a diverse society?' So, what can be learnt from a social model approach to the challenges posed by an ageing society?

There are several (not mutually exclusive) groups whose experiences are relevant to this discussion. Considering these groups demonstrates areas of overlap between experiences of older people and disabled people:

- People with lifelong impairments, in particular people with learning difficulties, who are living longer and experiencing age-related impairments in addition to previous impairments (Bigby 2004) as well as their 'family carers' who acquire impairments which impact on their caring role.
- Non-disabled people who acquire physical impairments and/or cognitive impairments as they age.
- People for whom the closure of long-stay institutions in the 1970s means that they are the first group of people with lifelong impairments to be ageing in the context of Care in the Community.
- Disabled people, including disability activists who campaigned as the 'first generation' of the Disabled People's Movement and who are now experiencing ageing. (Zarb and Oliver 1993; McFarlane 1994)

Further commonalities of experience between many older people and many disabled people in the UK include accessing health, social care and third-sector services as well as involvement in assessment and as recipients of benefits within the welfare state (Oldham 2002).

However, parallels between disabled people and older people pose conceptual and practical challenges, and are not necessarily embraced by disabled people and older people themselves. Older people with impairments do not necessarily identify themselves as disabled, and older disabled people do not necessarily identify with the experiences of people who acquire age-related impairments. Similarly, there are areas related to ageing – such as the need for care – which could be interpreted as increasing dependency and which do not sit comfortably alongside independence as promoted within the disabled people's movement (Fine and Glendinning 2005). Within a life-course approach to understanding impairment and disability, expectations around impairment being part of the normal ageing process also differentiate older people with impairments from younger disabled people (Priestley 2006), presenting the complexity in parallels between the two groups (Walker and Walker 1998). This is demonstrated in the conceptual difference between a 'disabling society' and an 'ageing society'.

As a demonstration of commonalities, however, let us take dementia as an example of an impairment related to ageing. Downs (1997) referred to the language that was, at that time, being used within dementia research, language which was grounded in an individual deficit approach to dementia: *dementia sufferers* or *dementia victims*, who place a *burden* of care on their families who are also *victims*. Conversely, Gilliard et al. (2005: 576) cite contributions which the social model has to make to understanding dementia, including: shifting the focus away from loss; a recognition of marginalisation and discrimination faced by people living with dementia; the importance of listening to people's views and experiences; and the significance of social and built environments in disabling experiences of people with dementia.

Perhaps the least problematic parallel between ageing and disability, and a site for dialogue between the two, is that of empowerment and participation in the form of collective action. Additionally, links between groups of disabled people and groups of older people are, potentially, strengthened as the first generation of activists within the disabled people's movement themselves become older people, leading to a potential application of disability rights ideals to ageism.

In relation to older people and ageing, the field of critical gerontology is significant in its conceptual shift away from thinking about older people as a drain on resources and a burden to society towards valuing the contribution that older people can make to society as active citizens (Bernard and Scharf 2007). This includes roles for older people as volunteers (Martinez et al. 2011) or as informal carers, in which they contribute significantly both to the economy and to health and social care provision, though this is often unacknowledged (Argyle 2001). Returning to the specific example of dementia, there are groups of people living with dementia who have developed a collective voice, similar to that of self-advocacy and the mental health user/survivor movement, through increasing awareness and influencing policy (Weaks et al. 2012; Williamson 2012).

In exploring commonalities and differences between ageing and disability, this chapter has outlined areas of potential dialogue between the two, at the same time as acknowledging the theoretical and practical challenges within any comparison. A challenge is posed to Disability Studies students and academics as well as practitioners and policy-makers to acknowledge disabling barriers faced by older people as well as the contribution they can make to the development of an inclusive society.

For Discussion

- What are the key challenges faced by people with lifelong impairments as they become older?
- In what way are the experiences of older people similar to those of disabled people? In what way are they different?
- How might the social model of disability be applied to the experiences of older people?
- What are the conceptual and practical commonalities and differences between 'a disabling society' and 'an ageing society'?

Further Reading

Bernard, M. and Scharf, T. (eds) (2007) *Critical Perspectives on Ageing Societies*. Bristol: Policy Press.

Bigby, C. (2004) *Ageing with a Lifelong Disability: A Guide to Practice, Program and Policy Issues for Human Services Professionals*. London: Jessica Kingsley.

Oldham, C. (2002) 'Later life and the social model of disability: a comfortable partnership?', *Ageing and Society*, 22 (6): 791–806.

References

Argyle, E. (2001) 'Poverty, disability and the role of older carers', *Disability & Society*, 16 (4): 585–95.

Bernard, M. and Scharf, T. (eds) (2007) *Critical Perspectives on Ageing Societies*. Bristol: Policy Press.

Bigby, C. (2004) *Ageing with a Lifelong Disability: A Guide to Practice, Program and Policy Issues for Human Services Professionals*. London: Jessica Kingsley.

Downs, M. (1997) 'The emergence of the person in dementia research', *Ageing and Society*, 17 (5): 597–607.

Fine, M. and Glendinning, C. (2005) 'Dependence, independence or inter-dependence? Revisiting the concepts of "care" and "dependency"', *Ageing and Society*, 25 (4): 601–21.

Gilliard, J., Means, R., Beattie, A. and Daker-White, G. (2005) 'Dementia care in England and the social model of disability: lessons and issues', *Dementia*, 4 (4): 571–86.

Martinez, I., Crooks, D., Kim, K. and Tanner, E. (2011) 'Invisible civic engagement among older adults: valuing the contributions of informal volunteering', *Journal of Cross-Cultural Gerontology*, 26 (1): 23–37.

McFarlane, A. (1994) 'On becoming an older disabled woman', *Disability & Society*, 9 (2): 255–56.

Oldham, C. (2002) 'Later life and the social model of disability: a comfortable partnership?', *Ageing and Society*, 22 (6): 791–806.

Oliver, M. (2004) 'The social model in action: if I had a hammer', in C. Barnes and G. Mercer (eds), *Implementing the Social Model of Disability: Theory and Research*. Leeds: The Disability Press, pp. 18–31.

Priestley, M. (2006) 'Disability and old age: or why it isn't all in the mind', in D. Goodley and R. Lawthom (eds), *Disability and Psychology: Critical Introductions and Reflections*. Basingstoke: Palgrave Macmillan, pp. 84–93.

Walker, A. and Walker, C. (1998) 'Normalisation and "normal" ageing: the social construction of dependency among older people with learning difficulties', *Disability & Society*, 13 (1): 125–42.

Weaks, D., Wilkinson, H. and McKillop, J. (2012) *Perspectives on Ageing with Dementia*. York: Joseph Rowntree Foundation.

Williamson, T. (2012) *A Stronger Collective Voice for People with Dementia*. York: Joseph Rowntree Foundation.

Zarb, G. and Oliver, M. (1993) *Ageing with a Disability: What do they Expect After all These Years?*, www.leeds.ac.uk/disability-studies/archiveuk/Oliver/ageing%20with%20 disability.pdf.

4

Alienation

Colin Cameron

Human existence is an ambiguous experience. Against a backdrop of awareness of our own finitude, each of us is confronted with the task of trying to make sense of who we are in the social, economic and cultural situations in which we find ourselves. We become who we are, for good or bad, through the decisions and choices we make and in terms of the way we deal with the identities ascribed and the opportunities available to us. Yet in different situations within each of our lives the meaning and point of who we are will be called into question. Illness, bereavement, accident and frailty are always possibilities.

While many meanings have been given to the term, I want here to draw on Schmitt's description of alienation as involving the denial of this ambiguity and the attempt to pretend that it has been overcome (Schmitt 2003). Alienation involves a concerted effort to brush out of the picture, at both personal and social levels, the difficult and challenging, odd and inconvenient aspects of what being human is about, and to focus instead on keeping up appearances; on maintaining a narrative which says that 'all is well with us'. In many ways, within contemporary capitalism alienation is inevitable, for maintaining a creditable appearance is a requirement for getting by: 'one must create a worklife of one's own, one must manage the different personalities that dwell in one's body, in order to present oneself to the world and to oneself as a reasonable person' (Schmitt 2003: 80).

This business of self-presentation as reasonable involves learning how to look as if one is in control and invulnerable, as if one knows what it's all about, to be pleasing and reliable, to have the appearance of success, to rub along without causing disturbance or going against the grain.

Alienation describes the anxiety experienced by many people which leaves them perpetually concerned 'not to be different from others, eager to conform and be accepted' (Schmitt 2003: 93). It describes the feeling that others wouldn't like us if they knew what we were really like and the readiness to be what others require us to be in order to be liked:

> The eagerness to create good impressions, even at the cost of deceiving others, arises from the thought that if others saw us as we are, they would not pay attention to us because we are such insignificant persons. They would not want to be seen in our company or consider being our friends because we are, behind the fronts we present to the world, neither likeable nor attractive.
>
> (Schmitt 2003: 87)

There is an economic function served by the creation of this sense of personal insecurity that requires being offset by others' approval. Appearing as reasonable requires investment in wearing the right clothes, playing the right games, using the right gadgets, having the right gear. Within contemporary capitalism the constant generation of needs, consumption and profit requires individuals to identify themselves as consumers, continually purchasing goods to sustain their 'strategic image-presentation' (Lodziak 2002: 58).

Disabled people pose a challenge to the idea of 'the reasonable person' as standard because their embodiment serves as an unwelcome reminder of the frailty, temporality and contingency of human life. For this reason they have been assigned a social role described by Shakespeare (1997) as 'dustbins for disavowal', onto whom are projected the anxieties of non-disabled people, perpetually anxious to deny their own mortality and physicality. As Shakespeare says: 'It is not just that disabled people are different, expensive, inconvenient, or odd; it is that they represent a threat ... to the self-conception of western human beings' (Shakespeare 1997: 235).

This role has involved the representation of disabled people as weak, passive, power-less, dependent, vulnerable, child-like, tragic, repulsive, hideous, malignant, bitter and devious. It has required the physical exclusion of people with impairments who have been cast out of the social body, just as it has required that the idiosyncrasies and falli-bilities of each 'reasonable person' are kept hidden from view.

Disability is the ontological price paid by people with impairments for the relative security and comfort of 'the reasonable person'. As well as being an oppressive social relationship, disability is an alienating social relationship in that it distorts the ways people are able to relate both to their own bodies and to each other. This goes not just for non-disabled people, who are encouraged and expected to hide their own infirmities and insecurities for fear of social ostracism and disapproval, but for disabled people too. Watermeyer and Swartz have commented that:

> A common experience described by disabled people is apprehension of a potent culturally condensed message which says that impairment is 'not OK'; in other words, it's not OK to not be fully able to see, hear, walk, speak or whatever. The motivation to obscure or disguise evidence of impairment, or of its severity, which flows out of this may serve to produce a form of human alienation not only between the disabled person and others, but also within the disabled individual.

> (Watermeyer and Swartz 2008: 602)

Alienation involves an inauthentic way of relating to oneself. It requires that individuals look not to find meaning in the conditions of their actual embodied existence, but that instead they should invest their energies in striving to be something they are not. It requires disabled people to disavow their impairments and to seek to deflect attention away from their impairments. But, as Schmitt points out, 'the eagerness to appear other than as we are denigrates ourselves' (Schmitt 2003: 88). Relating authentically to oneself depends on having the opportunity for mutual recognition, for friendship, for love, for a variety of group relations in which we see and are seen more or less as we are (Schmitt 2003). In the situation of disabled people, this requires recognising and valuing impairment on its own terms: not necessarily as a cause for exuberant celebration, nor as the most significant part of what makes an individual who they are, nor as a cause of perpetual regret. Rather, impairment should be regarded as what it is, a characteristic of the profound ambiguity of human existence.

Michalko has suggested that impairment is indicative of the fragility of the human body and subversive in its power to indicate the fragility of the body politic:

> The disruption of contemporary hegemonic ideas of reason over passion and mind over body is perhaps disability's greatest possibility. Disability disrupts society's carefully structured and multilayered façade behind which it hides the human body together with its fragility and vicissitudes.
>
> (Michalko 2002: 166)

Rather than being useless difference, there is much that impairment, and the experience of impairment, has to teach about what it means to be human. Much is heard about the need to 'change attitudes towards disabled people'. Perhaps the need is rather for 'the reasonable person' to change their attitudes towards themself.

For Discussion

There is nothing more alienating than being around people who do not share your values, idiosyncratic preferences, sensibilities, appetites, hope, anxieties or sense of humour. And these are just some of the incompatibilities one can label.

(Marar 2012: 26)

- Discuss the above quotation in relation to the experience of disability.

  - How important to you are looks? How important to you is the way you are looked at by others? Does what you see when you look at others say more about them or about your way of looking?
  - Reflect on the ways in which popular culture produces and reproduces alienation in your own life.

Further Reading

Schmitt, R. (2003) *Alienation and Freedom*. Oxford: Worldview Press.
Shakespeare, T. (1997) 'Cultural representation of disabled people: dustbins for disavowal', in L. Barton and M. Oliver (eds), *Disability Studies: Past, Present and Future*. Leeds: The Disability Press, pp. 217–366.
Watermeyer, B. (2012) 'Is it possible to create a politically engaged, contextual psychology of disability?', *Disability & Society*, 27 (2): 161–74.

References

Lodziak, C. (2002) *The Myth of Consumerism*. London: Pluto Press.
Marar, Z. (2012) *Intimacy: Understanding the Subtle Power of Human Connection*. Durham: Acumen Publishing Limited.
Michalko, R. (2002) *The Difference That Disability Makes*. Philadelphia, PA: Temple University Press.

Schmitt, R. (2003) *Alienation and Freedom*. Oxford: Worldview Press.

Shakespeare, T. (1997) 'Cultural representation of disabled people: dustbins for disavowal', in L. Barton and M. Oliver (eds), *Disability Studies: Past, Present and Future*. Leeds: The Disability Press, pp. 217–36.

Watermeyer, B. and Swartz, L. (2008) 'Conceptualising the psycho-emotional aspects of disability and impairment: the distortion of personal and psychic boundaries', *Disability & Society*, 23 (6): 599–610.

5

Barriers

Laurence Clark

Socially constructed barriers prevent disabled people from full participation in society. Barriers are present everywhere, from the steps going into a building, to the accessible toilet being used as a broom cupboard, to the passer-by who stops to tell a wheelchair user how brave and inspirational she is. Taking on an understanding which identifies the problem of disability as having to do with the barriers faced by disabled people involves a shift in thinking:

> When people identify disability as 'our problem' they will respond to us as victims in need of 'special' treatment and requiring 'special' services. When people identify disability as a problem with the way society is organised, they will work to remove the barriers by which we have been prevented from taking part in society.

(Oliver 1990: 4)

The cumulative effects of social barriers will be to exclude or restrict people with impairments from participating in numerous aspects of everyday life. Physical barriers can dictate where someone lives, works or chooses to spend time; and barriers to communication can prevent them from making informed decisions. The effects are compounded by multiple barriers, e.g. a lack of information can in turn limit someone's ability to identify accessible facilities.

Physical barriers play a significant role in the disabling process. They arise from architects and designers neglecting the physical access requirements of people with impairments. The vast majority of housing in the owner-occupation market is inaccessible, effectively forcing disabled people into social housing and residential institutions (Thomas 2004). Barriers can dictate where disabled people are educated because many schools, colleges and universities are not completely physically accessible (Barnes 1991). They can influence what disabled people buy, because designers need to consider how people with different impairments may use their products. They can prevent disabled people using planes, trains, buses and cars to travel where they want to go (Lawson and Matthews 2005). Even if they get to where they are going, physical barriers can still prevent them from socialising with friends, as many bars, clubs, restaurants and theatres are not accessible. Finally barriers can affect their chances of landing and retaining a job because many workplaces are still physically inaccessible. This in turn has negative consequences for an impaired person's income and quality of life.

Lack of information is just as disabling as a narrow door or a flight of stairs (Barnes 1991). Knowledge is power, and disabled people who lack access to information will be disadvantaged when making important decisions (Clark 2002). For example, it's impossible to decide what to have for dinner if you cannot read what is written on the menu. For this reason, 'information' was included as one of the fundamental requirements for removing the barriers to independent living (Davis 1990). People need information both at the onset of impairment and at various stages of life, for example, entering adulthood (Office for Disability Issues 2007).

In order to identify the various barriers disabled people face and the potential solutions to those barriers, some knowledge of impairment-related needs is essential (Barnes 2003). However, it should always be up to the individual to dictate their own access needs. People with visual impairments may need information in alternative formats such as large clear print, audiotape, Braille or assistive information technology like reader software. People who are deaf or have hearing impairments experience barriers around audible communication. Alternatives should be offered, such as sign language interpreters and transcribers, as well as technological solutions such as induction loop systems, telephones with texting facilities, videophones and audiovisual fire alarms. A person with a learning difficulty may require information to be explained verbally or written in simple language, with clear illustrations. Finally a person with speech impairments may require assistive technology such as text-to-speech software. Someone with more than one type of impairment will face a combination of these barriers, requiring a variety of flexible solutions.

Negative attitudes towards disabled people can be as much of a barrier to inclusion as an inaccessible building. Such attitudes may stem from misplaced pity, or from inaccurate stereotypes about disabled people, e.g. tabloid newspaper stories of benefit scroungers. Speaking slowly or loudly to someone with a speech impairment in the mistaken belief that they also have a learning or hearing impairment is another form of negative stereotyping, as is avoiding contact with disabled people altogether out of fear of offending them.

Impairments such as learning difficulties, mental health issues, epilepsy, cancer and arthritis are not immediately visible. This sometimes leads to unwillingness to make adjustments in the belief that these impairments are not bona fide. Even the very best of intentions can lead to attitudinal barriers, with disabled people held up to be brave, special or inspirational for just performing everyday tasks and getting on with their lives. Such attitudes come across as patronising and condescending.

Cultural or systemic barriers arise from inflexible laws, policies and practices which do not account for the fact that people with impairments may need additional support and different ways of doing things. For example, some of the major barriers to employment stem from the reluctance of employers to make adjustments for disabled workers. Research has shown that measures such as flexible working hours and job sharing help disabled people to stay in work (Branfield and Maynard Campbell 2000). Rigid rules and regulations around the systems for supporting disabled people also create barriers.

The traditional 'social care' system creates barriers to disabled people having choice and control over what they do with their lives, sometimes dictating when and, in some cases, where they can be supported (Morris 1993). In the UK, disabled people with high support needs face barriers to moving to a different area because they currently cannot take their support packages with them. In addition, the current care charging system creates barriers to wealth by financially penalising disabled people who need support and have savings and investments (Clark 2006). Similarly the 'benefits trap' is a barrier to employment whereby some disabled people choose not to work because the loss of their social housing support and income from benefits would mean that they are worse off overall.

For Discussion

Make two lists:

1. The causes of different types of impairments
2. The causes of disability (i.e. the social barriers)

- Which of the two lists would be the most practical for society to address and do something about?
- Addressing which list would yield the most positive results for the disabled community?

Further Reading

Hemmingway, L. (2011) *Disabled People and Housing: Choices, Opportunities and Barriers.* Bristol: Policy Press.

Imrie, R. (2014) 'Designing inclusive environments and the significance of universal design', in J. Swain, S. French, C. Barnes and S. Thomas (eds), *Disabling Barriers – Enabling Environments*, 3rd edn. London: Sage, pp. 287–97.

Oliver, M. (2009) *Understanding Disability: From Theory to Practice*, 2nd edn. Basingstoke: Palgrave Macmillan.

References

Barnes, C. (1991) *Disabled People in Britain and Discrimination*, 3rd edn. London: Hurst and Co.

Barnes, C. (2003) 'Disability studies: what's the point?' Notes for a verbal presentation at the Disability Studies: Theory, Policy and Practice Conference, University of Lancaster, 4 September.

Branfield, F. and Maynard Campbell, S. (2000) *Common Barriers and Their Removal: Report of Research into Barriers to Employment and Training Faced by Disabled People and their Employers and Training Providers.* Manchester: Breakthrough UK Ltd.

Clark, L. (2002) *Accessible Health Information.* Liverpool: Liverpool Primary Care Trust.

Clark, L. (2006) 'A comparative study on the effects of community care charging policies for personal assistance users'. Unpublished MA dissertation.

Davis, K. (1990) *Activating the Social Model of Disability: The Emergence of the 'Seven Needs'.* Derbyshire: Derbyshire Coalition of Disabled People.

Lawson, A. and Matthews, B. (2005) 'Dismantling barriers to transport by law: the European journey', in C. Barnes and G. Mercer (eds), *The Social Model of Disability: Europe and the Majority World*. Leeds: Disability Press, pp. 80–97.

Morris, J. (1993) *Independent Lives? Community Care and Disabled People*. London: The Macmillan Press.

Office for Disability Issues (2007) *Improving Information for Disabled People*. London: HMSO.

Oliver M. (1990) *The Politics of Disablement*. Basingstoke: Macmillan Press.

Thomas, P. (2004) 'The experience of disabled people as customers in the owner occupation market', *Housing Studies*, 19 (5): 781–794.

6

Bodies

Colin Cameron

Different approaches to understanding the body discussed in this chapter enable readers to call into question assumptions about the 'givenness' of the 'natural body' (Goodley 2011: 158). First, a historical view of ideas about the body helps problematise conventional understandings of impairment and disability.

Western thought has been profoundly influenced by Descartes. Writing in the seventeenth century, Descartes believed that the mind and the body are two distinct essences – the mind bestowing humanity, while the body is animal. While the mind is conceived as 'an indivisible thinking substance' (Shildrick 2002: 48), the body is regarded as determined by the laws of natural science, as the case which encloses the self: 'I (am) a substance whose essence or nature is to be conscious and whose being requires no place and depends upon no material thing' (Descartes, 1637, in Edwards 2005: 100).

The privileging of independence is embedded in Descartes' influence on thinking about the body, and became a key variable around which inequality was structured with the establishment of capitalism.

As medical knowledge and practice developed through the 'Enlightenment period' of the seventeenth and eighteenth centuries, the body was increasingly regarded as a piece of machinery judged in terms of what it should be able to do independently in its own environment. The expectation surfaced that if a body fails to operate independently then it needs to be fixed. It is important to understand the significance of the mind/body division in thinking about the body, because it has fundamentally shaped our perceptions of disability today. Where the 'legitimate person' is seen as 'one who owes their existence and individuality to no other thing' (Edwards 2005: 100), the association of disability with dependence means that people with impairments have been regarded as illegitimate and needing fixing. This way of thinking has also given rise to the perception that disabled people have 'true selves' trapped or imprisoned within broken bodies. The emphasis on recognising disabled people as 'people with disabilities', as if personhood and impairment can be separated, is a further intensely problematic outcome of historical thinking.

Drawing on different strands of sociological thought, many perspectives can be found which critique prevailing perceptions of the body and its relationship to disability. French (1993) discusses the pressures on disabled people to aspire to independence or, at least, to the appearance of independence. Her writing makes important connections between the perception of disabled people as transgressive in work situations, for example, and historic views of the body. She describes how it is sometimes made very difficult for disabled people to ask for help because of assumptions that any request for assistance is a sign of deficit arising from impairment. In this context, however, French continues, *everyone* has their own share of limitations, sometimes far outstripping those of a disabled person:

> The crucial difference is that able-bodied people's problems are regarded as normal and acceptable, and thus they can ask assistance of each other without feeling guilty or inferior. Disabled people can ask for help too as long as they steer clear of any problems directly associated with disability.

(French 1993: 47)

Her point is that while in the course of everyday life everybody is, in fact, dependent on other people – as human beings we are all interdependent – the nature of non-disabled people's reliance seems ordinary, while any reliance of disabled people is seen as extraordinary. While non-disabled people's needs are largely met in social contexts such as work environments, people with impairments are often faced with disabling barriers. Disabled people's problems are identified not with the fact that their access requirements have not been addressed, but with their 'faulty' bodies.

Other writers have argued that 'the body is produced by meaning and interpretation and is, therefore, best understood in terms of discourse or cultural representation' (Hughes 2014: 58). The body, and the way the body is experienced, understood, made sense of and related to, is not viewed as 'just' a naturally occurring physical entity, but as the product of 'certain kinds of knowledge which are subject to change' (Lupton 1998). What is considered acceptable or normal bodily comportment – the ways people use their bodies and move their bodies, the things they do *with* their bodies – is shaped by the requirements of different societies in different times and places and by the discourses of class, race, gender, sexuality, age and disability. People learn that some bodies are afforded more power than others, something Foucault terms 'bio-power' (Foucault 1998).

Bio-power is afforded through 'a series of practices or body techniques which represent and regulate bodies in time and space' (Lupton 1998). Doyle makes plain how easily disabled people can find bio-power diminished:

> I remember, on numerous occasions, lying on a couch in a school surgery with nothing on but my underpants with lots of student nurses and doctors talking about me and looking at me. Nobody asked my permission for this.

(Doyle 2013)

It is through these processes, of having our bodies measured, weighed, tested, assessed, checked-up on and gazed at, that bodies are controlled and difference becomes tangible. Rather than being expressive of an objective reality, terms like 'impairment' and 'disability' are arbitrary and conventional terms used to describe what appears when the body is looked at in a certain way (Hughes 2014).

The compulsion to monitor, to repair, to restore, to normalise, is a response that would not have been, and *is* not, made at all times and in all places, but becomes established when physical difference is viewed as abnormality. In the meantime, rather than being able to value their own difference, disabled people learn to regard their bodies as inconvenient burdens, impeding the fulfilment of their selves.

Through a different theoretical lens, phenomenologists reject the distinction between mind and body and regard selfhood as 'inseparable from material being-in-the-world' (Shildrick 2002: 49). The body is regarded not as just a fleshy object, but as

the 'place' in which we live and by which we are recognised ... (as) an object on which we can reflect. In all these incarnations, it is social. It is the where, why and when of our daily activities and experiences.

(Hughes 2014: 58).

Body and mind are not thought of as separate but as thoroughly related, as Charlesworth illuminates in reflections on the experience of social class:

We are not simply in the world, we are amidst it, our world comes to inhabit us because we come to know it through our socialisation into a way of being that discloses the world in a certain way.

(Charlesworth 2000: 91)

It becomes possible to understand that the oppressive nature of disability lies in the fact that the world is organised into a hierarchy in which the non-disabled body is advantaged and the impaired body is judged as incompetent:

The social and physical world has been made by and in the image and likeness of non-disabled people. It is a home for *their* bodies. Even the norms and codes of movement and timing which structure everyday communication are informed by and devised in an idiom that is based on the carnal and emotional needs of non-disabled people.

(Hughes 2014: 59)

Clearly there are material, social and political conditions associated with the representation and enablement of bodies, and the implications of these for disabled people are far-reaching.

Each of the alternative ways of understanding the body discussed here offers different understandings of the body. The tensions and intersections between different approaches suggest many questions which determine the relevance of discussion about the body within contemporary Disability Studies and show much further thinking is required.

For Discussion

- What goes through your head when you think about your own body?
- What is the historical, cultural and biographical context of your thinking?
- What are the implications of these reflections for your understanding of disability?

Further Reading

Aphramor, L. (2009) 'Disability and the anti-obesity offensive', *Disability & Society*, 24(7): 897–909.

Hughes, B. (2014) 'Disability and the body', in J. Swain, S. French, C. Barnes and S. Thomas (eds), *Disabling Barriers – Enabling Environments*, 3rd edn. London: Sage, pp. 55–61.

Peuravaara, K. (2013) 'Theorizing the body: conceptions of disability, gender and normality', *Disability & Society*, 28 (3): 406–15.

References

Charlesworth, S.J. (2000) *A Phenomenology of Working Class Experience*. Cambridge: Cambridge University Press.

Doyle, P. (forthcoming 2013) 'Beyond segregated school: voices of disabled school leavers'. PhD thesis to be submitted, University of Sheffield.

Edwards, S.D. (2005) *Disability: Definitions, Value and Identity*. Oxford: Radcliffe.

Foucault, M. (1998) *The History of Sexuality: The Will to Knowledge*. London: Penguin.

French, S. (1993) 'What's so great about independence?', in J. Swain, V. Finkelstein, S. French and M. Oliver (eds), *Disabling Barriers – Enabling Environments*. London: Sage, pp. 44–48.

Goodley, D. (2011) *Disability Studies: An Interdisciplinary Introduction*. London: Sage.

Hughes, B. (2014) 'Disability and the body', in J. Swain, S. French, C. Barnes and C. Thomas (eds), *Disabling Barriers – Enabling Environments*, 3rd edn. London: Sage, pp. 55–61.

Lupton, D. (1998) *Medicine as Culture: Illness, Disease and the Body in Western Societies*. London: Sage.

Shildrick, M. (2002) *Embodying the Monster: Encounters with the Vulnerable Self*. Sage: London.

7

Care

Colin Cameron

The idea that care is regarded by many disabled people as a problematic concept, or as a feature of their oppression, may initially seem quite challenging. The word is so prevalent in the contexts in which many disabled people live that it passes almost without notice. To take the time to enquire of its meaning might seem a strange and unnecessary thing to do. Unexamined, the idea of care seems unquestionably benign. It is a word that suggests concern, consideration for others and attentiveness to their needs (Swain and French 1998). The following two quotes, however, illustrate a divergence of perspectives:

> Let us state what disabled people do want by stating first what we don't want:
>
> WE DON'T WANT CARE!!!
>
> (Wood 1989: 201)
>
> One third of social care users are disabled adults of working age. Care allows them to get out of the house, have a cooked meal or take part in their community. Without access to care, disabled people are left utterly isolated.
>
> (Hawkes 2012)

The first statement, made a quarter of a century ago by Richard Wood, then the Chair of the British Council of Organisations of Disabled People, explicitly rejects the idea of care. The meaning of 'care', as this word is recognised by Wood, has come to encompass 'a relatively narrow range of social practices involved in "looking after" those deemed dependent' (Thomas 2007: 89). The second, written in a letter published in *The Guardian* newspaper in 2012 by Richard Hawkes, Chief Executive of Scope, one of the UK's largest disability charities, endorses the idea. Wood makes the point that the view of disabled people as people in need of care is most often held by governments and professionals, and that 'the concept of care seems to many disabled people a tool through which others are able to dominate and manage our lives' (Wood 1989: 199). Hawkes, on the other hand, suggests that without care disabled people's lives will be impoverished.

The issue is that the presumption that disabled people have a need for care, and that it is through care that their needs will be met, involves an association of impairment and disability with inability, incompetence, personal inadequacy, and dependence. The medical model, identifying these in terms of loss, abnormality, restriction and lack of ability, is clearly in evidence. Care has been conceived in terms of doing things for disabled people that they are unable to do for themselves. This has been criticised by disabled people as involving roles of 'doing' and 'being done to', involving carers who 'do' and disabled people who are 'done to'. As Wood has stated, 'disabled people's lives are often dominated by professionals and services which de-skill us and turn us into passive recipients of care' (Wood 1989: 199). Accessing benefits and services to meet their needs frequently requires disabled people to present themselves as abject sufferers. Care involves oppression because it has robbed disabled people of opportunities for agency and for developing skills in managing their own lives. Much abuse to disabled people has been carried out in segregated settings where they have been placed in the name of care (Young 2011).

Swain and French (1998: 90) have argued that 'the oppressive nature of caring lies in the pre-determination of identities of "cared for" and "carers", and their relationships and expectations of each other'. Particularly in situations where disabled people are reliant on having their needs met by family members, care often involves feelings of entrapment within situations from which there seems no escape. From the perspective of disabled people, Brisenden (in Hasler 2004: 227) argues that care 'exploits both the carer and the person receiving care. It ruins relationships between people and results in thwarted life opportunities on both sides of the caring equation.' The view that caring involves oppression is also expressed by carers' organisations. Referring to the 2012 report 'In Sickness and in Health', published by eight charities for National Carers

Week, Baroness Pitkeathley states that 83 per cent of carers surveyed said that caring had a negative impact on their physical health and 87 per cent said it had a negative impact on their mental health (cited in Pitkeathley 2012). Carers UK cite evidence that caring can cause ill health, poverty and social isolation (Carers UK 2012).

The paradox lies in what is proposed as a resolution to the problem of care. While carers' organisations demand 'a better deal for carers' (Pitkeathley 2012) and incremental changes in existing services, disabled people have argued for a complete re-think of the issue. As stated elsewhere in this book, disabled people do not deny the reality of impairment and impairment effects, but argue that the issue is to do with how society responds to these. In a society which prizes normality and identifies impairment principally as a departure from this ideal, normalising care has been considered an appropriate way of dealing with impairment. Disabled people have long proposed the notions of independent living and 'support needs' as an alternative (Harris and Roulstone 2011; Priestley 1999; Thomas 2007). Employment of their own personal assistants, for example, with appropriate support and training from disabled people's organisations, has replaced relationships of care in many disabled people's lives. This has enabled them to take control over the choices and decisions which impact on their lives, from the most mundane upwards.

The landscape of service provision in which Hawkes' letter was published has changed in many ways since Wood stated that disabled people do not want care. The current roll-out of personalisation and self-directed support, for example, is intended to transform the ways in which services for disabled people are delivered. Yet still, in the very language used to describe these services, 'the ethos of care lingers' (Thomas 2007). Terms such as 'adult social care', 'health and social care', 'respite care', and 'care packages' are pervasive. As Roulstone and Prideaux suggest, 'this runs the risk of confining debates within a "care" and "alleviation of burden"' approach' (Roulstone and Prideaux 2012: 71). It may also be that charities remain attached to the terminology of care because their income is in large part dependent on voluntary giving. Shifting this discourse looks set to remain a struggle.

For Discussion

- How much do you like to be a recipient of 'care'? What social parameters of care – such as personal relationships, interdependence, or coercion, for example – might make receiving care problematic for you?
- What amount of time do you like to spend providing care?
- How does care impact on family and social life?
- On reflection, do you think the discourse of care should be challenged? Why do you think this?

Further Reading

Swain, J., French, S. and Cameron, C. (2003) 'Policy, provision and practice: care or control?', *Controversial Issues in a Disabling Society*. Buckingham: Open University Press, pp. 141–50.

Wood, R. (1989) *Care of Disabled People*, www.psi.org.uk/publications/archivepdfs/Disability%20and%20social/WOOD.pdf.

Woodin, S. (2014) 'Care: controlling and personalising services', in J. Swain, S. French, C. Barnes and S. Thomas (eds), *Disabling Barriers – Enabling Environments*, 3rd edn. London: Sage, pp. 247–54.

References

Carers UK (2012) *What is Caring?* www.carersuk.org/about-us/what-is-caring, accessed 26 October 2012.

Harris, J. and Roulstone, A. (2011) *Disability, Policy and Professional Practice*. London: Sage.

Hawkes, R. (2012) 'Letters and emails', *The Guardian*, 6 October 2012.

Hasler, F. (2004) 'Disability, care and controlling services', in J. Swain, S. French, C. Barnes and S. Thomas (eds), *Disabling Barriers – Enabling Environments*, 3rd edn. London: Sage, pp. 226–30.

Pitkeathley, J. (2012) *A Better Deal for Carers*, www.epolitix.com/latestnews/article-detail/newsarticle/baroness-pitkeathley-a-better-deal-for-carers/, accessed 26 October 2012.

Priestley, M. (1999) *Disability Politics and Community Care*. London: Jessica Kingsley.

Roulstone, A. and Prideaux, S. (2012) *Understanding Disability Policy*. Bristol: Policy Press.

Swain, J. and French, S. (1998) 'Normality and disabling care', in A. Brechin, J. Walmsley, J. Katz and S. Peace (eds), *Care Matters: Concepts, Practice and Research in Health and Social Care*. London: Sage, pp. 81–95.

Thomas, C. (2007) *Sociologies of Disability and Illness: Contested Ideas in Disability Studies and Medical Sociology*. Basingstoke: Palgrave Macmillan.

Wood, R. (1989) *Care of Disabled People*, www.psi.org.uk/publications/archivepdfs/Disability%20 and%20social/WOOD.pdf, accessed 25 October 2012.

Young, A. (2011) *A Dying Breed*, www.disabilityartsonline.org/A-Dying-Breed-Ann-Young, accessed 26 October 2012.

8

Charity

Colin Cameron

Disabled people have long been critical of the role that large charities – organisations *for* rather than *of* disabled people – have had in their oppression. Charity advertising campaigns have been identified as playing a major part in perpetuating stereotypes of disabled people as poor, child-like victims, deserving of other people's pity and kindness (Rieser and Mason 1992). Charities' concerns with raising research funding into medical causes and the elimination of impairments have reinforced ideas associating disability with illness and sent out negative messages about the experience of living with impairment (Marks 1999). Charities have been heavily involved in perpetuating the myth that disability is an individual condition and that people with different impairments have nothing to do with each other (Cameron 2011). The slogan of the disabled people's movement, 'Rights Not Charity', expresses the antipathy felt about these big businesses.

In recent years, and in the light of public criticism from disabled people, many charities have attempted to re-brand themselves and to develop a more acceptable image. The Spastics Society in England, for example, has renamed itself *Scope* and The Scottish Council for Spastics has renamed itself *Capability Scotland*. Many disabled people, however, feel scepticism about these changes and argue they have little depth:

> Our history has taught us that in the recent past these organisations played a leading role in keeping us oppressed and out of society. Name changes, tidying up their language and employing token disabled people cannot disguise the underlying reality that these agencies are interested primarily in self-preservation and that they will say and do anything that is politically expedient in order to retain their influence in Government circles.

(Oliver and Barnes 2006: unpaged)

In an article in *Coalition*, published by the Greater Manchester Coalition of Disabled People, Carr critiqued the 'Enable' campaign run by the Leonard Cheshire Foundation (since renamed Leonard Cheshire Disability) in 2000. She talks about the way the organisation 'continues to appropriate our language as efficiently as it corrupts our image and commodifies our lives to ensure its thriving status' (Carr 2000: 29). She documents the repackaging of the charity to harness both the ideas of the disabled people's movement, such as Independent Living, and the co-operation of disabled people themselves through 'user involvement initiatives'. Such strategies, she argues, serve to strengthen the charity model and the charity's credentials in speaking on behalf of disabled people, whilst also rationalising continued segregated provision (Swain, French and Cameron 2003: 92).

While disabled people's organisations are often registered as charities for legal pur-poses, they are usually dependent for revenue on local authorities and grant-making trusts and unwilling to go down the collecting-tin route of income generation. Large charities have little problem with this. The Capability Scotland website, for example, informs people that:

> Your small change will make a big change! By having one of our collection boxes in your business or workplace, your customers and colleagues can start making a difference to the lives of disabled adults and children right now … When the box is emptied we will give you a 'thank you' receipt displaying the amount collected from the box. This thanks everyone and lets them know how valuable their support is.

(Capability Scotland 2012a)

An organisation which describes itself as 'a campaigning organisation working for political change' and as raising the profile of 'the issues that really matter to disabled people' (Capability Scotland 2012b) appears to see no incongruity between these aims and its continuing representation of disabled people as charity cases.

A 2009 story in *The Scotsman* newspaper was headlined 'Blind charity aims to raise awareness of visual impairment with tour'. The story reads:

> Instead of open-top buses and perfectly-poised binoculars, the only aide on the latest Edinburgh tour is a pair of dark glasses. The pilot, launched by the Royal National Institute of Blind People (RNIB), is aimed at making those who take the tour realise what it is like to move around one of Europe's most picturesque cities as a visually-impaired person … RNIB's

inclusive society group director, Fazilet Hadi, said: 'We are asking the general public to consider what they would lose from their lives if they lost their sight … The tours, launching next month, will be a really powerful way for people to experience first hand just how much losing your sight can impact upon your life.' As well as raising awareness of the impact of sight loss on everyday life, the RNIB hopes to boost its profile.

(*The Scotsman*, 2009: unpaged)

In 2007, in keeping with the re-branding of other large disability charities and in line with the preferred language of the disabled people's movement, the Royal National Institute for the Blind became the Royal National Institute of Blind People (RNIB 2012: unpaged). The announcement of this bus tour, however, reveals that the image of blindness being projected by the organisation is still rooted in terms of personal tragedy. Disabled people's organisations have long rejected the value of simulation exercises like this: 'Simulation exercises, by their very nature, focus on supposed difficulties, problems, inadequacies and inabilities of disabled people. They contribute to rather than challenge damaging stereotypes' (Swain and Lawrence 1994: 91).

Mary, a disabled woman I interviewed in Cameron (2010), discussed the use of children in charity advertising. She compared funding campaign posters produced in the 1960s by The Spastics Society and in 2005 by the same organisation, re-branded Scope. The 1960s poster bore the alarming statement 'It could have been your child' and depicted 'a lovely little girl, of course … hair in bunches and she's probably about … four, five … and she's on callipers … and behind her, in the background, are some other children with mobility aids' (Cameron 2010: 175).

Describing the 2005 poster, Mary says:

It's got nine little kids and they're all … you know, three, five … all dressed up … there's a paramedic … a doctor … painter … all these kinds of things … they're an ethnic mix and it's apparent that some of them have impairments … the strapline for this is *Want to Work? We Do.*

(Cameron 2010: : 175)

Both posters rely on images of cute disabled children to make money. Mary said she is annoyed because this kind of imagery involves 'the infantilising of disabled people … obviously you're using children because it's emotive and they're cuter than disabled adults' (Cameron 2010: 175).

The aspirations of disabled people to transform public discourse on disability are frustrated by the refusal of disability charities to move beyond the medical model. Medical model thinking is evidenced, for example, in the following statement by Shaw Trust, a UK charity working in the area of employment: 'Work Choice is a Government supported employment programme designed specifically for people who, due to their disability, may find it difficult to find or keep a job' (Shaw Trust 2012).

Impairment rather than structural barriers is identified here as the cause of disabled people's unemployment, revealing a stubborn attachment to thinking about and representing disability as a personal problem. While these organisations continue to be regarded within the public realm as speaking authoritatively on behalf of disabled people, transforming perceptions about disability remains difficult.

For Discussion

- Why are disabled people absent from powerful positions in large charities and why do agencies controlled by disabled people command fewer resources?
- Why are the images of disabled people used in advertisements by traditional charities unacceptable to disabled people?
- How can the situation of disabled people working for large charities be likened to that of women working in strip bars?

Further Reading

Barnes, C. and Mercer, G. (2010) *Exploring Disability*, 2nd edn. Cambridge: Polity.
Cameron, C. (2011) 'Whose problem? Disability narratives and available identities', in G. Craig, M. Mayo, K. Popple, M. Shaw and M. Taylor (eds), *The Community Development Reader: History, Themes and Issues*. Bristol: Policy Press, pp. 259–66.
Waltz, M. (2012) 'Images and narratives of autism within charity discourses', *Disability & Society*, 27 (2): 219–33.

References

Cameron, C. (2010) 'Does anybody like being disabled? A critical exploration of impairment, identity, media and everyday life in a disabling society'. PhD thesis, Queen Margaret University, http://etheses.qmu.ac.uk/258/1/258.pdf.
Cameron, C. (2011) 'Whose problem? Disability narratives and available identities', in G. Craig, M. Mayo, K. Popple, M. Shaw and M. Taylor (eds), *The Community Development Reader: History, Themes and Issues*. Bristol: Policy Press, pp. 259–66.
Capability Scotland (2012a) Collection Boxes, www.capabilityscotland.org.uk/ collectionboxes.aspx, accessed 24 September 2012.
Capability Scotland (2012b) About Us, www.capability-scotland.org.uk/what-can-capability-do-for-me/what-do-you-need-to-know/about-us/, accessed 15 November 2012.
Carr, L. (2000) 'Enabling our destruction', *Coalition*, August: 29–36.
Marks, D. (1999) *Disability: Controversial Debates and Psychosocial Perspectives*. London: Routledge.
Oliver, M. and Barnes, C. (2006) *Disability Politics and the Disability Movement in Britain*, www.leeds.ac.uk/disability.../Coalition%disability%20politics%20paper.pdf, accessed 26 October 2009.
Rieser, R. and Mason, M. (1992) *Disability Equality in the Classroom*. London: Disability Equality in Education.
RNIB (2012) *History of RNIB*, www.rnib.org.uk/aboutus/who/historyofrnib/Pages/rnibhistory.aspx, accessed 24 September 2012.
Scotsman, The (2009) 'Blind charity aims to raise awareness of visual impairment with tour', http://news.scotsman.com/health/Blind-charity-aims-to-raise.5768501.jp, accessed 27 October 2009.
Shaw Trust (2012) *Work Choice*, www.shaw-trust.org.uk/workstep, accessed 2 February 2013.
Swain, J. French, S. and Cameron, C. (2003) *Controversial Issues in a Disabling Society*. Buckingham: Open University Press.
Swain, J. and Lawrence, P. (1994) 'Learning about disability: changing attitudes or challenging understanding?', in S. French (ed.), *On Equal Terms: Working with Disabled People*. Oxford: Butterworth-Heinemann, pp. 87–102.

9

Citizenship

WaiYeen Peng

This chapter begins by defining the concept of citizenship. It then shows how contradictions between the perceived rights and responsibilities embedded in the concept of citizenship can contribute to disabled people's exclusion from society. For example, a disabled person may have the right to vote, but may be unable to take full advantage of this if their polling station is inaccessible.

Citizenship has a long history, dating back to the Ancient Greeks (fifth–fourth centuries BC). To them 'the optimum relationship between the individual and the state was embodied in the notion of the citizen' (Beckett 2006: 24).

Citizen literally means *member of the state* (Beckett 2006: 24). In Ancient Greece, there were penalties for those who failed to conform to the expectations arising from their status as citizens (Beckett 2006). Citizenship remains closely linked to the activities of individuals (especially men) within society. Through their involvement, they will be rewarded with certain entitlements, such as retirement benefits and healthcare (Turner 2009: 7).

People are also rewarded for the establishment of family units, as this will help the economy. However, social exclusion may occur for those with 'poor health, mental illness, poor education, disability or impairment' (Turner 2009: 7).

This produces the assumption that only 'able bodied individuals' are able to fulfil the requirements of being 'active citizens' (Turner 2009: 7). Those who do not conform to the cultural and social norms are labelled as outcasts (Watson 1998).

The most influential concept of citizenship is that of the sociologist T.H. Marshall (1950, cited in Turner 2009). Marshall stated that citizenship is associated with the possession of three specific rights – civil, political and social rights (Turner 2009). Civil rights include freedom of speech, the right to own property and the right to justice. Political rights include the right to vote in elections. Social rights include the possession of a degree of economic welfare, and the right to live in and be involved in society (Turner 2009).

Morris (2005, cited in Rankin 2009: 5) argues that these principles of citizenship are not sufficient to enable the full inclusion of disabled people (Rankin 2009; Morris 2005). This is because 'citizenship can hold different meaning depending on personal circumstance' (Roche (1992, cited in Rankin 2009: 5).

Morris (2005) believes that citizenship in terms of disability comes in three forms: self-determination, participation and contribution. Self-determination involves the possession of and the opportunity to exercise choice and autonomy, e.g. independent living. Participation includes political participation as well as participation in the community, with the aim of combatting social exclusion. Contribution includes involvement in the economic and social life of one's society. Barriers affecting these three areas inhibit both disabled people's equality and their opportunities for full citizenship (Morris 2005).

The current United Kingdom Coalition Government regards citizenship as the coming-together of individuals for the benefit of society as a whole (*The Telegraph* 2010). Not everyone is able to contribute equally, however – especially those who are disabled or, for reasons related to impairment, cannot work. This not only segregates them from other members of society, but reinforces social exclusion (Barnes and Mercer 2010). Sometimes disabled people refer to themselves as 'second-class citizens' because 'they regard their citizenship as being of a quality inferior to that enjoyed by the majority' (Drake 2001: 416).

Disabled people are socially excluded by disabling environmental, physical and social barriers. Bowie (1978, cited in Barnes and Mercer 2010) identifies six key areas of concern: the built environment, public attitudes, education, the labour market, the law and personal relations. These barriers contribute to disabled people's separation from mainstream society. This in effect challenges the notion of citizenship for disabled people (Barnes and Mercer 2010): it takes away their ability to fulfil their responsibilities as citizens (Watson 1998).

Social participation in society is a fundamental part of citizenship, but disabled people face many excluding barriers. These include inadequate support, communication problems, inaccessible buildings, equipment or facilities, inaccessible transport and lack of accessible information (Barnes and Mercer 2010). As a result of these restrictions, disabled people are unable to exercise the freedom to choose when and where they want to involve themselves in the community as rightful citizens (Barnes and Mercer 2010; Morris 2005). These factors can also constitute barriers to employment, education and politics. Such barriers affect disabled people, who may struggle to develop a sense of belonging in and contributing to society (Morris 2005). This highlights the weaknesses in Marshall's notion of social and civil rights.

The attitudes of non-disabled people also play a major part in social exclusion. The assumption that disabled people have nothing to contribute sets up a 'self-fulfilling prophecy', where disabled people are so constantly told this that they often start to believe it themselves (Morris 2005: 31). The dominance of this assumption leads to a failure to deliver the support needed to enable disabled people to make a contribution (Morris 2005: 31). For example, disabled people receiving benefits may be labelled as scroungers, because society simply assumes that they have nothing to contribute and ignores the reasons behind their exclusion. Therefore, how society views disabled people will shape the way they see themselves in society.

The Disability Discrimination Act 1995 (DDA) attempted to challenge the social exclusion and the denial of basic rights of citizenship for disabled people. However, Gooding (1995, cited in Marks 1999: 78) argues that the Act was 'full of loopholes and justifications that condone discrimination against disabled people'.

Citizenship is socially constructed and has many different interpretations. Sometimes it depends on the individual and how they perceive the concept of citizenship, but principally, it is society that establishes the inequality and exclusion disabled people face. This chapter has identified many barriers that limit disabled people from achieving full citizenship. These barriers prevent disabled people from becoming fully involved in their community and from being able to exercise choice and autonomy, thus questioning their status as citizens.

For Discussion

- What impact do you think that the 2012 Paralympics might have had on questions of citizenship for disabled people?
- Have a look at the texts of the Disability Discrimination Act 1995 and the Equality Act 2010. Do you think that the Equality Act successfully addresses the criticisms that Gooding and others have made of the Disability Discrimination Act?
- Do you agree with the three forms of citizenship which Morris has identified as being applicable to disabled people?

Further Reading

Jaeger, P.T. and Bowman, C.A. (2005) *Understanding Disability: Inclusion, Access, Diversity, and Civil Rights*. Westport, CT: Praeger Publishers.

Nussbaum, M.C. (2006) *Frontiers of Justice: Disability, Nationality, Species Membership*. Cambridge, MA: Harvard University Press.

Rummery, K. (2002) *Disability, Citizenship and Community Care: A Case for Welfare Rights?* Aldershot, Hampshire: Ashgate, University of Michigan.

References

Barnes, C. and Mercer, G. (2010) *Exploring Disability*, 2nd edn. Cambridge: Polity Press.

Beckett, A.E. (2006) *Citizenship and Vulnerability*. Basingstoke: Palgrave Macmillan.

Drake, R.F. (2001) 'Welfare states and disabled people', in G.L. Albrecht, K.D. Seelman and M. Bury (eds), *Handbook of Disability Studies*. Thousand Oaks, CA: Sage, pp. 412–29.

Marks, D. (1999) *Disability: Controversial Debates and Psychosocial Perspectives*. London: Routledge.

Morris, J. (2005) *Citizenship and Disabled People: A Scoping Paper Prepared for the Disability Rights Commission*, http://disability-studies.leeds.ac.uk/files/archiveuk/morris-Citizenship-and-disabled-people.pdf, accessed 16 September 2012.

Rankin, J.C. (2009) *Disability, Citizenship and Identity*, www.leeds.ac.uk/disability-studies/archiveuk/rankin/Final%20Citizenship%20Disability%20Identity.pdf, accessed 16 September 2012.

Telegraph, The (2010) 'David Cameron's Conservative Conference speech in full', www.telegraph.co.uk/news/newstopics/politics/david-cameron/8046342/David-Camerons-Conservative-conference-speech-in-full.html, accessed 16 September 2012.

Turner, B.S. (2009) *Thinking Citizenship Series: T.H. Marshall, Social Rights and English National Identity*, www.tandfonline.com/doi/full/10.1080/13621020802586750, accessed 16 September 2012.

Watson, N. (1998) 'Enabling identity: disability, self and citizenship', in T. Shakespeare (ed.), *The Disability Reader: Social Science Perspectives*. London: Continuum, pp. 147–63.

10 Disability Arts

Colin Hambrook

Disability Arts has been defined as:

> art by disabled people for disabled people that speaks the truth about the disability experience.

(Masefield 2006: 22)

Masefield's definition suggests that Disability Arts involves the portrayal of the experience of living in a disabling world, but the term has become a catch-all for work by disabled individuals and companies of disabled artists, whose arts production does not necessarily exemplify Disability Arts within a political context.

The Disability Arts movement began in the mid-1970s, as part of the growing surge of political activism by disabled people during this period. By the mid-1990s Disability Arts Fora (DAFs) had been set up in many major cities within the UK. Largely disability-led, they provided training to make the arts more inclusive, and also gave support to a burgeoning community of disabled artists – providing opportunities to perform, exhibit and develop artistic practice.

Williamson (2008) comments that 'disability politics and art have evolved a deeply symbiotic relation to the funding institutions that might be described as a top-down structural relationship'. The result is that while the disabled people's movement has achieved much, Disability Arts has moved away from its original political intentions.

By the beginning of the new millennium funding criteria had changed. Support for a community of emerging disability artists gave way to the idea of 'mainstreaming' disability. The DAFs that still exist today are obliged to nurture 'mainstream' collaborations in order to justify their funding agreements. Unsurprisingly, many DAFs have foundered, unable to compete with larger arts production companies.

A few key disabled artists and creatives have, however, continued to see themselves, their work and the role of Disability Art as provocateur, setting a challenge to notions of 'normality' and upbraiding the absurdities of discriminatory attitudes and practices.

Live Art challenges the normalisation of disabled people through transgressive acts of art production. In November 2007, disabled avant-garde artists Aaron Williamson and Katherine Araniello gave an unsolicited performance at Birkbeck College, London. They staged a satirical public protest, inventing a story that budget airlines had refused to fly Katherine to Zurich, having blacklisted her for purchasing an 'assisted death' in a clinic there. The public were requested to support Katherine's right to fly/die by signing a petition. Without question or debate 37 people signed the petition, illustrating how easily convinced the general public is of the worthlessness of disabled people's lives.

Artist and film-maker Liz Crow's film project *Resistance: which way the future?* (2005) outlines the Aktion-T4 Nazi mass murder programme, which targeted disabled people. Crow's film centres on a character named Ellie Blick, based on a real-life disabled woman referred to by her initials – EB. Crow found that venue programmers labelled the work as 'worthy' or 'depressing' as an excuse for not engaging with it. So when an opportunity arose to participate in Antony Gormley's Fourth Plinth project *One and Other* at Trafalgar Square in 2009, Crow took it. Sitting in her wheelchair dressed in full Nazi regalia, she created an arresting image that provoked much interest. She then lifted a flag, bearing Niemoeller's words: 'First they came for the sick, the so-called incurables and I did not speak out – because I was not ill ...' (Roaring Girl Productions 2009).

In 2009, Rita Marcalo attempted to induce an epileptic seizure in a 12-hour live performance *Involuntary Dances* (Disability Arts Online 2012). The piece was inspired by a number of YouTube videos of epileptic seizures, filmed without the consent of the people with epilepsy in question. The piece attracted a lot of adverse media attention, highlighting how uncomfortable and angry people feel about invisible impairments being put on a stage. In terms of disability the performance raised issues about how the rights of disabled people to make our own decisions are often negated. In response to a review on Disability Arts Online (DAO), Allan Sutherland asked

> Why should not following the doctor's orders be such a transgressive act? ... Why should we not make our own decisions on such things? What right does anyone else have to tell us what to do with our own bodies?

> (Verrent 2009)

On 28 May 2012 Noëmi Lakmaier set out from Toynbee Studios in Tower Hamlets towards the Gherkin building in the City of London. This one-mile stroll was a slow and exhausting test of endurance, as she did it on her hands and knees. Smartly dressed in business attire she crawled through the streets of London, her clothes getting increasingly dirty and torn. After seven hours she crossed the border from the Borough of Tower Hamlets to the City of London. Through her live performance work, Noëmi has continually pushed the boundaries of the disabled body as 'object', challenging notions of the 'norm'. *One Morning in May* illustrates the lengths of endurance to which she will go to elicit responses and to challenge attitudes:

> I wanted to cross over the border of these worlds (poverty of Tower Hamlets versus affluence of City of London) in a slow and strenuous way, dressed as Them while clearly being Other, socially, politically, economically and physically.

> (Cleary 2012)

Lakmeier describes her piece as a 'role-play with the viewer who is forced into the dominant role through my action, forced to react in one way or another' (Cleary 2012).

Through its affirmation of impaired lives, Kaite O'Reilly's 2012 play *In Water I'm Weightless*, commissioned by Unlimited as part of the Cultural Olympiad, involves the audience in examining their own assumptions. The play opens with the lines:

I'm so, so sorry. It will happen to you. It will happen on a specific date at a fragmented hour and immediately everything you know will change. It will happen slowly, so inconsequentially that you will not notice until a moment before it is upon you and there is nothing you will be able to do to avoid it.

An acknowledgement is required that impairment is an inevitable part of life; that aspects of our physical, sensory and mental experience of the world will inevitably be altered by the ageing process, if not by circumstance. The five characters are played by disabled performers who delve into the lived experience of disability and impairment. The final monologue in the piece, 'A short history of fear', challenges the fear that the disabled body provokes in others:

the mongs, the spazzies, the shunned, the feared ... those intellectually challenged by hate and prejudice, not by brain circuitry. The schizos, the deafies, the crippled ... you threaten the narrow definition of human variety, you broaden the scope of *homo-sapiens* possibilities, you challenge normalcy, the normative, Norm ... and he hates you for it.

(O'Reilly 2012)

The speech addresses the centuries-old fear of disabled people expressed through myths and folklore which perpetuate notions of hatred and of pity.

The foregoing are clear examples of artistic practice inspired by the social model and affirming the identities of disabled people. The crucial point about Disability Arts is that it is informed by the experience of disability as a social role. Performing arts organisations like Graeae Theatre or CandoCo Dance Company emphasise accessible communication and performance techniques, but are nevertheless working within mainstream arts production genres. Though disabled performers/artists play a key role, these companies are producing arts for a mainstream setting. Disability Arts today is still, however, produced almost exclusively by and for disabled people.

For Discussion

- What role do you think Disability Arts has in empowering disabled people to take control of their lives?
- What impact do you think Disability Arts has in creating a framework for the way disabled people understand their experience?
- What do you think the value of Disability Arts is to a wider non-disabled audience?

Further Reading

Keidan, L. and Mitchell, C.J. (eds) (2012) *Access All Areas: Live Art and Disability*. London: Live Art Development Agency.

O'Reilly, K. (2002) *Peeling*. London: Faber and Faber Ltd.

Wilde, A. (2014) 'Disability culture: the story so far', in J. Swain, S. French, C. Barnes and S. Thomas (eds), *Disabling Barriers – Enabling Environments*, 3rd edn. London: Sage, pp. 114–121.

References

Cleary, M. (2012) *Preview: One Morning in May – Noëmi Lakmaier*, www.disabilityartsonline. org.uk/One-Morning-In_May-Noemi-Lakmaier, accessed 9 October 2012.

Disability Arts Online (2012) *Waking Up, Shaking Up*, www.disabilityartsonline.org.uk/ creativecase-live-art, accessed 9 October 2012.

Masefield, P. (2006) *Strength: Broadsides from Disability on the Arts*. Stoke-on-Trent: Trentham Books Ltd.

O'Reilly, K. (2012) *In Water I'm Weightless*. Unpublished. First produced Wales Millennium Centre/Southbank Centre, National Theatre Wales/Cultural Olympiad, August 2012.

Roaring Girl Productions (2009) *Resistance on the Plinth*, www.roaring-girl.co.uk/productions/ resistance-on-the-plinth/, accessed 9 October 2012.

Verrent, J. (2009) 'Review: Rita Marcalo's Involuntary Dances', www.disabilityartsonline. org/?location_id=1110, accessed 9 October 2012.

Williamson, A. (2008) Performance/Video/Collaboration. London: Live Art Development Agency and KIOSK.

11 Disability Research

Colin Cameron

While social scientists and sociologists have been researching disability since at least the 1950s (Barnes 2014), much of this research has been criticised by Disability Studies academics for taking an unexamined medical model as its foundation. That is, it is based on the view that disability and disadvantage are the direct outcomes of impairment. This can be seen, for example, in a series of questions developed during the 1980s by the UK Office of Censuses and Population Surveys (OPCS) to gather information about the lives of disabled people:

Are your difficulties in understanding others mainly due to a hearing problem?

Does your health problem/disability prevent you from going out as often or as far as you would like?

Does your health problem/disability affect your work in any way at present?

Does your health problem/disability mean that you need to live with relatives or someone else who can help or look after you?

Does your present accommodation have any adaptations because of your health problem/ disability?

(Oliver 1990, in Barnes and Mercer 2010: 33)

These questions are framed so that any information produced in response to them is bound to reinforce a way of thinking which regards disability as an individual problem. Oliver (1990) critiqued the OPCS survey, arguing that the questions here do not allow those asked to think about or indicate how far, if at all, social and environmental barriers are part of their everyday experience. Responding to the OCPS survey, Oliver developed a series of alternative, parallel questions rooted in the social model:

> Are your difficulties in understanding people mainly due to their inability to communicate with you?
>
> What is it about the local environment that makes it difficult for you to get about in your neighbourhood?
>
> Do you have any problems at work because of the physical environment or the attitudes of others?
>
> Are community services so poor that you need to rely on relatives or someone else to provide you with the right level of personal assistance?
>
> Did the poor design of your house mean that you had to have it adapted to suit your needs?
>
> (Oliver 1990, in Barnes and Mercer 2010: 33)

If we accept that the purpose of research is the production of new knowledge to illuminate decisions and actions, we can see that a different response would be required on the basis of disabled people's answers to this second set of questions. Rather than suggesting rehabilitative action aimed at adjusting disabled individuals to their environments, it is likely that responses to the social model questions would identify the need for change within the environments in which disabled people live.

The point is that research does not provide objective knowledge about the world from a neutral standpoint outside it, but always produces results implicit in its underlying assumptions. Research is always a creative and productive process which helps to produce the world (Oliver and Barnes 2012). Medical model research which treats as 'natural' and uncontroversial the understanding that disability is something 'wrong' with individual bodies is underpinned by the ideology of normality (Oliver 1996) and plays a part in maintaining disabling social relations. Disability Studies academics have criticised the myth of objectivity that has characterised much traditional disability research and have proposed an emancipatory paradigm for its development. Priestley has identified six core principles of emancipatory disability research:

1. The adoption of a social model of disability as the ontological and epistemological basis for research production (1997: 91)

This requires a shift not only in deciding about the nature of what we are looking at but about how we look for answers. As Barnes and Mercer (2010) have put it, the task of critical disability research is to examine the character and extent of social exclusion and the disadvantages facing disabled people. Involved here is a requirement to shift the focus of social research away from 'the problems of impairment' to identifying and understanding disabling physical and social barriers.

2. The surrender of falsely-premised claims to objectivity through overt political commitment to the struggles of disabled people for self-emancipation.

(Priestley 1997: 91)

This involves a rejection of the idea of researcher neutrality and of positivist claims that there is a world out there waiting to be 'revealed' through research (Mercer 2002). This is offset by a requirement to recognise and engage with the socially created nature of disability so that research challenges rather than sustains oppressive social relations.

3. The willingness only to undertake research where it will be of some practical benefit to the self-empowerment of disabled people and/or the removal of disabling barriers.

   (Priestley, 1997: 91)

Much disability research has been undertaken as a result of the academic interests of non-disabled researchers. Priestley here identifies the need for research to be linked to transformational activity identified by disabled people. Studies such as Beckett's survivor-led evaluation of a survivor-led crisis centre or Valentine's evaluation of a mental health service in North East Scotland (in Sweeney et al. 2009) are good examples of user-led research.

4. The devolution of control over research production to ensure full accountability to disabled people and their organisations.

   (Priestley, 1997: 91)

Whereas traditional research has involved unequal power relationships, viewing disabled people as the subjects of research carried out by expert researchers, there is a need for researchers to put their experience and skills in the hands of those involved, identifying with them as participants and collaborators, actively involved in determining the aims, methods and uses of research.

5. The ability to give voice to the personal while endeavouring to collectivise the commonality of disabling experiences and barriers.

   (Priestley, 1997: 91)

While traditional research has focused on disability as an individual problem, emancipatory research focuses on disability as a social issue experienced by individuals. The personal is political, and the impact of structural social relations is felt at the individual level. The voices of disabled people are key to understanding how disabling barriers are experienced both personally and collectively.

6. The willingness to adopt a plurality of methods for data collection and analysis in response to the changing needs of disabled people.

   (Priestley, 1997: 91)

'Methods' refer to the specific techniques used in data collection, for example, surveys, focus groups or interviews (Mercer 2002). In emphasising the importance of accessibility in emancipatory disability research, this principle places a responsibility on the researcher to be creative and inventive in research design. As Mercer suggests (2002: 242), there is a responsibility 'to make transparent how the research unfolds, from design through data collection, analysis and recommendations'.

Attention has been drawn by Disability Studies scholars to the challenging issues raised when translating these ideas into practice (Mercer 2004). As research can only be judged to be emancipatory in terms of its outcomes, in hindsight and whether it has brought about positive changes to the lives of disabled people, for a researcher to say 'I am doing emancipatory research' is perhaps to speak over-confidently. It could be argued that the principles identified here should be most usefully regarded as a set of guidelines while emancipatory research remains an aspiration.

For Discussion

- Esterberg (2002: 9) suggests that 'If theories are stories about the way the world (or some portion of it) works, then they are always in a state of revision, and there are always other, alternative stories that could be told'. What significance might emancipatory research principles have in the development of new stories about disability?
- What is the difference between being a research *subject* and a research *participant*?
- What is meant when it is said that the idea that there is a world out there waiting to be 'revealed' through research is rejected? What implications does this have for disability research?

Further Reading

Barnes, C. (2014) 'Reflections on doing emancipatory research', in J. Swain, S. French, C. Barnes and C. Thomas (eds), *Disabling Barriers – Enabling Environments*, 3rd edn. London: Sage, pp. 37–44.
Barnes, C. and Mercer, G. (2010) *Exploring Disability*, 2nd edn. Cambridge: Polity.
Sweeney, A., Beresford, P., Faulkner, A., Nettle, M. and Rose, D. (eds) (2009) *This is Survivor Research*. Ross-on-Wye: PCCS Books.

References

Barnes, C. (2014) 'Reflections on doing emancipatory research', in J. Swain, S. French, C. Barnes and C. Thomas (eds), *Disabling Barriers – Enabling Environments*, 3rd edn. London: Sage, pp. 37–44.
Barnes, C. and Mercer, G. (2010) *Exploring Disability*, 2nd edn. Cambridge: Polity.
Esterberg, K.G. (2002) *Qualitative Methods in Social Research*. Maidenhead: McGraw-Hill.
Mercer, G. (2002) 'Emancipatory disability research', in M. Barnes, M. Oliver and L. Barton (eds), *Disability Studies Today*. Cambridge: Polity, pp. 228–49.
Mercer, G. (2004) 'From critique to practice: emancipatory disability research', in C. Barnes and G. Mercer (eds), *Implementing the Social Model of Disability: Theory and Practice*. Leeds: The Disability Press, pp. 118–37.
Oliver, M. (1990) *The Politics of Disablement*. Basingstoke: Macmillan.
Oliver, M. (1996) *Understanding Disability: From Theory to Practice*. Basingstoke: Macmillan.
Oliver, M. and Barnes, C. (2012) *The New Politics of Disablement*. Basingstoke: Palgrave Macmillan.
Priestley, M. (1997) 'Whose research? A personal audit', in C. Barnes and G. Mercer (eds), *Doing Disability Research*. Leeds: The Disability Press, pp. 88–107.
Sweeney, A., Beresford, P., Faulkner, A., Nettle, M. and Rose, D. (eds) (2009) *This is Survivor Research*. Ross-on-Wye: PCCS Books.

12   Disability Studies

Colin Cameron and Michele Moore

It might be helpful in defining Disability Studies to state, first of all, what it is not. Disability Studies does not involve the study of bodies or 'conditions'. Just as Women's Studies does not involve the study of women's biology to critique the social construction and experience of gender and gender inequality, neither does Disability Studies regard impairment as being a relevant starting point for the analysis of disabling social relations. Disability Studies does not deal with how to 'care' for disabled people. Rather, it offers a distinct critical perspective on the mechanisms society has used to exclude disabled people and on how these can be challenged.

Disability Studies emerged as a discipline in the UK through the research and teaching of disabled scholar Mike Oliver in the early 1980s. As Barton (2010) describes, Disability Studies evolved at a time when 'both nationally and internationally disabled people and their organisations were involved in serious struggles over the establishment of empowering conceptions of disability, rights, citizenship and independent living'. The pioneering advocacy of disabled people was significant in establishing Disability Studies within higher education and accordingly Mike Oliver later became the first Professor of Disability Studies in the UK (see Oliver 1993).

Oliver's ideas on the social model of disability were at the heart of the newly emerging discipline, enabling disability to be understood as a form of social oppression and so linked to issues of equity, social justice and human rights. As Disability Studies began to gain influence in higher education it developed as an interdisciplinary academic discipline, drawing on sociology, social policy, linguistics, economics, anthropology, politics, history, psychology and media studies (Swain et al. 2003). Nowadays Disability Studies is the basis for foundation degrees, first degrees, postgraduate, doctoral and research programmes around the world, extensively researched, debated and theorised but most important of all, applied. It was always part of Mike Oliver's teaching that Disability Studies should seek to bridge the gap between the academy and the actuality of disabled people's lives (Moore 2010). He insisted that Disability Studies should have direct impact on the dismantling of disabling barriers and that it would not be sufficient for its teachings to make a difference solely within the world of the academy.

In 1986 the journal *Disability & Society* was founded by Mike Oliver and Len Barton, providing a forum for the development of critical debate that is intended always to privilege the voices and experience of disabled people in a critique of models, assumptions, policies and practices relating to disability based on individualised deficit views and assumptions. The journal's sustained impact on the actuality of disabled people's lives is known across the world (Moore 2012). There are regular academic conferences concerned with Disability Studies, and a growing list of new scholarly journals, including *The Scandinavian Journal of Disability Research*, *The Journal of Literary and Critical Disability Studies*, and *Disability Studies Quarterly*.

The social model approach at the centre of Disability Studies courses enables students to critically contest ideas enshrined in traditional teaching and training courses which emphasised individualised 'problems' of impairment. Before Disability Studies, teaching and training which dealt with disability typically focused on instruction in the recognition of 'defects', testing for 'defect', and instruction in categories of defect and intervention, mostly with a focus on cure, therapy, rehabilitation and control. This education failed to reconcile programme content with the knowledge and aspirations of disabled people themselves (Moore and Slee 2012). Through Disability Studies, the failure to address institutional causes of disablement was addressed. The interrogation of policy frameworks and the analysis of power and injustice became key. Gradually the implications of the social model of disability itself have been critiqued and new affirmative and other models of disability emerged, offering a wide range of 'social' perspectives on the nature of impairment and disability (Cameron 2008; Thomas 2007).

It has remained essential within Disability Studies that the voices of disabled people must always be enlisted in the building of ideas, theories and practices (Barton 2003; Moore 2000; Moore and Slee 2012; Oliver 2009). Barton (2010) insists that the voices of disabled people must be raised and that Disability Studies scholars are always concerned with 'the issue of change and the development and maintenance of an inclusive, non-discriminatory and non-oppressive social world'.

Since Disability Studies emerged through disabled people's struggles, it is desirable that it should continue to be a site for open disagreements and creative tensions between different commentators. There are some disturbing agendas and challenges relating to genetic engineering, bioethics and euthanasia, for example, that must be explored. Of course impairment is not the only determinant of disability and so the relationship and difference between disability, class, race, gender, sexuality, religion, work and poverty must be rigorously examined. The role of research in disabled people's lives has to be scrutinised to ensure disabled people play a meaningful role in the inception, conduct, analysis and dissemination of enquiries that will impact on their lives.

Increasingly the global agenda for Disability Studies is expanding, with more work in the field emanating from the majority world (Moore 2012). This has forged new imperatives for critical attention to the challenges of cross-cultural issues in relation to disablist assumptions, language and processes of empowerment, for example. The scope of Disability Studies is ever-expanding to keep up with new situations and to sustain forms of resistance associated with global conflicts and crises faced by disabled people in the twenty-first century. Deepening global conflicts and crises, and how these impact on disabled people's lives, are many and complex and in need of constant engagement. These include widening inequality associated with deepening poverty in some parts of the world and multiple financial, industrial, agrarian and economic challenges. Social revolutions and transformations, conflict and war impact on disabled people's lives in hitherto unknown ways. Environmental challenges, upheavals in cultures and beliefs, new global activism and alliances, all require responsive approaches to theorising disability in challenging contexts informed by the perspectives of disabled people themselves.

Such concerns affirm the critical importance of keeping Disability Studies at the forefront of academic life. Disability Studies involves not just the study of disabled people's lives, but the interdependency between all lives. As an academic discipline, Disability Studies is not only concerned with revealing that disability impacts on the lives of people with impairments. It establishes new modes of inclusion in which each individual's sense of self is enmeshed and entwined with knowledge of what has been excluded. Disability Studies is about you and about the world you aspire to be part of.

For Discussion

- Think about your own world of scholarship; discuss the most contentious disability issues you feel need to be addressed. Is there agreement amongst your peers on the importance of these issues?
- There are bi-annual Special Issues of *Disability & Society* which address selected themes and, from 2012 onwards, Virtual Special Issues in which retrospective collections of some of the most significant papers to have been published in the history of the journal are pulled together by serving Executive Editors. Have a look at some of these and consider the new insights and questions that these resources give you.
- What are your aspirations for the future of Disability Studies and how can you work towards these?

Further Reading

Barnes, C. (2014) 'Disability, disability studies and the academy', in J. Swain, S. French, C. Barnes and S. Thomas (eds), *Disabling Barriers – Enabling Environments*, 3rd edn. London: Sage, pp. 17–23.

Goodley, D. (2011) *Disability Studies: An Interdisciplinary Introduction*. London: Sage.

Oliver, M. and Barnes, C. (2012) *The New Politics of Disablement*. Basingstoke: Palgrave Macmillan.

References

Barton, L. (2003) *Inclusive Education and Teacher Education: A Basis for Hope or a Discourse of Delusion*. London: Institute of Education University of London.

Barton, L. (2010) 'Interview with Professor Len Barton', editor of *Disability & Society*. Transcription version of record first published 4 January 2010, www.educationarena.com/pdf/lbarton_transcript.pdf.

Cameron, C. (2008) 'Further towards an affirmation model', in T. Campbell, F. Fontes, L. Hemingway, A. Soorenian and C. Till (eds), *Disability Studies: Emerging Insights and Perspectives*. Leeds: The Disability Press, pp. 14–30.

Moore, M. (2000) *Insider Perspectives on Inclusion: Raising Voices, Raising Issues*. Sheffield: Philip Armstrong.

Moore, M. (2010) 'Personal reflections', *Disability & Society*, 25 (1): 1–2.

Moore, M. (ed.) (2012) *Moving Beyond Boundaries in Disability Studies: Rights, Spaces and Innovation*. Abingdon: Taylor & Francis.

Moore, M. and Slee, R. (2012) 'Disability studies, inclusive education and exclusion', in C. Thomas, N. Watson and A. Roulstone (eds), *Routledge Handbook of Disability Studies*. Routledge, pp. 225–39.

Oliver, M. (1993) 'What's so wonderful about walking?' Inaugural Professorial Lecture University of Greenwich, London, http://disability-studies.leeds.ac.uk/files/library/Oliver-PROFLEC.pdf.

Oliver, M. (2009) *Understanding Disability: From Theory to Practice*. Basingstoke: Macmillan.

Swain, J. French, S. and Cameron, C. (2003) *Controversial Issues in a Disabling Society*. Maidenhead: Open University Press.

Thomas, C. (2007) *Sociologies of Disability and Illness: Contested Ideas in Disability Studies and Medical Sociology*. Basingstoke: Palgrave Macmillan.

13

The Disabled People's Movement

Colin Cameron

While the 1960s are looked back on as a decade of radical social change, little seemed to happen during this decade to progress the rights and freedoms of disabled people. As Oliver noted (2009), Bob Dylan may have sung '*the times they are a-changin*', but this was not the experience of disabled people incarcerated within residential homes and institutions; effectively positioned as 'socially dead', their impairments identified as being the cause of their social problems and restrictions (Mercer 2002). Nevertheless, and although there is evidence of a longer radical tradition among groups of disabled people in Britain (Humphries and Gordon 1992), it is during the 1960s that the beginnings of a self-organised social movement of disabled people are found.

Pivotal to the development of the disabled people's movement was Paul Hunt who, on the basis of his own experiences in a residential home, had begun to develop an understanding of disability as social oppression:

> We are challenging society to take account of us, to listen to what we have to say, to acknowledge us as an integral part of society itself. We do not want ourselves, or anyone else, treated as second-class citizens and put away out of sight and mind.

> (Hunt 1966: 157).

By the late 1960s disabled people were beginning to collectively question the purposes and legitimacy of large charities organised to speak on behalf of people with specific impairments and seeking to organise disabled people's lives. Charities began to be identified as part of the problem of disability rather than as part of the solution. Hunt became increasingly involved in acts of resistance, organising and encouraging disabled people in residential homes to take over the management or to break out. In September

1972 he had a letter published in the *Guardian* newspaper, inviting other disabled people to write to him:

> Severely physically handicapped people find themselves in isolated, unsuitable institutions, where their views are ignored and they are subject to authoritarian and often cruel regimes. I am proposing the formation of a consumer group to put forward nationally the views of actual and potential residents of these successors of the workhouse.

(in Campbell and Oliver 1996: 65)

Many disabled people responded to this letter, and their correspondence led to the formation of the Union of the Physically Impaired Against Segregation (UPIAS). UPIAS was established as a forum for debate about disability issues *by* disabled people living in residential homes. UPIAS rejected the idea that organisations *for* disabled people – led by non-disabled people – were able to comprehend or promote the best interests of disabled people. While the key aim of UPIAS was the eradication of all segregated 'special' homes, perhaps the most important and lasting contribution this group made to the development of the disabled people's movement was the establishment of definitions of impairment and disability that would become known as the social model (Barnes 2004).

From the late 1970s, more and more organisations formed and led by disabled people emerged to add to increasingly loud demands for equality. The British Council of Organisations of Disabled People (BCODP) was formed in 1981 in a day centre in London by representatives of nine of these organisations. Only organisations at least 51 per cent controlled by disabled people were eligible for membership of BCODP (Campbell 1997).

Gradually the social model of disability was extended beyond the interests of people with physical impairments to include those with sensory, emotional and cognitive impairments (Barnes 1994). Deaf people, blind people, people with mental health issues and people with learning difficulties, for example, became increasingly active in the disability movement. This involved the development of an understanding that the interests of people with different impairments are not separate, and that disabled people have much to gain by talking to each other:

> We break through the idea, presented to us by the medical profession and disability charities in particular, that our situations are different and unrelated, and come together not as the blind or the deaf or the epileptic, or the spastic or the arthritic, but as disabled people.

(Sutherland 2004: unpaged)

The 1980s saw the appearance of various forms of social action and political activity carried out by organisations of disabled people across Britain, uniting under the BCODP umbrella. Following the establishment in Derbyshire of the first Coalition of Disabled People and Centre for Integrated Living (CIL) (Derbyshire Coalition of Disabled People 2007), further coalitions of disabled people emerged across the UK in which disabled people came together to collectively debate and raise issues; around housing, education, employment, public transport, information and leisure opportunities. The coalitions ensured these issues were drawn to the attention of local service providers and politicians. The Campaign for Independent Living saw new CILs being organised. A national network of disability arts forums developed. Organisations such as Disability Equality in

Education and the Alliance for Inclusive Education emerged to promote inclusion in school education. Disability Studies grew as a distinct academic discipline, critiquing the ways in which society has been organised to exclude people with impairments.

During the early 1990s media attention was drawn to a number of demonstrations in which disabled people came together to make their voices heard. Handcuffing themselves to buses and throwing themselves out of their wheelchairs, campaigners blocked London rush-hour traffic in order to draw attention to the lack of accessible public transport. In 1992 there was a major demonstration by 2,000 disabled protestors who successfully called on a major UK TV station to scrap an annual fund-raising event that represented disabled people as tragic charity cases. The success of such activity led to the formation in 1993 of the Disabled People's Direct Action Network (DAN). Using 'tactics of non-violent civil disobedience to promote the full participation and equality of disabled people in society' (Bowler and Rose 2007), DAN continues to demonstrate for accessible transport, affordable, accessible homes, and against benefit cuts.

Campbell has said that 'the disability movement is a jigsaw – each piece is vital for the true picture to emerge' (Campbell and Oliver 1996: 199). I have given a condensed, introductory outline of where the disabled people's movement has come from, what it has been about, and what it has achieved. Further reading will reveal complex struggles within the movement over issues relating to gender and disability; ethnicity and disability; and the rights of impairment groups to develop their own cultures and organisations and yet retain solidarity with the wider disabled people's movement. While it could be argued that the biggest achievements of the movement have included the establishment of anti-discrimination legislation and the shift in the delivery of local services towards self-directed support, it needs to be remembered that the best way to kill a movement is to give it a little of what it demands. While some progress has been made, much remains to be done. The ascendance of neo-liberal individualism at the expense of collectivist politics means the future of the movement will require commitment and determination in the face of complacency.

For Discussion

- Why is disability a political issue?
- Why have disabled people argued that only their own organisations, rather than organisations controlled by non-disabled people, can speak authentically about issues that affect their lives?
- Why might it be considered troubling to see disabled people involved in political demonstrations?

Further Reading

Campbell, J. and Oliver, M. (1996) *Disability Politics: Understanding Our Past, Changing Our Future*. London: Routledge.

Hunt, P. (2014) 'A critical condition', in J. Swain, S. French, C. Barnes and S. Thomas (eds), *Disabling Barriers – Enabling Environments*, 3rd edn. London: Sage, pp. 3–5.

Manchester Mule (2010) 'Interview – Disabled People's Direct Action Network', http://manchestermule. com/article/interview-disabled-peoples-direct-action-network, accessed 5 October 2012.

References

Barnes, C. (1994) *Disabled People in Britain and Discrimination: A Case for Anti-Discrimination Legislation*. London: Hurst and Co.

Barnes, C. (2004) 'Reflections on doing emancipatory disability research' in J. Swain, French, S., Barnes, C. and Thomas, C. *Disabling Barriers – Enabling Environments*, 2nd edn. London: Sage, pp. 47–53.

Bowler, E. and Rose, D. (2007) Who is DAN? www.bbc.co.uk/ouch/news/btn/danqa.shtml, accessed 21 January 2007.

Campbell, J. (1997) 'Growing pains: disability politics – the journey explained and described', in L. Barton and M. Oliver (eds), *Disability Studies: Past, Present and Future*. Leeds: Disability Press, pp. 78–89.

Campbell, J. and Oliver, M. (1996) *Disability Politics: Understanding Our Past, Changing Our Future*. London: Routledge.

Derbyshire Coalition of Disabled People (2007) *About DCDP*, www.dcil.org.uk/AboutDCDP, accessed 22 January 2010.

Humphries, S. and Gordon, P. (1992) *Out of Sight: The Experience of Disability*. Plymouth: Northcote House.

Hunt, P. (ed.) (1966) *Stigma: The Experience of Disability*. London: Geoffrey Chapman.

Mercer, G. (2002) 'Emancipatory disability research', in C. Barnes, M. Oliver and L. Barton (eds), *Disability Studies Today*. Cambridge: Polity, pp. 228–49.

Oliver, M. (2009) *Understanding Disability: From Theory to Practice*, 2nd edn. Basingstoke: Macmillan.

Sutherland, A. (2004) *What is Disability Arts?* www.disabilityarts.com/dao/what-is-disarts, accessed 30 November 2007.

14

Discrimination

Colin Cameron

At its most basic level, discrimination is about the identification of difference. This is an ordinary and uncontroversial part of life. When we decide every day what clothes to wear or what food to eat we discriminate in favour of some things over others. As Thompson puts it, we would experience major difficulty if we were unable to distinguish between, say, safety and danger or friendship and hostility (Thompson 2010: 5). There is nothing inherently wrong in identifying differences, moreover, between, for example, men and women, black or white, young and old or disabled and non-disabled people. Difference is what makes humanity diverse and interesting. In the context of Disability Studies and disabled people's lives, however, discrimination becomes a problem when difference forms the basis for privileging one group over another and for treating people unequally and unfairly.

Thompson suggests that discrimination takes two main forms, personal and institutional. Of personal discrimination, he says:

> This can be deliberate, for example, when someone is acting on the basis of an overt dislike of, or prejudice towards, a particular individual or group. However, it can also be unwitting – for example, when someone makes a discriminatory assumption about someone else (acting on the basis of a misleading stereotype perhaps) without necessarily intending to discriminate against that person.

(Thompson 2010: 6)

I recall while working in my first job as a residential social worker, going with Keith (not his real name), a young man with autism, to a bar in Windsor. It was a bar that was popular with young people and Keith enjoyed it. We had been there a few times before the manager asked us to leave, saying he had received complaints that Keith's rocking movements were upsetting other customers. We had no choice but to get out. This was one form of personal discrimination, where Keith was excluded because of prejudice against disabled people.

I cannot begin to recollect the number of times when, as a young man, I walked into bars with a friend or two and went to order drinks, only to be told 'I'm not serving you … You've had enough to drink already.' On the basis of the fact that I walked with a limp and talked slowly as a result of brain injuries acquired years earlier, I was taken to be drunk. It was not that bar staff intended to discriminate against me as a disabled person, nevertheless this was the outcome.

Thompson describes institutional discrimination as meaning 'that discrimination can often arise, not so much as a result of personal prejudice, but because of the way an organisation works' (Thompson 2010: 6). He outlines two types of institutional discrimination, cultural and structural. Cultural refers to:

> sets of taken-for-granted assumptions, shared meanings or 'unwritten rules' that develop amongst groups of people … These can be very powerful because they often influence us without our knowing that they are doing so (as a result of the fact that we have become 'socialised' into a particular culture over time and thus internalised it to the extent that it shapes how we see the world – it becomes our 'normality').

(Thompson 2010: 6)

A disabled friend of mine recently told teachers at her son's school that she was uncomfortable about her boy having to participate in planned Children in Need activities. Children in Need is an annual BBC television charity fundraising event involving 'celebrities' recycling images of 'tragic', 'needy', 'grateful' disabled children. My friend was met with bafflement and some hostility, as the teachers regarded Children in Need as being principally about 'fun' and could see nothing wrong with it. Taking a stand against practices which reinforce disablism can involve disabled people having to become involved in unwanted confrontation and being labelled as complainers, impacting on how they are regarded by service providers.

Structural institutional discrimination refers to:

the set of inter-relationships that influence power and opportunities. This includes hierarchies within organisations ... as well as broader social structures ... and established sets of relationships that influence the distribution of power and life chances.

(Thompson 2010: 7)

A postgraduate student with experience of mental health issues was advised a few years back by a disability officer at a UK university not to tick the 'disabled' box on a job application form (Cameron 2011). The thinking behind this was that to disclose her mental health issues would be to prejudice this student's chances of getting a job interview. Yet in this advice the disability officer not only colluded in and left discriminatory practices unchallenged, but reinforced for the student the perception that impairment is something to be hidden and denied. The student was at a loss about how to regard her situation as anything other than negative when even those meant to support her confirmed this.

Thompson points out that discrimination is a matter of outcomes, rather than intentions. It is easy, he states, for people to discriminate unfairly against others without realising they are doing it because discrimination is not simply a matter of overt prejudice (Thompson 2010: 7). Because dominant perceptions are so thoroughly wrapped up with assumptions about the tragic nature of disability, discriminatory judgements set the context for everyday life as experienced by disabled people and very often pass without remark.

It might be hoped that, since the passing of the Disability Discrimination Act in 1995, things must have become better in the UK. The situation with Keith described above happened in the 1980s. My being refused drinks in bars happened mostly in the 1980s and '90s. Such things are illegal now and, surely, don't happen today?

Sarah, a young wheelchair-user I interviewed in Cameron (2010), described discriminatory judgements she was subjected to when out for a meal in a restaurant in Edinburgh with a boyfriend who is also disabled:

You'd go into a restaurant and stuff, and it'd be like 'Oh, is there someone with you?' ... why can't you see us just like any ordinary couple going out ... why is there this big palaver which then makes us feel more ... abnormal, if you like.

(Cameron 2010: 125)

The query 'is there someone with you?' indicates puzzlement at the fact that two young disabled people are out on their own without a 'carer'. This is discrimination, for the question would not be asked of other people; it has an undermining impact on a disabled person's sense of self, suggesting their competence and right to be present is in doubt.

Discrimination can be present in both large and small judgements experienced by disabled people, for example, in decisions made about employment opportunities or the ways in which goods and services are delivered. It has a corrosive influence because it places unequal limitations on life opportunities and possibilities. As

Oliver and Barnes have observed, the prohibition of disability discrimination by law has done little to eliminate this (2012: 175). Just as race and gender discrimination are still institutionalised in organisational cultures and structures throughout society some forty years after the introduction of legislation to outlaw these, so it seems likely that disability discrimination will take a long time to disappear.

For Discussion

The Equality Act 2010 identifies and makes illegal seven types of discrimination:

- direct discrimination
- associative discrimination
- perceptive discrimination
- indirect discrimination
- harassment
- third-party harassment
- victimisation.

What kinds of behaviour does each of these descriptions refer to? Think of examples from your own experience.

In what way was disability discrimination often institutionalised in organisational culture and practice?

Why do you think diability discrimination is sometimes hard to identify?

Further Reading

Johnson, M. (2003) *Make Them Go Away: Clint Eastwood, Christopher Reeve and the Case Against Disability Rights*. Louisville, KY: Advocado Press.

Thompson, N. (2012) *Anti-Discriminatory Practice: Equality, Diversity and Social Justice*, 5th edn. Basingstoke: Palgrave Macmillan.

Wilson-Kovacs, Ryan, M., Haslam, S. and Rabinovich, A. (2008) '"Just because you can get a wheelchair in the building doesn't necessarily mean that you can still participate": barriers to the career advancement of disabled professionals', *Disability & Society*, 23 (7): 705–17.

References

Cameron, C. (2010) 'Does anybody like being disabled? A critical exploration of impairment, identity, media and everyday experience in a disabling society'. PhD thesis, Queen Margaret University, http://etheses.qmu.ac.uk/258/1/258.pdf.

Cameron, C. (2011) 'Not our problem: impairment as difference, disability as role', *The Journal of Inclusive Practice in Further and Higher Education*, 3 (2): 10–25.

Oliver, M. and Barnes, C. (2012) *The New Politics of Disablement*. Basingstoke: Palgrave Macmillan.

Thompson, N. (2010) *Promoting Equality, Valuing Diversity: A Learning and Training Manual*. Lyme Regis: Russell House.

15

Education (Post-compulsory)

Nicola Martin

UK providers of post-compulsory education are subject to The Equality Act (2010). This incorporates previously separate strands of legislation, including the Disability Discrimination Act (1995). The Equality Act serves students and others covered by nine protected characteristics – age, disability, gender reassignment, marriage and civil partnership, pregnancy and maternity, race, religion and belief, sex and sexual orientation.

Before the 1980s there was minimal provision for disabled students in further and higher education (FE and HE) (Borland and James 1999). While the OFFA (the Office for Fair Access to higher education) scrutinizes the engagement of universities with disabled students, The Children and Families Bill (2012–13), going through the House of Lords at the time of writing, deemphasizes higher education as a viable post-school destination. While the number of disabled students in UK universities is increasing (Equality Challenge Unit 2012), FE colleges struggle to offer equal access to learners carrying the 'learning difficulty' label – particularly those with profound multiple impairments (National Union of Students, 2011). Developing an appropriate curriculum for students who are deemed a challenge to conventional notions of adult learning requires imagination (Tomlinson 1996). FE disengaged from the requirements of such individuals can hardly claim to comply with the spirit of The Equality Act, but progressing to a specialist segregated college for disabled students is still a common trajectory for learners thought to present too many challenges to mainstream FE (Chown and Bevan 2011).

Finance is available to assist UK disabled students to access FE (Additional Support Funding) and HE (The Disabled Student Allowance, DSA). Joint funding arrangements involving Social Services are necessary when personal care is required (National Union of Students 2010). With very rare exceptions international disabled students cannot get funding for personal care. Students with expensive requirements are vulnerable, particularly in the present economic climate. DSA is insufficient, for example, to cover full costs of British Sign Language interpretation, although institutions should cover shortfall and students should not incur disability-related costs.

Though the social model requires that disabling barriers should be identified and minimised (Barnes 2004), disability is often problematised rather than celebrated as a valued strand of diversity. While equality legislation has theoretically evolved to recognise multiple identities (Parken 2010), terms like 'special needs' still insult and oppress disabled students (Valentine 2002).

Disabled students and Critical Disability Studies academics co-exist in institutions, yet there is scant evidence of cross-fertilisation of ideas (Cameron 2011). Peer reviewed publications like *The Journal of Inclusive Practice in Further and Higher Education* (which aims explicitly to further disability equality post-school) have no status within the Research Excellence Framework (REF). Critical Disability Studies theory is rarely related practically to college and university contexts in ways which challenge the requirement for a 'diagnosis' (disabled naming) as a gateway to services.

Disabled students with unseen impairments (Equality Challenge Unit 2012) often did not identify as disabled until undertaking diagnostic interventions in order to access services dependant on disabled naming. Labels, such as *dyslexic*, may be acquired as a result of a student having failed an aspect of their course.

Many students fear discrimination and it is incumbent on the institution to address this concern. Aspects of 'competency standards' defined by certain professional bodies (social work, teaching, and branches of medicine) may indeed represent institutional disablism (Murphy 2008).

Emancipatory research principles (Oliver 2009) could underpin proactive change as required by The Equality Act. An approach in which 'researchers engage in explicit, self-aware analysis of their own role' (Finlay 2002: 531) may enlighten staff who work with disabled students. Foucault's understanding of power relationships is certainly relevant for staff undertaking research on student experience (Foucault 1982; McIntosh 2002).

Inclusive practice entails developing community by promoting a sense of belonging (Tomlinson 1996). The 2010 guidance from the Higher Education Funding Council (HEFCE) and Quality Assurance Agency for HE (QAA) encourages a culture in which the whole student journey, from pre-entry to post-exit, models anti-discriminatory practices. In reality, 'special' resources accessed following 'disclosure' run counter to inclusive practice and disenfranchise those wishing to keep their diagnosis private (Griffin and Pollak 2009). Stereotyping by impairment label (e.g. 'this is the package for deaf students') is also a concern (Atkinson et al. 2011).

Incorporating impairment-related student services into a well-being agenda alongside financial support, childcare and similar services (Marshall and Morris 2011) treats impairment as ordinary (Cameron 2008, 2011) and addresses disabling barriers alongside other obstacles (such as lack of affordable childcare). Disability and impairment are not automatic bedfellows, and disabling barriers need not be inevitable.

For Discussion

- What might be the benefits of a post-compulsory education in which emancipatory research principles apply and disabled students, staff and critical Disability Studies scholars work together to improve the student experience?
- Consider potential tensions between inclusive practice and student services which are dependent on disabled naming. Think about possible improvements.
- What more could be done to consistently promote equality for disabled students in post-compulsory education?

Further Reading

HEFCE (2010) *Key Outcomes of HEFCE Review of Policy as it Relates to Disabled Students*, December 2009/49. Bristol: Higher Education Funding Council for England.

QAA (2010) *Code of Practice for the Assurance of Academic Quality and Standards in Higher Education. Section 3. Disabled students*. London: QAA.

Tomlinson, J. (1996) *Inclusive Practice*. London: Further Education Funding Council.

References

Atkinson, R., Evans, S., Gandy, C., Graham, C., Hendrick, S., Jackson, V. and Martin, N. (2011) 'A buddy scheme – supporting transition and progression for students identified with Asperger syndrome', *Journal of Inclusive Practice in Further and Higher Education*, 3 (2): 109–24.

Barnes, C. (2004) 'Disability, disability studies and the academy', in J. Swain, S. French, C. Barnes and C. Thomas (eds), *Disabling Barriers – Enabling Environments*. London. Sage, pp. 28–34.

Borland, J. and James, S. (1999) 'The learning experience of students with disabilities in higher education. A case study of a UK university', *Disability & Society*, 14 (1): 85–101.

Cameron, C. (2008) 'Further towards an affirmative model', in T. Campbell, P. Dawson, P. Eyre, F. Fontes, L. Hemingway and C. Till (eds), *Disability Studies: Emerging Insights and Perspectives*. Leeds: The Disability Press, pp. 14–30.

Cameron, C. (2011) 'Not our problem: disability as role', *Journal of Inclusive Practice in Further and Higher Education*, 3 (2): 10–25.

Children and Families Bill (2012–13), http://services.parliament.uk/bills/2012-13/childrenand families. html.

Chown, N. and Bevan, N. (2011) 'Intellectually capable but socially excluded? A review of the literature and research on students with autism in further education', *Journal of Further and Higher Education*, 35 (4): 1–17.

Disability Discrimination Act 1995, www.legislation.gov.uk/id/ukpga/1995/50.

Equality Act 2010, homeoffice.gov.uk/equalities/equality-act/.

Equality Challenge Unit (2012) *Higher Education Statistical Report*. London: Equality Challenge Unit, www.ecu.ac.uk/publications/equality-in-he-stats-11.

Finlay, L. (2002) 'Outing the researcher: the provenance, process and practice of reflexivity', *Qualitative Health Research*, 12 (4): 531–45.

Foucault, M. (1982) 'The subject and power', *Critical Enquiry*, 8 (94): 777–95.

Griffin, E. and Pollak, D. (2009) 'Student experiences of neurodiversity in higher education: insights from the BRAINHE project', *Dyslexia: An International Journal of Research and Practice*, 15 (1): 23–41.

HEFCE (2010) *Key Outcomes of HEFCE Review of Policy as it Relates to Disabled Students*, December 2009/49. Bristol: Higher Education Funding Council of England.

Marshall, L. and Morris, C. (2011) *Taking Wellbeing Forward in Higher Education: Reflections on Theory and Practice*. Brighton: University of Brighton Press.

McIntosh, D. (2002) 'An archi-texture of learning disability services: the use of Michel Foucault', *Disability & Society*, 17 (1): 65–79.

Murphy, F. (2008) *The Clinical Experience of Dyslexic Healthcare Students*, www.sciencedirect. com/science.

National Union of Students (2010) *Life not Numbers: The Experience of Disabled Students in Higher Education Using Personal Care Packages*. London: NUS.

National Union of Students (2011), www.nus.org.uk/en/campaigns/disability/finding-the-way-in-fe/.

Office for Fair Access (OFFA) www.offa.org.uk/.

Oliver, M. (2009) *Understanding Disability, from Theory to Practice*, 2nd edn. Basingstoke: Palgrave Macmillan.

Parken, A. (2010) 'A multi-strand approach to promoting equalities and human rights in policy making', *Policy and Politics*, 38 (1): 79–99.

Tomlinson, J. (1996) *Inclusive Practice*. London: Further Education Funding Council.

Valentine, J. (2002) 'Naming and narrating disability in Japan', in M. Corker and T. Shakespeare (eds), *Embodying Disability Theory: Disability and Postmodernism*. London: Continuum, pp. 213–27.

16   Education (School)

Dawn Benson

In writing this short chapter about education and disability I draw upon my own experiences as a disabled person, as an academic in both Disability Studies and inclusive education, and as a parent of disabled children. In particular I attempt to outline the position of disabled children in education and relay their perspectives.

Access to, and the quality of, education for disabled children has been politicised by the disabled people's movement. Writers such as Barton and Armstrong (2007), Moore and Slee (2012) and Oliver and Barnes (2012) have argued that education for disabled children is a civil/human rights issue which should not be separated from other sociological debates, and that failure to provide all children with meaningful educational experiences denies them citizenship. As with other social structures, such as family and employment, disabling factors which militate against education and citizenship involve exclusion, oppression and discrimination rather than impairment (Barton 2012). It is for this reason that I refer to 'disabled children', dispensing with the commonly used term 'special need' or 'special educational need' (SEN), except in reference to policy documents.

It is important to note that 'special' education is not the same as inclusive education, although they are often associated with one another, particularly by those people who support the principles of 'special' education. The distinction lies in the fact that special education aligns itself to diagnoses and labels which are in turn levied alongside notions of being 'special' and having 'need'. The idea that a child has a 'special' need is then used in attempts to justify their separation and segregation from their non-disabled peers (Rioux and Pinto 2012). Such separation is what perpetuates their exclusion and marginalisation from mainstream society (Armstrong and Barton 2007; Barnes and Mercer 2010). Inclusive education, however, is built upon the idea that children are entitled to an education that is equitable to that of their non-disabled peers (Corbett and Slee 2000). Any notion of need is therefore associated with the school, as it can then be seen that schools have a responsibility to provide inclusive and equitable education to all children irrespective of impairment or other factors such as race, gender, religion, parental background or economic circumstance (Barton 2012). It is important to note that impairment is not the sole determinant of exclusion, nor does being a disabled child make exclusion inevitable, however a combination of factors increase the likelihood of neither gaining qualifications and employment or of marginalisation from mainstream society (Burchardt 2005). Therefore, schools might 'need' to acquire resources, alter practice or engage in staff training to enable them to be inclusive.

The principle of inclusive education has become part of an international movement (Alur and Timmons 2009; Barton and Armstrong 2007). Cross-cultural ideas about what constitute good practice vary and are constructed within individual historical, cultural, political and economic contexts, but despite this there is a shared belief that inclusion is an ongoing process (Barton and Armstrong 2007). For the children of Britain the journey towards inclusive education can be mapped across a policy landscape, often referred to as the 'SEN legal framework', with the most progress taking place since the 1970 Education Act when all children gained the right to education (see Armstrong 2007 for a detailed history).

There has been a myriad of policy and legislation both nationally and internationally that advocates for disabled children to have access to meaningful education. Yet arguably it is attitudes, willingness and the sheer determination of individuals that makes inclusion possible (Barton 2012). It is to my children and their perspectives that I now turn to demonstrate that inclusion is only achieved through excellence, which according to writers such as Barton (2012) and Moore and Slee (2012), is only possible through partnership between children, professionals and parents. My children have experience of mainstream, segregated/'special' and hospital/residential schools, split placements, integrated units and independent schools and have all attended school outside their local community. They are therefore perfectly positioned to provide valuable perspectives on what excellence is in relation to inclusive education.

For Jack (who is 17 and is deaf) inclusion is about being part of a community, in particular having an opportunity to make and develop *friendships*. For him inclusion is 'being together [with] other people who sign and aren't teachers – friends teach me important stuff'.

For Matty (who is 16) inclusion is about *being listened to* and having people respond to him:

> it's like when the teacher understood when I said an extra class early in the morning with loads of people was hopeless for me, so now I get an hour of one-to-one, it's like they listened to me and respected what I said.

For Michael (who is 18) being included was about *being wanted*, which was demonstrated by the headmaster of his new school, who said, 'What do we need to do to make it possible for Michael to join us in September?' and then went ahead and made changes.

For Simon (who is 13) being included is about *being valued*. When talking about a school that some of his friends were going to, he said:

> I like being good at some things. I know I am not good at everything like football and geography but I like being good at art and English and if I go there [different school] I won't be good at anything and the teachers wouldn't know what I am good at.

The themes that evolved from the conversations I had with my children included friendship, being listened to, feeling wanted and knowing they are valued. The fact that their responses are different highlights the fact that inclusive education means different things to each child and those things are likely to change over time. It is therefore essential that policy-makers and practitioners strengthen their collaboration with children, families and communities to find evidence of what they want. Inclusion can only be realised through inclusive practice and that requires partnership and giving voice to those people that it affects (Barton 2012). Professionals need to see education as a lifelong process that touches whole communities. Finally, it is essential that we prioritise children's voices and perspectives, as their worlds will constantly change our minds.

For Discussion

- What are the things that make you feel included?
- What is inclusive practice?
- Who is responsible for developing inclusive practice?

Further Reading

Clough, P. and Corbett, J. (2000) *Theories of Inclusive Education: A Student's Guide*. London: Sage.

Moore, M. and Slee, R. (2012) 'Disability studies, inclusive education and exclusion', in N. Watson, A. Roulstone and C. Thomas (eds), *Routledge Handbook of Disability Studies*. London: Routledge, pp. 225–39.

Rioux, M. and Pinto, P. (2012) 'A time for the universal right to education: back to basics', in M. Arnot (ed.), *The Sociology of Disability and Inclusive Education: A Tribute to Len Barton*. London: Routledge, pp. 92–113.

References

Alur, M. and Timmons, V. (eds) (2009) *Inclusive Education Across Cultures: Crossing Boundaries, Sharing Ideas*. London: Sage.

Armstrong, F. (2007) 'Disability, education and social change in England since 1960', *History of Education Society*, 36 (4): 551–68.

Armstrong, F. and Barton, L. (2007) 'Policy, experience and the challenges of inclusive education: the case of England', in L. Barton and F. Armstrong (eds), *Policy, Experience and Change: Cross-cultural Reflections on Inclusive Education*. Dordrecht: Springer, pp. 5–18.

Barton, L. (2012) 'Response', in M. Arnot (ed), *The Sociology of Disability and Inclusive Education: A Tribute to Len Barton*. London: Routledge, pp. 114–22.

Barton, L. and Armstrong, F. (eds) (2007) 'Introduction', in *Policy, Experience and Change: Cross-cultural Reflections on Inclusive Education*. Dordrecht: Springer, pp. 1–4.

Barnes, C. and Mercer, G. (2010) *Exploring Disability*, 2nd edn. Cambridge: Polity Press.

Burchardt, T. (2005) *The Employment of Disabled Young People*, www.jrf.org.uk/publications/education-and-employment-disabled-young-people, accessed 1 January 2013.

Corbett, J. and Slee, R. (2000) 'An international conversation on inclusive education', in F. Armstrong and L. Barton (eds), *Inclusive Education: Policy, Contexts and Comparative Perspectives*. London: David Fulton, pp. 133–46.

Moore, M. and Slee, R. (2012). 'Disability studies, inclusive education and exclusion', in N. Watson, A. Roulstone and C. Thomas (eds), *Routledge Handbook of Disability Studies*. London: Routledge, pp. 225–39.

Oliver, M. and Barnes, C. (2012) 'Disability studies, disabled people and the struggle for inclusion', in M. Arnot (ed), *The Sociology of Disability and Inclusive Education: A Tribute to Len Barton*. London: Routledge, pp. 20–33.

Rioux, M. and Pinto, P. (2012) 'A time for the universal right to education: back to basics', in M. Arnot (ed), *The Sociology of Disability and Inclusive Education: A Tribute to Len Barton*. London: Routledge, pp. 92–113.

17 Eugenics

Emmeline Burdett

Seventy years ago, the Nazis' ... first official programme of murder targeted disabled people and became the blueprint for the Final Solution. Today, the development of pre-natal screening and a rush to legal rights for newly disabled people to assisted suicide, show that disabled people's right to life still needs to be defended ... Disabled people still experience those historical values as a daily threat.

(Crow 2009)

On 8 August 2009, the disabled artist and activist Liz Crow sat on the Fourth Plinth of Trafalgar Square as part of Antony Gormley's *One and Other* project (Crow 2009). Crow wanted to increase public awareness of the Nazi 'euthanasia' programme of 1939–1945, in which hundreds of thousands of disabled people were murdered, as well as highlighting its contemporary relevance. The programme was the culmination of eighty years' international interest in eugenics. Horror at the Nazi genocide is often said to mark the point at which eugenics became indelibly tainted (e.g. Kevles 1995). Some Disability Studies scholars have, however, identified eugenic resonances in modern-day practices (Asch 2001; Kumari Campbell 2000). Others (e.g. Shakespeare 1998) warn that describing modern-day measures as straightforwardly eugenic is unhelpful. Bioethicists argue that their proposals are humanitarian, and owe nothing to the eugenic ideas of the past (e.g. Rachels 1986; Singer 2001).

Eugenics entails the affecting of reproductive practice through the application of theories of heredity – public health reforms, inducements for 'desirable' parents, sterilization and 'euthanasia' (Bashford and Levine 2010). The main point to keep in mind is the judgemental nature of eugenics: 'Eugenics always had an evaluative logic at its core. Some life was of more value – to the state, the nation, the race, future generations – than other human life' (Bashford and Levine 2010: 4).

Though recognisably eugenicist ideas have been in circulation from ancient times, modern eugenics theory originated with Francis Galton (1822–1911), Charles Darwin's cousin. In his book *Hereditary Genius* (1869), Galton showed that a disproportionately large number of notables in fields as diverse as politics and poetry were related to each other. He concluded that some families were much more likely than others to make positive contributions to society (Kevles 1995). Galton's theories won widespread favour at the beginning of the twentieth century, fuelled by such concerns as the 'physical unfitness' of volunteer soldiers during the Boer War (1899–1902). Consequently, in 1903, Parliament established a committee on 'national deterioration' and the Eugenics Record Office at University College London (Kevles 1995). The Mental Deficiency Act 1913 introduced IQ tests to identify 'feeble-minded' children, who were then sent to segregated schools (Kerr and Shakespeare 2002). In 1912, the first International Eugenics Conference, held in London, was attended by four hundred delegates from twelve countries.

The Great War of 1914–18 intensified support for eugenics. Asylum inmates were considered to enjoy a pampered existence while the cream of the country's young men fought and died at the Front. In fact, insanitary conditions and insufficient nourishment caused the death rate in asylums to rise sharply (Kemp 2002). In Germany, this occurred to an even more pronounced degree (Burleigh 1994). Institutionalisation encouraged the perception that the inmates were a burden on society but not a part of it (Morris 1991), as evidenced by such texts as Binding and Hoche's *The Granting of Permission for the Destruction of Worthless Life* (Leipzig 1920).

With *Buck v. Bell* (1927) the US sterilisation laws reached the Supreme Court. The case involved three generations of 'hereditary feeblemindedness'. Supreme Court Judge Oliver Wendell Holmes declared '[T]he public welfare may call upon the best citizens for their lives. It would be strange if it could not call upon those who already sap the strength of the State for these lesser sacrifices' (quoted in Kevles 1995: 111).

Upon coming to power in 1933, the Nazis passed the Law for the Prevention of Hereditarily Diseased Offspring, under which around 375,000 persons were sterilised against their will (Gallagher 1990). The reasons for the law were explained in a propaganda film:

> In the last seventy years our population has increased by 50%, while ... the number of hereditarily ill has risen by 450% ... the Law for the Prevention of Congenitally Diseased Offspring is ... the restoration of a natural order which mankind has disrupted because of a false sense of humanity.

(Quoted in Burleigh 1994: 191)

Such emphasis on the counter-selectivity of modern society, and on the 'unrestrained fecundity' of the 'hereditarily ill', echoes the arguments of earlier eugenicists. Killing was a logical next step, and one which Hitler had already envisaged, both in *Mein Kampf*, and at the 1929 Nuremberg party rally (Gallagher 1990). The Nazi 'euthanasia' programme began in summer 1939. It involved 'the systematic and secret execution of the aged, insane, incurably ill, of deformed children and diverse other persons, by gas, lethal injections and diverse other means, in nursing homes, hospitals and asylums' (Nuremberg Medical Trial Transcript, Paragraph 9).

By 1945, hundreds of thousands of people had been murdered (Evans 2007). Indeed, institution inmates continued to be murdered after the defeat of the Nazis. Internationally, eugenics policies continued until decades after the end of the Nazi regime (Gallagher 1990). There was nothing uniquely Nazi about viewing disabled people as antithetical to the rest of society (Gallagher 1990). Nowadays, bioethicists such as Peter Singer advocate 'euthanasia' of impaired newborns. They demonstrate 'an implicit (and troubling) view that ranking individuals according to quality of life is not only possible but inevitable' (Goering 2008: 126). These ideas concur with many current in society at the moment, such as the high rates of abortion of impaired foetuses.

For Discussion

- How would you decide whether a measure should be described as part of the 'new eugenics'?
- How do you think adherence to either the medical or the social model of disability might impact on whether life with an impairment is seen as 'worth living'?
- Do you think that the high death rates at asylums during WW1 were connected to the prevalence of eugenic theory at the time?

Further Reading

Kerr, A. and Shakespeare, T. (2002) *Genetic Politics: From Eugenics to Genome*. Cheltenham: New Clarion Press.

Smith, A. (2011) *Hideous Progeny: Disability, Eugenics, and Classic Horror Cinema*. New York: Columbia University Press.

Snyder, S. and Mitchell, D. (2006) *Cultural Locations of Disability*. Chicago, IL and London: University of Chicago Press.

References

Asch, A. (2001) 'Disability, bioethics and human rights', in Albrecht, G.L., Seelman, K.D. and Bury, M. (eds), *The Disability Studies Handbook*. Thousand Oaks, CA: Sage, pp. 297–326.

Bashford, A. and Levine, P. (eds) (2010) *The Oxford Handbook of the History of Eugenics*. Oxford: Oxford University Press.

Burleigh, M. (1994) *Death and Deliverance: 'Euthanasia' in Germany 1900–1945*. Cambridge: Cambridge University Press.

Crow, L. (2009) *On the Plinth*, www.roaring-girl.com/productions/resistance-on-the-plinth.

Evans, S.E. (2007) *Hitler's Forgotten Victims: The Holocaust and the Disabled*. Stroud: Tempus.

Gallagher, H.G. (1990) *By Trust Betrayed: Patients, Physicians, and the License to Kill in Nazi Germany*. New York: Henry Holt and Company.

Goering, S. (2008) '"You say you're happy, but…" contested quality of life issues in bioethics and disability studies', *Bioethical Enquiry*, 8: 125–35.

Kemp, N.D.A. (2002) *'Merciful Release': The History of the British Euthanasia Movement*. Manchester: Manchester University Press.

Kerr, A. and Shakespeare, T. (2002) *Genetic Politics: From Eugenics to Genome*. Cheltenham: New Clarion Press.

Kevles, D.J. (1995) *In the Name of Eugenics: Genetics and the Uses of Human Heredity*. Cambridge, MA: Harvard University Press.

Kumari Campbell, F. (2000) 'Eugenics in disguise? Law, technologies and negotiating the "problem" of disability', *Australian Feminist Law Journal*, 14: 55–70.

Morris, J. (1991) *Pride Against Prejudice: Transforming Attitudes to Disability*. London: The Women's Press.

Nuremberg Medical Trial Transcript FO 646 Case 1 Medical (*U.S. v Karl Brandt* et al). Twenty-three volumes.

Rachels, J. (1986) *The End of Life: Euthanasia and Morality*. Oxford and New York: Oxford University Press.

Shakespeare, T. (1998) 'Choices and rights: eugenics, genetics and disability equality', *Disability & Society*, 13 (5): 665–81.

Singer, P. (2001) *Writings on an Ethical Life*. London: Fourth Estate.

18   Families

Alison Wilde and Adele Hoskison-Clark

Many of the Internet resources brought up when searching for the term 'disabled family' reflect medical or individual models of disability.[1] These models tend to portray disabled families as a 'problem' in need of special help. This perpetuates the image of disabled families as dependant and deviant. Images of disabled children often promote stereotypes about tragedy, charity, segregation and parental heroism (Barnes 1992) or blame (Rawls 2012). Disabled parents are likely to be seen as incompetent and/or selfish (Wilde 2011).

In contrast, social model understandings of disabled families refer to individual and collective family experiences of disabling attitudes and social circumstances. Disablement may arise from the poor material circumstances of many disabled families (Wood 2011); from the 'courtesy stigma' often associated with those related to people with impairments (Wilde 2010); or from cultural attitudes which value individualism and competition above social support and the recognition of a diversity of individual needs. These attitudes are bolstered by the political and media rhetoric of austerity (Briant et al. 2011).

Many disabled parents feel excluded from the Government's family strategies (Goodinge 2000). Prospective parents also encounter stereotypes of asexuality, dependency and incompetency (Wilde 2011). Maternity support emphasises risks to mother or child from parental impairments and the ability to provide children with a 'normal' childhood (Kallianes and Rubenfield 1997). Training and practice of doctors, nurses and midwives is dominated by medical model understandings of disabled parents as pathological and lacking (Crow 2003).[2]

Disabled parents are an 'administratively invisible' group (Olsen and Wates, 2003): outside the range of policy-making and services for both disabled people and parents and prospective parents (Morris and Wates 2006). Due to this official invisibility disabled parents are 'misrecognised' (Fraser 1997): seen, at best, in terms of 'special needs'. Attitudes towards disabled parents are informed by an 'unacknowledged distinctiveness', invariably portraying them as 'pathological' and 'difficult', rather than implementing affirmative forms of support for personalised and interdependent needs.

Disabled parents (Olsen and Clarke 2003) and parents of disabled children (Cerebra 2012) both fear that their family life will become a cause for professional and public scrutiny and that they may be deemed incompetent. The removal of children from their parents has been of particular concern for women accredited with learning difficulties, and such fears are common both before and during parenthood (Wilde 2011).

This assumption of deficit is reflected in more abstract eugenicist ideas about preventing the births of disabled children. Abortions until the end of pregnancy are often justified on the grounds of children's impairments (Beckford 2011; Hern, 2012). The training of clinicians to focus on such questions reflects wider trends and perpetuates the perception of disabled people as undesirable and unnecessary 'others' (Shakespeare 1994).

Dominant cultural attitudes about 'normal parents' and 'normal children' influence interactions with the wide range of service providers and health professionals, who populate the everyday lives of each member of the family. Such value-laden assumptions often lead to the children of disabled parents being labelled as 'young carers'. It is often assumed that the children of disabled people will adopt a caring role and this is deemed to flout the normative principles of childhood. Conversely, patterns of interdependency existing in disabled families – e.g. the amounts of time engaged in talking to children (Olsen and Clarke 2003: 132) and co-operative ways of achieving family goals (Williams 2004: 3) – are often overlooked.

The 'administrative invisibility' and cultural stigmatisation of disabled families often perpetuates the barriers they face. The separation of adult and children's welfare services means that collective and intersecting family issues are seldom adequately addressed. For example, the individualistic 'special needs' approach to education often works on a case-by-case basis. Schools are often unprepared for disabled families, making disabled parents' participation in school events impossible due to unmet access needs (Brunner et al. 2009).[3] Despite Fair Access to Care's statement that parental roles and responsibilities should be considered when individuals are being assessed for community care services, disabled parents are still inadequately supported with parenting (Commission for Social Care Inspection 2009).

The misrecognition of disabled people and families often lies at the heart of barriers to inclusion. The ideal of the nuclear family is invoked in the stigmatisation of young 'carers'. Disabled parents are expected to fit to into increasingly demanding and selective work roles (framed in individualistic, neo-liberalist terms) while confronted with attitudes which deny their competencies to do so.

Notes

1   Google search, 11 November 2012.

2   However in the UK the Royal College of Nursing (RCN) *Pregnancy and Disability Guidance for Midwives and Nurses* (2007) is comprehensive and based (according to the document itself) on a social model approach.

3   From personal experience as a volunteer, this type of barrier is one which is reported to organisations such as Disabled Parents' Network, UK.

For Discussion

- How might the experience of disabled families contribute to a critique of normative theorisations of 'the family' and models of service provision?
- Do disabled families face a common oppression, given the diversity of family forms, impairments, social values and disabling barriers?
- Do disabled families offer distinctive modes of interdependency which can be used to inform ways of approaching family relationships? What are the benefits and dangers in taking this approach?

Further Reading

Brunner, R., Maguire, R., Stalker, K. and Mitchell, J. (2009) *Supporting Disabled Parents' Involvement in their Children's Education: Good Practice Guide for Schools*, www.leeds.ac.uk/disabilitystudies/archiveuk/maguire/2500_Guidance_5.pdf.

Morris, J. and Wates, M. (2006) *Supporting Disabled Parents and Parents with Additional Support Needs*. Bristol: Social Care Institute for Excellence.

Olsen, R. and Clarke, H. (2003) *Parenting and Disability: Disabled Parents' Experiences of Raising Children*. Bristol: Polity Press.

References

Barnes, C. (1992) *Disabling Imagery and the Media: An Exploration of the Principles for Media Representation of Disabled People*. Keele: Keele University Press.

Beckford, M. (2011) 'More than 120 abortions after upper time-limit', *The Telegraph*, 9 April, www.telegraph.co.uk/health/healthnews/8438261/More-than-120-abortions-after-upper-time-limit.html.

Briant, E., Watson, N. and Philo, G. (2011) *Bad News for Disabled People: How the Newspapers are Reporting Disability. Project Report*. Glasgow: Strathclyde Centre for Disability Research and Glasgow Media Unit, University of Glasgow.

Brunner, R., Maguire, R., Stalker, K. and Mitchell, J. (2009) *Supporting Disabled Parents' Involvement in their Children's Education: Good Practice Guide for Schools*, www.leeds.ac.uk/disabilitystudies/archiveuk/maguire/2500_Guidance_5.pdf.

Cerebra (2012) *Dealing with Stigma as the Parent of a Child with Disabilities*, www.cerebra.org.uk/English/getinformation/dailyliving/Pages/Dealingwithstigmaastheparentofachildwithdisabilities.aspx.

Commission for Social Care Inspection (2009) *Supporting Disabled Parents: A Family or Fragmented Approach?* London: Commission for Social Care Inspection.

Crow, L. (2003) 'Invisible and Centre-Stage'. Paper presented to Department of Health Open Forum Event of the Children's National Service Framework (Maternity Module), 15 January.

Fraser, N. (1997) *Justice Interruptus: Critical Reflections on the 'Post-Socialist' Condition*. New York: Routledge.

Goodinge, S. (2000) *A Jigsaw of Services: Inspection of Services to Support Disabled Adults in their Parenting Role*. Department of Health.

Hern, A. (2012) 'MENCAP slam UKIP candidate who called for "compulsory abortion of disabled people"', *The New Statesman*'s rolling politics blog, 18 December, www.newstatesman.com.

Kallianes, V. and Rubenfield, P. (1997) 'Disabled women and reproductive rights', *Disability & Society* 12 (2): 203–21.

Morris, J. and Wates, M. (2006) *Supporting Disabled Parents and Parents with Additic   Needs*. Bristol: Social Care Institute for Excellence.

Olsen, R. and Clarke H. (2003) *Parenting and Disability: Disabled Parents' Experienc ,   Children*. Bristol: Polity Press.

Olsen, R. and Wates, M. (2003) *Disabled Parents: Examining Research Assumptions*. Dartington: Research in Practice.

Rawls, K. (2012) 'Don't blame parents for an education system that fails US children', *The   Guardian*, 11 December.

Shakespeare, T. (1994) 'Cultural representations of disabled people: dustbins for disavowal',   *Disability & Society*, 9 (3): 283–99.

Thomas, C. (1997) 'The baby and the bath water: disabled women and motherhood in social   context', *Sociology of Health and Illness*, 19 (5): 622–43.

Wilde, A. (2010) 'Sisters aren't doing it for themselves: the negotiation of special identities', in   B. Cumberland and B. Mills (eds), *Siblings and Autism*. London: Jessica Kingsley Publishers,   pp. 193–202.

Wilde, A. (2011)'Great expectations: the significance of concepts of normality, care, and social   support in cultural discourses of disabled motherhood', unpublished paper for Breakthrough UK.

Williams, F. (2004) *Rethinking Families*. London: Calouste Gulbenkian Foundation.

Wood, C. (2011) *Tracking the Lives of Disabled Families Through the Cuts: Destination Unknown: Autumn 2011*. London: Demos.

19   Feminist Disability Studies

Ana Bê

In this chapter, I present a brief summary of a growing interdisciplinary field that articulates feminist theory with Disability Studies. Rosemarie Garland-Thomson has termed this *feminist Disability Studies* (Garland-Thomson 2005, 2006).

Since the inception of the disabled people's movement, women writing about disability have been very keen to show that the experiences of disabled women often placed them behind a double curtain described in terms of invisibility. On the one hand, they have often been invisible within the disabled people's movement, which has largely presented the experiences of disabled men as universal. On the other, feminism has also frequently excluded the experiences and contributions of disabled women, as well as being distinctly ableist in outlook (Asch and Fine 1988; Begum 1992; Driedger 1989; Garland-Thomson 2006; Morris 1991, 1996).

The 1980s and 1990s saw the publication of a number of first-person narratives by disabled women (Driedger and Gray 1992; Morris 1989, 1991, 1996; Rousso et al. 1988).

CHAPTER 19

More recently, research that gives voice to disabled women has also contributed to combat the invisibility that had been forced upon them (Thomas 1999). Personal narratives are still a fundamental tool for disabled women in particular (Rousso 2013), since for a long time our lives were not valued or even acknowledged as significant. These aspects set feminist Disability Studies apart from other Disability Studies' perspectives – women writing about disability have always asserted the feminist motto that the personal is political, whereas, for instance the social model of disability has traditionally focused more on the physical and social barriers that are experienced (Barnes et al. 1999; Bê 2012; Thomas 1999, 2007). Disabled feminists have proposed that engaging with the body actually allows disabled people the possibility of *reconceptualising existing and prevalent negative notions about impairment in their own terms* (Crow 1996; Morris 1991, 1996). This argument has by no means found favour with everyone, particularly with proponents of the social model of disability, many of whom have expressed the belief that a focus upon impairment and the body might encourage traditional 'medical model' ideas of impairment as tragedy.

Despite this, since the 1990s, a number of important theoretical contributions have arisen that establish feminist Disability Studies as a central sub-field with an important body of work (Garland-Thomson 1997; Morris 1991; Thomas 1999, 2007; Wendell 1996). Sociologist Carol Thomas has proposed the notion of *psycho-emotional disablism* to reflect the ways in which negative words and actions impact on disabled people's emotional well-being and impose restrictions that shape their identity (Thomas 2007). She has also proposed the notion of impairment effects, defined as the '*direct and unavoidable impacts that impairments (physical, sensory, intellectual) have on individuals' embodied functioning in the social world*' (Thomas 2010: 37, author's emphasis). Both concepts introduce important theoretical tools shaped by a feminist Disability Studies perspective.

Both concepts introduce important theoretical tools shaped by a feminist Disability Studies perspective. Philosopher Susan Wendell has also added to this body of work by noting that disabled people have been historically constructed as *other* by the non-disabled world, which has tended to 'support the paradigm of humanity as young and healthy' (Wendell 2006: 245).

However, this is only an idealised notion. Particularly in old age, disability is a category into which anyone can enter. Wendell argues that this is exactly why disabled people's knowledge of the body and of pain should be cherished and shared instead of suppressed. Her discussion of chronic illness and disability identity remains an excellent introduction to the topic, and reflects the willingness in feminist Disability Studies to discuss issues other traditions prefer not to engage with (Wendell 1996).

Rosemarie Garland-Thomson's work has established vital bridges between feminist Disability Studies and the humanities (Garland-Thomson 1997). She argues that disability should in fact be seen as another legitimate category of inquiry:

> The informing premise of feminist disability theory is that disability, like femaleness, is not a natural state of corporeal inferiority, inadequacy, excess, or a stroke of misfortune. Rather, disability is a culturally fabricated narrative of the body, similar to what we understand as the fictions of race and gender. The disability/ability system produces subjects by differentiating and marking bodies.

> (Garland-Thomson 2006: 259)

This allows us to think about how disability, like gender or race, is constructed through complex processes of relationality that create and help structure power relationships which, in turn, form the basis for both privilege and marginalisation.

For Discussion

- Why did disabled women feel invisible both in the disabled people's movement and within feminist perspectives?
- What is the importance of feminist contributions to debates about the place of the body in Disability Studies?
- Can you name three key concepts proposed by authors in feminist Disability Studies?

Further Reading

Bê, A. (2012). 'Feminism and disability: a cartography of multiplicity', in N. Watson, A. Roulstone and C. Thomas (eds), *Routledge Handbook of Disability Studies*. London: Routledge, pp. 363–75.

Thomas, C. (1999). *Female Forms: Experiencing and Understanding Disability*. Buckingham: Open University Press.

Garland-Thomson, R. (2006). 'Integrating disability, transforming feminist theory', in L.J. Davis (ed.), *Disability Studies Reader*. New York: Routledge, pp. 257–75.

References

Asch, A. and Fine, M. (1988) 'Introduction: beyond pedestals', in M. Fine and A. Asch (eds), *Women with Disabilities: Essays in Psychology, Culture, and Politics*. Philadelphia, PA: Temple University Press, pp. 1–39.

Barnes, C., Mercer, G. and Shakespeare, T. (1999) *Exploring Disability: A Sociological Introduction*. Cambridge: Polity.

Begum, N. (1992) 'Disabled women and the feminist agenda', *Feminist Review*, (40): 70–84.

Bê, A. (2012) 'Feminism and disability: a cartography of multiplicity', in N. Watson, A. Roulstone and C. Thomas (eds), *Routledge Handbook of Disability Studies*. London: Routledge, pp. 363–75.

Crow, L. (1996) 'Including all of our lives: renewing the social model of disability', in J.E. Morris (ed.), *Encounters with Strangers: Feminism and Disability*. London: Women's Press, pp. 206–26.

Driedger, D. (1989) *The Last Civil Rights Movement: Disabled People's International*. New York: St. Martin's Press.

Driedger, D. and Gray, S. (1992) *Imprinting Our Image: An International Anthology by Women with Disabilities*. Charlottetown: Gynergy.

Garland-Thomson, R. (1997) *Extraordinary Bodies: Figuring Physical Disability in American Culture and Literature*. New York: Columbia University Press.

Garland-Thomson, R. (2005) 'Feminist disability studies', *Signs: Journal of Women in Culture and Society*, 30 (2): 1577–87.

Garland-Thomson, R. (2006) 'Integrating disability, transforming feminist theory', in L.J. Davis (ed.), *Disability Studies Reader*. New York: Routledge, pp. 257–75.

Morris, J. (1989) *Able Lives: Women's Experience of Paralysis*. London: Women's Press.

Morris, J. (1991) *Pride against Prejudice: A Personal Politics of Disability*. London: Women's Press.

Morris, J. (1996) *Encounters with Strangers: Feminism and Disability*. London: Women's Press.

Rousso, H., Gushee O'Malley, S. and Severance, M. (1988) *Disabled, Female, and Proud! Stories of Ten Women with Disabilities*. Boston, MA: Exceptional Parent Press.

Rousso, H. (2013) *Don't Call Me Inspirational: A Disabled Feminist Talks Back*. Philadelphia, PA: Temple University Press.

Thomas, C. (1999) *Female Forms: Experiencing and Understanding Disability*. Buckingham: Open University Press.

Thomas, C. (2007) *Sociologies of Disability and Illness: Contested Ideas in Disability Studies and Medical Sociology*. Basingstoke: Palgrave Macmillan.

Thomas, C. (2010) 'Negotiating the contested terrain of narrative methods in illness contexts', *Sociology of Health and Illness*, 32 (4): 647–60.

Wendell, S. (1996) *The Rejected Body: Feminist Philosophical Reflections on Disability*. New York and London: Routledge.

Wendell, S. (2006) 'Toward a feminist theory of disability', in L.J. Davis (ed.), *The Disability Studies Reader*. New York and Abingdon: Routledge, pp. 243–54.

20   Harassment and Hate Crime

Colin Cameron

In this chapter I am going to use the affirmation model to develop an explanation of disability-related harassment and hate crime. I will distinguish between these and the related concept of discrimination, but suggest that they share a common characteristic of violence. Violence may be verbal, psychological or physical (Rosenberg 2003), but it is always used to diminish. The affirmation model identifies impairment as 'physical, sensory, emotional and cognitive difference, divergent from socially valued norms of embodiment, to be expected and respected on its own terms in a diverse society', and disability as 'a personal and social role which simultaneously invalidates the subject position of people with impairments and validates the subject position of those identified as normal' (Cameron 2010: 113).

Disability-related harassment is defined by the Equality and Human Rights Commission (EHRC) as 'unwanted, exploitative or abusive conduct against disabled people which has the purpose or effect of either violating the dignity, safety, security or autonomy of the person experiencing it, or creating an intimidating, hostile, degrading or offensive environment' (EHRC 2011a). Disability hate crime is any criminal offence perceived, by the victim or by any other person, to be motivated by hostility or prejudice based on a person's being disabled or perceived to be disabled (CPS 2010). While most everyday harassment of disabled people – bullying, name-calling, being spat at – the 'drip, drip, nag, nag ... so-called "low-level" harassment' that ruins many disabled people's lives (EHRC 2011b: 5) – is not regarded as hate crime, all hate crime involves harassment. Harassment and hate crime must, of course, be distinguished from discrimination which is often unintentional and can involve instances, for example, of 'people talking to you as if you were stupid; talking to the person with you instead of to you; overtly treating you less favourably' (EHRC 2011b: 5).

Nevertheless, I suggest that the toleration and institutionalisation of disability discrimination in ordinary life establishes the basis for harassment and hate crime.

Quarmby (2011: 4) states that in her many interviews on the subject, police officers, disabled activists, academics and prosecutors all struggled 'to understand why disability hate crime exists and what can be done to stop it'. Given this, I want to use the affirmation model as an analytical tool to try and make sense of disability-related harassment and hate crime, particularly in situations where multiple perpetrators are involved; or in instances of 'mate crime', where hostile incidents are carried out by relatives or by one or more people considered by the disabled person to be their friends (Thomas 2012).

Hate crimes, and by extension harassment, often involve multiple perpetrators (Sherry 2010). An example of this can be seen in the murder of Steven Hoskin in 2006. Steven was a young disabled man with the learning difficulties label who was found dead at the bottom of a 100-foot high railway viaduct in St Austell, Cornwall, who had been:

> tortured for hours before his death, suffering various injuries inflicted on him by a number of perpetrators. He had been tied up, dragged round by a lead, imprisoned, burnt with cigarettes, humiliated and repeatedly violently abused in his own home over a period of time ... Finally he was taken to the viaduct and forced over the railings before one of the perpetrators stamped on his fingers until he let go.

(EHRC 2011b: 39)

Five people in their teens and twenties, including two who had lived in the same flat as Steven, were convicted on charges related to his imprisonment and murder.

I suggest that at least some of the reasons underlying the harassment of disabled people involve perpetrators' own personal needs and issues to do with their own sense of power and identity. Identifying impairment as undesirable difference, perpetrators validate each other's identities and inappropriately meet each other's esteem needs by confirming each other's worth when measured against those they victimise. In personal situations where they may not receive much validation from society at large, their own worth/normality is confirmed by those around them shouting encouragement. The impaired person takes on a role as a devalued, disabled object. Perpetrators don't need to come up with the idea that disabled people are of less value by themselves. That is a lesson society has already taught them.

Stuart Jack murdered Laura Milne, a young disabled woman with the learning difficulties label, in an Aberdeen flat in 2007, repeatedly slashing her throat with a knife while his two friends Debbie Buchan and Leigh Mackinnon demanded that he 'finish her off'. He later said that he had enjoyed cutting her throat and that he had murdered her because she was 'worthless' (EHRC 2011b: 42). His comment appears to reflect a sense of self-identity based on comparing his own worth against a disabled person's.

Quarmby (2011) cites research which shows that disabled people themselves have broadly similar attitudes towards other disabled people as the rest of the general population. In Cameron (2010) I have argued that society structures experience so that most disabled people learn to regard impairment as something that can only be lived negatively, that must be endured or overcome. There is plenty of symbolic encouragement for those who sign up to the goal of overcoming. An affirmation model analysis suggests that, in taking on self-identities which can only relate negatively to impairment, disabled people perform social roles which acknowledge the superiority and desirability of normality. The need for people to aspire to normality is a requirement for the functioning of the social and economic system.

Levin and McDevitt (2002: 51) have argued that 'hate crimes have a basis in what society's members are normally taught when they are growing up'. Perry (2009) describes bias-motivated violence as having an important role in maintaining social inequality and states elsewhere that 'hate crime is not abnormal, it is a normal (albeit extreme) expression of the biases that are diffused throughout the culture and history in which they are embedded' (Perry 2001: 37). My conclusion is that rather than being incomprehensible, disability-related harassment and hate crime can be understood as involving a ritualistic, if perverted, enactment of values many would consider perfectly acceptable.

To explain this is, however, far from excusing it. An affirmation model understanding of impairment as difference to be expected and respected on its own terms allows us to refuse to accept the inevitability of disabling social relations. Stryker (2002: 66) has argued that if it is social structure that shapes possibilities for interaction and so shapes, ultimately, the person, then conversely, if the social person creatively alters patterns of interaction, those altered patterns can change social structure. Owning impairment involves transgression and audacity when impairment is typically regarded as a mark of inferiority, but is a necessary step towards transforming experience.

For Discussion

- The most recent evidence suggests that disability hate crime is on the increase. There were 1,788 recorded incidents of disability hate crime in England and Wales in 2011, an increase of more than 18 per cent on the total for 2010 (*The Guardian* 2012).
- When were figures for disability hate crimes first recorded in England and Wales? Do you think this increase reflects an actual increase in disability hate crime or only in the recorded incidence?
- Do you think some impairment groups are more likely than others to be targeted for harassment and, if so, why?
- Quarmby (2011: 136) has characterised harassment and hate crime against disabled people as something that 'has happened while society has looked the other way'. What do you think she means by this?

Further Reading

Quarmby, K. (2011) *Scapegoat: Why We Are Failing Disabled People*. London: Portobello.
Thomas, P. (2012) 'Hate crime or mate crime? Disablist hostility, contempt and ridicule', in A. Roulstone and H. Mason-Bish (eds), *Disability, Hate Crime and Violence*. London: Routledge, pp. 135–46.
Thomas, P. (2014) 'Hate crime and the criminal justice system', in J. Swain, S. French, C. Barnes and S. Thomas (eds), *Disabling Barriers – Enabling Environments*, 3rd edn. London: Sage, pp. 312–19.

References

Cameron, C. (2010) 'Does anybody like being disabled? A critical exploration of impairment, identity, media and everyday experience in a disabling society'. PhD thesis, Queen Margaret University, http://etheses.qmu.ac.uk/258/1/258.pdf, accessed 2 April 2013.
Crown Prosecution Service (CPS) (2010) *Policy for Prosecuting Disability Hate Crime*. London: CPS.
Equality and Human Rights Commission (EHRC) (2011a) *Hidden in Plain Sight: Inquiry into Disability-related Harassment. Terms of Reference*, www.equalityhumanrights.com/legal-and-policy/

inquiries-and-assessments/inquiry-into-disability-related-harassment/background-to-the-inquiry/terms-of-reference/, accessed 2 April 2013.

Equality and Human Rights Commission (EHRC) (2011b) *Hidden in Plain Sight: Inquiry into Disability-related Harassment*. London: EHRC.

Guardian, The (2012) 'Disability hate crime is at its highest level since records began', www.guardian.co.uk/news/datablog/2012/aug/14/disability-hate-crime-increase-reported-incidents-data, accessed 2 April 2013.

Levin, J. and McDevitt, J. (2002) *Hate Crimes Revisited: America's War on those who are Different*. Cambridge, MA: Westview.

Perry, B. (2001) *In the Name of Hate: Understanding Hate Crimes*. New York: Routledge.

Perry, B. (2009) 'The sociology of hate: theoretical approaches', in B. Perry (ed.), *Hate Crimes: Understanding and Defining Hate Crime*. Westport, CT: Greenwood, pp. 55–76.

Quarmby, K. (2011) *Scapegoat: Why We Are Failing Disabled People*. London: Portobello.

Rosenberg, M. (2003) *Nonviolent Communication: A Language of Life*. Encinitas, CA: PuddleDancer Press.

Sherry, M. (2010) *Disability Hate Crimes: Does Anyone Really Hate Disabled People?* Farnham: Ashgate.

Stryker, S. (2002) *Symbolic Interactionism: A Social Structural Version*. Caldwell, NJ: Blackburn Press.

Thomas, P. (2012) 'Hate crime or mate crime? Disablist hostility, contempt and ridicule', in A. Roulstone and H. Mason-Bish (eds), *Disability, Hate Crime and Violence*. London: Routledge, pp. 135–46.

21

The Historical Construction of Disability

Colin Cameron

If we acknowledge all social knowledge as historically and culturally specific (Burr 2003), we understand that the way we look at things is structured by both the times and places in which we find ourselves. Theories that underpin the knowledge, assumptions and practice of professionals working with disabled people, for example, cannot be regarded as 'true', fixed-for-ever descriptions, but must be recognised as having been produced within specific social contexts and as reflecting specific social interests.

While people with impairments have been part of every human society since the beginning of recorded history, disabled people have only been around for about the past two hundred years or so. If this statement sounds contentious or confusing, a historical consideration of the emergence of disability as a social relationship may be illuminating. As

Oliver and Barnes have remarked (2012), an understanding of history is essential when considering questions such as 'How does disability arise?'

While there is much evidence that people with impairments have been on the receiving end of hostility and prejudice throughout the history of Western civilisation (Barnes 1997), there is a consensus among Disability Studies theorists that 'prior to the Industrial Revolution of the late eighteenth century, disabled people were part of an undifferentiated mass poor, and hence clustered at the lower reaches of society, but not excluded from it' (Borsay 2002: 103). People with impairments had a difficult and not particularly enjoyable life, but this was the experience of the majority of people. The point, however, is that people with impairments had a place in the midst of things. This can be surmised, for example, by considering various groups of crippled beggars in Peter Brueghel's sixteenth-century paintings, e.g. *The Fight Between Carnival and Lent* (1559). As Brendan Gleeson notes, these 'seem to signify that those with physical "maladies" had a place within the pre-modern social order' (Gleeson 1999: 61). Impairment was commonplace, regarded as inevitable and ordinary rather than as something separate from everyday life.

Prior to the industrialisation of society most work was agrarian or involved small-scale cottage industry. Individuals, with impairments or otherwise, worked co-operatively with the family and the community, contributing what they could (Oliver and Barnes 2012: 82). The shift in the circumstances of people with impairments arrived with the advent of the factory system of production and the establishment of new production norms.

With the coming of the factories there arose a need for a standard-shaped, standard-sized 'able-bodied' worker, capable of seeing, hearing, comprehending and moving quickly enough to operate standard-sized machines in order to generate capital for manufacturers. People with impairments, who had not previously been thought of as representing a distinct section of society, became regarded as problematic, as unable to meet the requirements of the new system. Finding themselves excluded from employment on the grounds of being unable to keep pace with these requirements, many found themselves removed from the mainstream of economic and community life and placed in a range of institutional settings (Barnes 1997). It is within these institutions that people with impairments fell under the gaze of the medical profession and that disability first became regarded as a medical issue (Oliver 1990).

Having been removed from everyday life, there was no perceived reason to take the needs of people with impairments into account in the planning and development of the rapidly expanding cities and towns that grew during the nineteenth century. Public buildings, schools, houses, transport systems, places of leisure and worship were built without regard for the needs of people with impairments.

Profound changes accompanied industrialisation, the development of capitalism and the shift of the population from the land to towns and cities. From having had fixed roles and certainty of place within an established feudal order, workers now had to compete to sell their labour in precarious economic circumstances. This competition required ever-greater attentiveness to the presentation of self, necessitating conformity, body consciousness and regulation of personal behaviour in terms of self-constraint. It is by this attentiveness that the individual comes into focus. As Michel Foucault (1987) has explained, through increasingly intrusive disciplinary mechanisms the individual is required to become his own moral surveyor.

Norbert Elias has argued that the increased need for self-governance corresponds with the increased size of societies and the greater number of networks typically experienced by individuals. Standardised modes of thinking and behaving become the only acceptable practice when large numbers congregate and interact. In this lies the paradox that the more uniquely one is made to sense his own individuality, the more he conforms with what is required of him and becomes like all the other individuals around him, all of whom

> [are] compelled to adopt a very high degree of restraint, affect, control, renunciation and transformation of instinct, and ... accustomed to relegating a large number of functions, instinct-expressions and wishes to private enclaves of secrecy withdrawn from the gaze of the 'outside world', or even to the cellar of their own psyche.

(Elias 2001: 28)

It is only with the requirement for standardisation that the non-standard becomes identifiable. Any sign of weakness, idiosyncrasy or blemishment is required to be hidden. The bodies of impaired people began to be regarded as markers of disorder and disruption, of unruly nature threatening to hold back and destroy the achievements of civilised society (Davis 1995).

Representations of people with impairments were used to evoke pity or sensations of horror in the readers of novels by Charles Dickens, Wilkie Collins, Mary Elizabeth Braddon and many other Victorian writers. Garland-Thomson (1997) has talked about the way in which disabled characters were used in nineteenth-century fiction to highlight the virtues of conforming heroes and heroines. Newly emerging charities played a further role in establishing a moral discourse around impairment, entrenching ideas that viewed impairment as a trial to be endured and overcome (Borsay 2002). Impairment was no longer considered ordinary and inevitable, it had become a metaphor harnessed in the business of establishing the boundaries of what was acceptable in the new social order of industrialised society.

It is being made the subject of regulation, coupled with the lack of thought for the needs of people with impairments in the planning and development of social environments, which produces disablement. Throughout the twentieth century the supervision of disabled peoples' lives became an increasingly sophisticated business (Albrecht 1992), requiring the development of a complex body of 'scientific' theory and knowledge, and the emergence of new professions to manage what were identified as their 'special needs' (Oliver 1990). People may be born with or acquire impairments, but being or becoming disabled involves being part of a society still emerging from its history.

For Discussion

- 'While people with impairments have been part of every human society since the beginning of recorded history, disabled people have only been around for about the past two hundred years or so.' What is meant by this?
- Whose social interests are served by the representation of disabled people's bodies as markers of disorder and disruption?
- In what ways can the management of disabled people's lives by professionals be described as 'a business'?

Further Reading

Borsay, A. (2002) 'History, power and identity', in C. Barnes, M. Oliver and L. Barton (eds), *Disability Studies Today*. Cambridge: Polity, pp. 98–119.

Burr, V. (2003) *Social Constructionism*. London: Routledge.

Oliver, M. and Barnes, C. (2012) *The New Politics of Disablement*. Basingstoke: Palgrave Macmillan.

References

Albrecht, G. (1992) *The Disability Business: Rehabilitation in America*. London: Sage.

Barnes, C. (1997) 'A legacy of oppression: a history of disability in Western culture', in L. Barton and M. Oliver (eds), *Disability Studies: Past, Present and Future*. Leeds: The Disability Press, pp. 3–24.

Borsay, A. (2002) 'History, power and identity', in C. Barnes, M. Oliver and L. Barton (eds), *Disability Studies Today*. Cambridge: Polity, pp. 98–119.

Burr, V. (2003) *Social Constructionism*. London: Routledge.

Davis, L.J. (1995) *Enforcing Normalcy: Disability, Deafness and the Body*. London: Verso.

Elias, N. (2001) *The Society of Individuals*. London: Continuum.

Foucault, M. (1987) *Discipline and Punish*. London: Penguin.

Garland-Thomson, R. (1997) *Extraordinary Bodies: Figuring Physical Disability in American Culture and Literature*. New York, NY: Columbia University Press.

Gleeson, B. (1999) *Geographies of Disability*. London: Routledge.

Oliver, M. (1990) *The Politics of Disablement*. Basingstoke: Macmillan.

Oliver, M. and Barnes, C. (2012) *The New Politics of Disablement*. Basingstoke: Palgrave Macmillan.

22

Humour

Colin Cameron

Disabled people have long been regarded as fair game for comedy. Clark (2003) has drawn attention to examples of the way they have been ridiculed, describing Shakespearian 'Fool' characters, public visits to Bedlam and other eighteenth-century 'mental' institutions, and numerous stereotyped characters with 'amusing' impairments in modern TV sitcoms. Stand-up comedians continue to find disabled people easy targets for cheap laughs (Delingpole 2012). While disability is often still regarded as an acceptable subject for humour, little is heard about the distinctive humour that has emerged from disabled people's own subculture (Barnes 1992). This in itself is unsurprising as disability culture is a suppressed culture, struggling to establish itself in the face of non-disabled hegemony.

Mainstream ways of thinking about disability, associating impairment with personal tragedy, might presume that disabled people have little to laugh about. The experience of oppression, however, allows for a different gaze at everyday life. The absurdity inherent in the behaviour of many non-disabled people towards disabled people is the subject of much disability humour. This humour is typically dark and involves a way of dealing with the oppression experienced through, for example, inappropriate professional officiousness or unwanted, patronising interference from nosey do-gooders.

Like all good humour, disability humour draws on observations about everyday life. It does this in order to illuminate what is going on and to draw attention to the ridiculous way in which power relations operate in encounters with non-disabled people. In the context of disability politics it provides a valuable outlet for the expression of anger in a way less directly confrontational than other forms of protest (Branagan 2007). For many disabled people, watching another disabled person at a disability comedy event, highlighting the absurdity involved in disabling encounters and managing to do so in a way that makes these seem funny, has been a transformative experience: 'Having someone on stage communicating ideas and feelings that an isolated disabled person never suspected were shared by others can be a turning point for many' (Morrison and Finkelstein 1993: 127).

In his performance poem 'Where D'ya Get That Leg?' (Holdsworth 1989), Johnny Crescendo uses humour to cock a snook at those who persistently inappropriately question him about his impairment and who pester him as an object of curiosity and fascination:

I've known you now for how long is it?

And where d'ya get that leg?

Are you alright on the stairs?

And where d'ya get that leg?

Why d'you walk silly?

And where d'ya get that leg?

Have you got a willy?

And where d'ya get that leg?

The lyrics of Ian Stanton's song 'Chip On Yer Shoulder' (Stanton 1989) involve laughing at the stereotyped responses disabled people are used to hearing when they draw attention to physical barriers and lack of access:

You've got a chip on your shoulder

Got a really bad attitude

Is it any wonder

That people treat you the way they do

You really should be grateful

For all we do for you

And be a quiet little crip without a chip.

The sketch 'What We Really Think' by the theatre group Get Off Our Backs (1998) takes a wry look at assumptions about normality and at the knots non-disabled people sometimes get themselves into over language in relation to disability. It discloses the insight that disabled people, comfortable together in their own bodies and with their own identities, do not always regard normality as something to aspire to. The sketch involves two disabled people sitting in a park talking to each other:

'Well, look at that! A normal person!'

'Don't be cruel! They can't help it. Do you want people to think you're prejudiced?'

'No, I suppose not. So what should I call them?'

'Well, language is important. I would stick with non-disabled ... tosser ... prat...'

Using the insulting terms *tosser* and *prat*, the actors undermine the assumption that disabled people spend their lives wishing to be like the non-disabled. The standard view that disabled people are to be pitied for the tragedy of their impairments is reversed as it is disclosed that disabled people often pity the non-disabled for their conventionality. In Paula Greenwell's words, 'People say to me wouldn't you want to be normal and I say I wouldn't want to lower my standards' (in Swain, French and Cameron 2003: 106). To a disabled audience, the exchange above is funny because in a few lines it expresses something often felt but rarely spoken.

The Best Fake Charity Collection Buckets (2007) is a film shown by disabled comedian Laurence Clark. It shows footage of Clark in his wheelchair on a busy London shopping street with a series of increasingly bizarre statements printed on the charity collection bucket he is holding: 'Pay off my mortgage'; 'Please don't put money in here, I will get a criminal record if you do'; 'Sucker! This is a scam!'; 'I am not a charity case'; 'Kill the puppies'. The humour lies in watching the variety and number of passers-by who, in spite of Clark's protests, insist on putting money into his bucket. The film demonstrates the need felt by many non-disabled people to respond with misplaced sympathy to the appearance of impairment, revealing clearly also their unwillingness to actually listen to what disabled people have to say.

Meet the Superhumans Part 2 (Araniello 2012a) is a satirical film in which, over incessant dramatic background music, Katherine Araniello appears, sweating, medal bedecked and wearing a track suit, spouting the kinds of cliched statements made with great frequency and intensity on television by disabled athletes during the 2012 London Paralympic Games. Her performance emphasises and mocks the tautological effect produced:

It was the toughest day of my life

I had to dig deep to achieve what I have achieved

And that was to be the best

And I am the best

It was an amazing experience

And I know that I have inspired a future generation

I want to say a big thank you

To everyone who has supported me

My family, friends, all of you,

Thank you so much

I couldn't have done it without you

I never knew someone like me

Could be of such sporting excellence

And achieve what I have achieved

I have set a legacy.

Commenting on the film, Araniello states that 'I find the terminology that the Paralympians use repetitive and the opposite to inspiring. The sentimentality of heroic status is not an association that I personally adopt or want to be identified with' (Araniello 2012b).

Araniello's point was to satirise Paralympians' use of 'repetitive uplifting language coupled with the heroic sentiments of triumph over tragedy' (Araniello 2012b) to draw attention to the fact that, in spite of the fact that during the Paralympics there was heightened media focus on disabled people, this actually delivered nothing new. This becomes clearer as the film continues:

Get down to your local sport centre

And get involved with sport

It's the only thing that there is

For people like us ...

Disability humour is a shared emotional response to the particular forms of oppression that disability involves. It offers not just an opportunity for the strengthening of collective identity among those who have experiences in common, but the possibility of balancing critical insights with an amused understanding.

For Discussion

- Relating this to other marginalised social groups, can you think of reasons why humour often emerges as a response to oppression?
- Is there anything controversial about the idea that disabled people laugh at the non-disabled?
- Can you think of instances of behaviours by the non-disabled towards disabled people that might be described as absurd?

Further Reading and Viewing

Araniello, K. (2012) *Meet the Superhuman Part 2 (subtitled)*, www.youtube.com/watch?v= KjRaN3iahyM.

Cameron, C. (2009) 'Tragic but brave or just crips with chips? Songs and their lyrics in the Disability Arts Movement in Britain', *Popular Music*, 28 (3): 381–96.

Clark, L. (2012) *The Best Fake Charity Collection Boxes*, www.youtube.com/watch?v=_U_byvTzW4w.

References

Araniello, K. (2012a) *Meet the Superhuman Part 2 (subtitled)*, www.youtube.com/watch?v=KjRaN3iahyM, accessed 9 January 2013.

Araniello, K. (2012b) *Superhuman Part 2*, www.araniello-art.com/recentfilms.html, accessed 9 January 2013.

Barnes, C. (1992) *Disabling Imagery and the Media: An Exploration of the Principles for Media Representations of Disabled People*. Halifax: Ryburn Publishing/BCODP.

Branagan, M. (2007) 'The last laugh: humour in community activism', *Community Development Journal*, 42 (4): 470–81.

Clark, L. (2003) *Disabling Comedy: Only When We Laugh*, http://disability-studies.leeds.ac.uk/files/library/Clark-Laurence/clark-on-comedy.pdf, accessed 3 March 2013.

Clark, L. (2007) *The Best Fake Charity Collection Buckets*, www.youtube.com/watch?v=_U_byvTzW4w, accessed 3 March 2013.

Delingpole, J. (2012) *Frankie Boyle: National Treasure*, http://blogs.telegraph.co.uk/news/jamesdelingpole/100178780/frankie-boyle-national-treasure/, accessed 3 March 2013.

Get Off Our Backs (1998) *What We Really Think*. Wallsend: Tyneside Disability Arts.

Holdsworth, A. (1989) *Johnny Crescendo Revealed*. London: Self-published.

Morrison, E. and Finkelstein, V. (1993) 'Broken arts and cultural repair: the role of culture in the empowerment of disabled people', in J. Swain, V. Finkelstein, S. French and M. Oliver (eds), *Disabling Barriers – Enabling Environments*. London: Sage, pp. 122–27.

Stanton, I. (1989) *Shrinkin' Man* cassette. Manchester: GMCDP.

Swain, J. French, S. and Cameron, C. (2003) *Controversial Issues in a Disabling Society*. Buckingham: Open University Press.

23

Identity

Colin Cameron

Given the overwhelmingly negative representation of disability encountered in daily life, it is unsurprising that many people with impairments seek to distance themselves from identifying personally, or being identified by others, as disabled. The following statement made by a disabled woman expresses this fairly clearly:

> People have expected me to take the nicely paved path laid out for the disabled. They expected me not to try, not to accomplish, and not to succeed. That map was tossed out long ago. I have followed my own path as a person, a woman, who happens to have a physical disability.

(Hyatt 2008: unpaged)

In this chapter, however, I will argue that acknowledging disabled identity orientates disabled people differently, from a position of strength, in relation to choices and decisions to be made about situations encountered in life's course. Drawing on the phenomenologist Schutz's ideas of imposed and intrinsic relevances, I will suggest that taking on a disabled identity necessitates becoming involved in making assertions about both the right to be different and the ordinariness of difference. This involves a rejection of the thinking expressed typically in Hyatt's words above. Claims for recognition as people 'who happen to have a physical disability' involve a response to the experience of impairment in a disabling society that is just as predictable, stereotyped and conformist as the passive lifestyle usually rejected. Hyatt's is a position which involves an attempt to live with a sense of one's own difference as undesirable misfortune, but hopes to compensate well enough so that others will tolerate or overlook impairment. It is a position which takes pleasure when people say 'I never think of you as disabled' and gives assent to a dominant cultural view which categorises impairment as 'useless difference' (Michalko 2002: 97).

By the term *relevances*, Schutz describes things in life that happen around us and which have to be dealt with in the business of getting on. He used the term imposed relevances to describe 'situations and events which are not connected with interests chosen by us, which do not originate in acts of our discretion, and which we have to take just as they are' (Schutz 1970: 114).

In terms of disability, examples of imposed relevances include barriers preventing equal participation within community life; inadequate and badly designed housing; lack of access or convenient access to public transport; low educational expectations; few employment opportunities; lack of information; lack of control over personal decision-making processes; inaccessible leisure facilities; experiences of oppressive care and unwelcome intrusion; experiences of being objectified as objects of pity, curiosity or hatred; being made the subject of stereotyping judgements and condescending assumptions. These are part and parcel of the experience of being disabled. This is the case for people with impairments whether they accept or reject disability as a basis for identity.

Schutz suggests that 'we have no power to modify them by our spontaneous activities except by transforming the relevances thus imposed into intrinsic relevances' (Schutz 1970: 114). Intrinsic relevances he describes as 'the outcome of our chosen interests, established by our spontaneous decision to solve a problem by our own thinking, to attain a goal by our own action, to bring forth a projected state of affairs' (Schutz 1970: 114).

I contend that there is much to be gained by identifying as disabled if this involves transforming imposed relevances into intrinsic relevances in order that these can be addressed. Involved here is a process Freire has described in terms of agents singling out elements from their 'background awareness' and reflecting upon these, making them objects of consideration and objects of action and cognition (Freire 1974: 56). This requires an altered subjectivity and a naming of disability as oppression, and is part of a process that Linton has called 'claiming disability' (Linton 1998).

For so long as disability is rejected as a foundation on which to build identity people with impairments are unable to resist oppression. Oppression is unrecognised as such but is rather treated as an inevitable part of experience, being the ordinary outcome of impairment. Imposed relevances remain 'unclarified and incomprehensible' (Schutz 1970: 114). Each disabled person continues to internalise ideological conventions and requirements and learns to regard and adjust both identity and physicality in the light of these standards (Cameron 2008). Pressures to discourage people with impairments from identifying collectively are embedded within everyday life practices. Those who talk about injustice are labelled as 'complainers ... who cannot deal with the problems related to their disabilities' (Murphy 2005: 161) and are identified and treated as bitter people who have just not come to terms with their limitations.

Collective identification, underpinned by the social model, has transformed the meaning of what it is to be disabled. To say, with conviction rooted in a social model understanding, *I am a disabled person* – as opposed to *I am a person who happens to have a disability* – is not to say *I have an impairment* but is to make a statement about the marginalised situation of people with impairments in a disabling society. Furthermore, to say *I am disabled* collectively with other disabled people as an expression of anger turns this into a statement of pride.

Transforming imposed relevances into intrinsic relevances in this context involves a realistic appraisal of one's material situation. It involves bringing the surroundings within which one experiences life to the forefront of consciousness and critically holding them up for interrogation.

Stevens distinguishes between 'real' disabled people and politically active disabled people involved in 'the movement': 'I would argue from experience that many disabled people do not understand the social model or become involved in the politics of disability because they are too busy getting on with their lives' (Stevens 2008: 10).

It is, however, at the everyday level – at which people busily get on with their lives – that oppression is experienced. The misrecognition of oppression does not mean that oppression does not exist. As Lefebvre points out, objective social reality functions beyond the individual's 'subjectivity', beyond his own private consciousness (Lefebvre 2008: 165). The imposition of the idea of impairment and disability as personal deficiency is resisted by those who do not consider themselves personally deficient, but unless this resistance acknowledges the structural relations which are served by this idea, it is empty protest. To say 'I don't see myself as disabled' does not mean that one does not experience physical or social barriers.

Identifying as disabled is not a decision that suddenly somehow means everything is all right, but involves a new understanding of the relationship between disabled people and the contexts in which they live. It does not imply there is no longer a need for struggle, but that the focus of struggle is shifted from one's own physicality to the disabling environments and assumptions which oppress.

For Discussion

- Many people with impairments prefer not to think of themselves as disabled. Why?
- How might other people's responses to impairment impact on a disabled person's sense of identity?
- In what ways might the development of a positive disability identity change the way a disabled person sees the world?

Further Reading

Cameron, C. (2010) 'Does anybody like being disabled? A critical exploration of impairment, identity, media and everyday experience in a disabling society'. PhD thesis, Queen Margaret University, http://etheses.qmu.ac.uk/258/1/258.pdf.

Islam, Z. (2009) 'Negotiating identities: the lives of Pakistani and Bangladeshi disabled young people', *Disability & Society*, 23 (1): 41–52.

Saltes, N. (2012) 'Disability identity and disclosure in the online dating environment', *Disability & Society*, 28 (1): 96–109.

References

Cameron, C. (2008) 'Further towards an affirmation model', in T. Campbell, F. Fontes, L. Hemingway, A. Soorenian and C. Till (eds), *Disability Studies: Emerging Insights and Perspectives*. Leeds: The Disability Press, pp. 14–30.

Freire, P. (1974) *Pedagogy of the Oppressed*. London: Penguin.

Hyatt, G.W. (2008) *Resuming my Misbehaving Woman Role*, www.doitmyselfblog.com/2008/resuming-my-misbehaving-woman-role/, accessed 15 June 2009.

Lefebvre, H. (2008) *Critique of Everyday Life: Vol. 1*. London: Verso.

Linton, S. (1998) *Claiming Disability*. New York: New York University Press.

Michalko, R. (2002) *The Difference that Disability Makes*. Philadelphia, PA: Temple University Press.

Murphy, J.W. (2005) 'Social norms and their implications for disability', in J.W. Murphy and J.T. Pardeck (eds), *Disability Issues for Social Workers and Human Service Professionals in the 21st Century*. New York, NY: Haworth, pp. 153–63.

Schutz, A. (1970) *On Phenomenology and Social Relations*. Chicago, IL: University of Chicago Press.

Stevens, S. (2008) 'Movement doesn't move me', *Community Care*, 13 November.

24 Impairment

Colin Cameron

Identified within the social model as 'the loss or limitation of physical, mental or sensory function on a long-term or permanent basis' (DPI 1981, in Rieser 2008: 24), or as 'a medically classified biophysiological condition' (Barnes and Mercer 2010: 11), the subject of impairment has been at the centre of controversial debates in Disability Studies. One area of contention, between social modelists and feminists, has been around the extent to which impairment is an appropriate focus for the discipline, while postmodernists have questioned the descriptive value of the term itself.

An 'orthodox' early position held that to include impairment as a focus of Disability Studies would be to undermine the social model, allowing critics to argue that disability has all along, after all, been an individual problem rather than a structural issue. This view held that the restrictions of activity experienced by disabled people are created by disabling physical and social environments and that these, rather than people's impairments, should be the focus of analysis. Oliver has stated that the social model 'is not about the personal experience of impairment but the collective experience of disablement' (Oliver 2004: 8).

An alternative view established by disabled feminists including, e.g. Crow (1992), French (1993) and Thomas (1999), argues, however, that impairment must be acknowledged as part of the experience of disability, and that even if all social barriers were removed, some impairments will continue to exclude disabled people from some activities. The personal is political, they argue, and the analysis of the subjective experience of impairment in a disabling society is a legitimate line of Disability Studies enquiry.

Postmodernists have criticised the way in which 'impairment has for the most part circulated in disability discourse as some objective, transhistorical and transcultural entity which biomedicine accurately represents' (Tremain 2002: 34). This is to suggest that what is regarded as impairment is not fixed for all time but changes as different discourses emerge, as ways of thinking and talking about the body transform. Impairment, it is argued, is no less a social construction than disability. Drawing on the French philosopher Foucault, Tremain has argued that rather than involving an uncontroversial description of physical reality, impairment is a naturalised *effect* of disciplinary knowledge/power.

From this view, impairment only appears when it is named by regulatory systems. 'Anomalies' in the social body appear when individual bodies become the subject of medicalising scrutiny and classification. The rituals which organise everyday life impose boundaries and categories on the ways individuals are able to think about and experience themselves. We think about impairment *as* impairment because social life is structured and reinforced through everyday interaction in ways which make it very difficult to consider how it could be regarded differently.

Postmodernists regard impairment less as a material 'fact' than as a representation of physicality used to give legitimacy to a particular form of social organisation. From this perspective, the social model treatment of impairment as 'a real thing' is problematic. An example of the use of postmodern analysis in Disability Studies would be to allow consideration of the way impairments 'appear' at different historical junctures. The inability to read, for example, would not have been regarded as indicative of having learning difficulties in a pre-literate society. It is only when literacy becomes a social requirement that this inability shows up and becomes identified as a problem, subject to the gaze and intervention of an array of medical, psychological and 'special' educational professionals. Yet what are labelled learning difficulties or learning disabilities are treated as indisputable facts, defining characteristics possessed by an individual as part of their core being. The description 'learning disabilities', moreover, draws us back into medical model discourse which identifies disability as a discreditable personal characteristic.

The materialist feminist Thomas (1999) made an important contribution to the discussion of impairment by introducing the notion of 'impairment effects'. By this term she describes:

> restrictions of activity [which] may be directly related to, or caused by, having a physical, sensory or intellectual impairment (not being able to do certain things because of the absence of a limb or the presence of chronic pain or fatigue, for example).

> (Thomas, 1999: 42)

Thomas is very clear, however, that these restrictions are not *disabilities*. 'The fact that I cannot hold a spoon or a saucepan in my left hand is an effect of my impairment and does not constitute disability,' she writes (Thomas 1999: 43). This may, though, become the marker for other restrictions of activity which do constitute disability if other people decide that because she cannot perform such actions, she is unfit to be a paid care worker or a parent and should be denied employment or the privilege of becoming a mother. Thomas argues that disability resides in the denial of rights, or the refusal to assist me in overcoming functional limitations, by allowing me to do things in an unconventional way, or by helping me to access instruments and technologies which would compensate for not being able to hold things 'normally'.

(Thomas 1999: 43)

Thomas argues, moreover, that impairment and impairment effects should not be regarded as 'natural' or as pre-social, 'biological' phenomena (Thomas 1999). She makes the point that the way in which impairment and impairment effects are perceived by others and, as a consequence, experienced by disabled people, is shaped by the interaction of biological and social factors. The meaning attributed to impairment profoundly determines the sense that can be made of the experience of living with impairment. In this sense, at the level of everyday experience, disability and impairment effects interact, which is why it is important to be clear about the distinction between the two. This is a view endorsed by Hughes and Paterson, who have suggested that 'disability is experienced in, on and through the body, just as impairment is experienced in terms of the cultural narratives that help to constitute its meaning' (Hughes and Paterson 2006: 101).

It should be noted, finally, that people with different impairments and impairment effects will often experience different aspects of disability. A wheelchair user, for example, is more likely to face barriers in the physical and social environment in terms, say, of encountering doors in public buildings which are too heavy to be opened or steps preventing access. A deaf person will encounter barriers because the organisers of an event have failed to provide a British Sign Language interpreter or an electronic note-taker. Someone labelled as having learning difficulties may be excluded within a meeting because a service provider uses complicated jargon. Somebody with a speech impairment may experience condescension because of other peoples' impatience and unwillingness to listen. It may also be the case as well that somebody will have a number of impairments and experience various forms of disablism simultaneously. What is common in each of these situations, however, is the experience of being placed at a disadvantage – in other words, disabled – because society is still not very good at including people with impairments as equals.

For Discussion

- Identify barriers that are likely to be encountered in everyday life by somebody who:

  - is a wheelchair user
  - has a visual impairment
  - is deaf or has a hearing impairment
  - experiences mental health issues
  - has been labelled as having learning difficulties
  - has a hidden impairment.

- Identify as many ways as you can of addressing and removing these barriers.
- Do you think it is the responsibility of disabled people to come to terms with their impairments?

Further Reading

Crow, L. (2014) 'Lying down anyhow – impairment, difference and identity', in J. Swain, S. French, C. Barnes and S. Thomas (eds), *Disabling Barriers – Enabling Environments*, 3rd edn. London: Sage, pp. 85–91.

Pueraveera, K. (2012) 'Theorising the body: conceptions of disability, gender and normality', *Disability & Society*, 28 (3) 408–17.

Thomas, C. (2014) 'Disability and impairment', in J. Swain, S. French, C. Barnes and S. Thomas (eds), *Disabling Barriers – Enabling Environments*, 3rd edn. London: Sage, pp. 9–16.

References

Barnes, C. and Mercer, G. (2010) *Exploring Disability*, 2nd edn. Cambridge: Polity.

Crow, L. (1992) 'Renewing the social model', *Coalition*, July: 5–9.

French, S. (1993) 'Disability, impairment or something in-between', in J. Swain, V. Finkelstein, S. French and M. Oliver (eds), *Disabling Barriers – Enabling Environments*. London: Sage, pp. 17–25.

Hughes, B. and Paterson, K. (2006) 'The social model of disability and the disappearing body: towards a sociology of impairment', in L. Barton (ed.), *Overcoming Disabling Barriers*. London: Routledge, pp. 91–107.

Oliver, M. (2004) 'If I had a hammer: the social model in action', in J. Swain, S. French, C. Barnes and S. Thomas (eds), *Disabling Barriers – Enabling Environments*, 2nd edn. London: Sage, pp. 7–12.

Rieser, R. (2008) *Making It Happen: Implementing the Duty to Promote Disability Equality in Secondary Schools and Local Authorities*. London: Disability Equality in Education.

Thomas, C. (1999) *Female Forms: Experiencing and Understanding Disability*. Buckingham: Open University Press.

Tremain, S. (2002) 'On the subject of impairment', in M. Corker and T. Shakespeare (eds), *Disability/Postmodernity: Embodying Disability* Theory London: Continuum, pp. 32–47.

25   Inclusion

Colin Cameron

The concept of *inclusion* needs first to be distinguished from that of *integration*. Education and social welfare policies with integration as their aim have usually been underpinned by deficit models of disability and have regarded it as desirable that disabled people are drawn into society and its processes. In this view the exclusion of disabled people from the social mainstream has been the unplanned consequence of society's historic develop-ment, and can be amended through paternalistic policy (Oliver and Barnes 2012). It is not seen that society is 'at fault', or in need of change, but that disabled people need to become assimilated within existing social norms and adjusted to social environments developed by and for a non-disabled population (Drake 1999). The onus for change within such policies is placed on disabled people. It is they who need to become 'more like' non-disabled people in order to gain acceptance. This can be seen, for example, in Wolfensberger's (1982) doctrine of normalisation or social role valorisation, which required disabled people – particularly people with the learning difficulties label – to gain socially valued behaviours and appearances (extending as far as plastic surgery to alter facial characteristics) as the price of community participation. Integration implies a tolerance of disabled people, whose presence may be accepted though they will never be regarded as equals. Disabled people are expected to strive to emulate the non-disabled while recognising that their best efforts will never be good enough.

Inclusion involves the view that the responsibility for change lies with society. In Oliver's words (1996: 90), inclusion is not something that can be delivered by politicians, policy-makers or educators, but is rather 'a process of struggle that has to be joined'. Taking school education as an example, whereas integration has traditionally assumed the assimilation of the disabled child into a mainstream school which is largely unchanged, inclusion requires a school to re-think the way it does everything. The school is required to identify and address the barriers within its environment, teaching and learning strategies, attitudes, organisation and management that prevent the full participation of disabled children (Rieser 2010). It is about creating opportunities for all children to learn together. Whereas integration has been conceived as a state to be achieved by setting targets in terms of numbers, inclusion is thought of as a process and as an aspiration. Inclusion involves the creation of settings in which difference is encouraged and valued. Similarly, social inclusion on a wider basis involves moving away from a set of assumptions which identify disability as a problem to be accommodated, instead identifying and addressing the barriers which have prevented the full involvement of disabled people as equal citizens.

Critically, inclusion needs to be regarded not just as a disability issue but as one which concerns everybody. Confronting the oppression experienced by disabled people involves confronting the cultural values by which other forms of oppression, e.g. racism, sexism, heterosexism, ageism and discrimination on the basis of social class, are created and sustained. Recognising the ways in which capitalism has marked and excluded impaired bodies as worthless produces a recognition of ways in which other categories of difference have been similarly marked and devalued. The struggle for inclusion makes alignment with other marginalised social groups necessary.

It is a sign of the success of the disabled people's movement in Europe that practices of inclusion have, over the past decade or so, been the focus of policies to 'mainstream' disability at local, national and European levels of government. Disability mainstreaming involves:

> the process of assessing the implications for disabled people of any planned action, including legislation, policies and programmes, in all areas and levels. It is a strategy for making disabled people's concerns and experiences an integral part of the design, implementation, monitoring, and evaluation of policies and programmes in all political, economic and social spheres so that disabled people benefit equality and inequality is not perpetuated.

(Disability KaR, in Social Economy Europe Disability Group 2008)

What this indicates is that considerable effort has been invested in trying to remove barriers to disabled people's participation in society and that there has been an acknowledgement of the need for social rather than individual change. Co-production, for example, draws on the principle that those affected by services are best placed to design them and involves partnership working between service providers and users (People and participation.net 2012). While there have been significant developments in terms of the greater inclusion of disabled people within the social mainstream over the past few years, however, to regard this process as one of untrammelled progress would be a mistake.

While access is a major part of moving towards equality, inclusion will always remain partial for as long as impairment is still regarded as deficit. The recycling of cultural narratives representing disability as something 'wrong' with disabled people prevents us from moving forward. Disabled people may be more frequently encountered within ordinary community life than they were a decade or two ago but, rather than being allowed to affirm difference, they are expected to perform a role which validates conformity (Cameron 2010). Inclusion has ended up being not so very different from integration, and disabled people are still more likely to be met with patronising tolerance than with respectful acknowledgement as equals. Tregaskis (2004) describes the way in which, while practising inclusion in terms of providing access, service providers often continue to hold stereotyped and belittling attitudes towards disabled people, and these shape their words and behaviours.

The problem with being mainstreamed is that this is conditional upon disabled people's willingness to downplay the significance of their impairments. There is an expectation that once barriers have been removed, impairment will be continue to regarded as an inconvenience, something it would still be better not to have, or to which reference should be avoided. This requires disabled people's acquiescence in normative ways of thinking about impairment and the de-politicisation of disability, effectively leading to capitulation rather than struggle. This is very different from the idea of regarding impairment as something valuable in and of itself, as a core part of someone's individuality.

Michalko (2002) has described the potentiality of impairment to disrupt conventional ways of thinking about the world and about being in the world. This is an opportunity which has been missed in manifestations of inclusion as these have transpired. As Tregaskis (2004: 151) remarks, the way forward towards real social inclusion 'depends on our ability to engage in dialogues that acknowledge and respect people's differences from each other'. Without access there can be no inclusion, but access is not an end in itself.

For Discussion

- What is the difference between integration and inclusion?
- Is being different something to be feared or something to be celebrated?
- 'Respecting difference means that we have to try and like everybody.' Do you agree or disagree with this statement?

Further Reading

Davis, J. (2014) 'Disability and childhood: a journey towards inclusion', in J. Swain, S. French, C. Barnes and S. Thomas (eds), *Disabling Barriers – Enabling Environments*, 3rd edn. London: Sage, pp. 157–64.

Rieser, R. (2010) *Integration and Inclusion*, www.worldofinclusion.com/integration_inclusion.htm.

Tregaskis, C. (2004) *Constructions of Disability: Researching the Interface Between Disabled and Non-disabled People*. London: Routledge.

References

Cameron, C. (2010) 'Does anybody like being disabled? A critical exploration of impairment, identity, media and everyday experience in a disabling society'. PhD thesis, Queen Margaret University, http://etheses.qmu.ac.uk/258/1/258.pdf, accessed 26 November 2012.

Drake, R. (1999) *Understanding Disability Policies*. Basingstoke: Macmillan.

Michalko, R. (2002) *The Difference that Disability Makes*. Philadelphia: Temple University Press.

Oliver, M. (1996) *Understanding Disability: From Theory to Practice*. Basingstoke: Macmillan.

Oliver, M. and Barnes, C. (2012) *The New Politics of Disablement*. Basingstoke: Palgave Macmillan.

People and participation.net (2012) *Co-Production*, www.peopleandparticipation.net/display/Methods/Co-production, accessed 27 November 2012.

Rieser, R. (2010) *Integration and Inclusion*, www.worldofinclusion.com/integration_inclusion.htm, accessed 26 November 2012.

Social Economy Europe Disability Group (2008) *Creating an Inclusive Society Mainstreaming Disability Based on the Social Economy Example*, www.ms-in-europe.com/w3p_dokumentearchiv/reykjavik_2008__workshop_iv_25.05.08.pdf, accessed 26 November 2012.

Tregaskis, C. (2004) *Constructions of Disability: Researching the Interface Between Disabled and Non-disabled People*. London: Routledge.

Wolfensberger, W. (1982) *Normalisation: The Principle of Normalisation in Human Services*. Toronto: National Institute on Mental Retardation.

26 Independent Living

Florence Garabedian

The idea of independent living, which emerged in the US and UK in the 1970s as a direct response to disabled people's experiences of institutionalisation and segregation, fundamentally challenged culturally normative views on 'caring'. It also shook up uncritical assumptions about independence, such as the idea that disabled people should aspire to physical independence or self-reliance. Disabled people define independent living as a means to having meaningful choices and control over their own lives:

> Independent living means all disabled people having the same freedom, choice and control as other citizens at home, at work, and in the community. It does not mean living by yourself or fending for yourself. It means rights to practical assistance and support to participate in society and live an ordinary life.

(Independent Living in Scotland 2012)

While arrangements for independent living can vary, they often involve direct cash payments to a disabled person in lieu of community care services. The disabled person is then able to employ their own personal assistants to support them with tasks they have prioritised, retaining self-determination and control over decisions in their life rather than becoming dependent on directly-provided services (Glasby and Littlechild 2009). Social responses and frameworks are required to make this possible:

> Independent living is a cross-silo, corporate issue, concerning the whole of disabled people's interactions with society; its organisations, facilities and structures; in every aspect of their quality and equality of life.

> (Elder-Woodward 2012)

The independent living movement locates independent living firmly within a human rights agenda. Entitlement to independent living is enshrined in the UN Convention on the Rights of Persons with Disabilities (UNCRPD) and recognised by the UK Government. For disabled people the right to independent living, where it is shored up by adequate resource commitment, means they can get on with their lives without having to negotiate continuous processes and obstacles imposed by society:

> [Funding for independent living] has completely changed my life. I now have a life again. Before going on to independent living I thought life had finished. I get out a lot more and all my daily requirements are met. What a remarkable change to my life and mental state.

> (Lothian Centre for Inclusive Living 2010)

However, despite significant promotion of the right to independent living by disabled people and their representative organisations in recent decades, real consolidation of automatic entitlement is hampered by competing majority interests in society. Any policy shift directing professionals to develop new assessments that continue to focus on limiting definitions of 'needs' of disabled people cannot enable the radical changes necessary to eradicate the social barriers that create disablement. Funding cuts introduced as austerity measures have taken hold across Europe and have decimated allowances and services. Independent living for millions of disabled people is threatened unless critical questions about how and where their rights are met are confronted.

Elsewhere in the context of service delivery for health and social care, 'personalisation' is presented as the key to independent living for disabled people. Yet making personalisation an aim for current changes in any sector such as community care, health, education, housing or accessible transport is likely to be reductive rather than progressing independent living. Arguably in the UK the rising personalisation agenda obfuscates the goals of the independent living movement. Shifting attention to issues of individual benefit is not conducive to developing the wider vision of entitlement to independent living. As Dodd (2013) states:

> To be clear, by concentrating solely on personalising services to individual needs, personalisation holds the danger of taking the focus away from disabling barriers that affect all disabled people, and obscuring possible alternative policy agendas.

Personalisation and person-centred approaches have an important role to play in giving disabled people a say in their own lives, including a say in the way organisations deliver services that will enable independent living. However, personalisation policy can be deeply divisive and disabling if it is rolled out without clear direction to ensure the goal of independent living is not diminished. This concern explains why disabled people's organisations seeking routes to independent living fight to uphold a more ambitious entitlement agenda than the personalisation agenda allows for. Independent living is not simply about addressing need, it strives to facilitate independent lives.

It is also important to note that independent living is the outcome of much more than an individual service user's relationship with any particular services. The achievement of independent living requires the removal of barriers within services and across services. It demands innovative approaches to the creation of service responses which transcend organisational boundaries that frequently constrain service delivery and support. To forge a service sector which will facilitate independent living, every nuance of ideology, policy and practice has to be interrogated in response to what disabled people themselves say about what they feel will be effective and relevant for their choices regarding independent living.

In my experience as Chief Executive of a user-led Centre for Inclusive Living I have found that when independent living becomes the aim of service development, embedded in policies and operational strategies, the aspirations of service providers change and broaden. This is because the focus is no longer on how a particular service responds to the needs of individual users. Wider consideration of how it responds to the whole lives of its community of users has come into play. Where transformation of services towards independent living is at its most enabling, disabled people's lives are not engaged with through a series of 'person-centred' interactions with individual services. They are viewed instead through a holistic lens that prioritises not 'what a service can offer in its own terms' but the desire for independence and freedom expressed by service users. The goal of independent living is not subsumed within a personalisation agenda and requires service providers to ally themselves with disabled people as agents of change. The idea of personalisation has, however, gained power within UK social policy contexts so that while it is oppositional to notions of independent living it must be an idea assimilated rather than ignored. Finding ways to connect ideas about personalisation of services and funding with social model thinking is vital to ensure practitioners do not find themselves eroding the core principles of control, choice and self-governance expressed in the key assumptions underpinning the philosophy of the independent living movement:

- All human life is of value
- Anyone, whatever their impairment, is capable of exercising choices
- People who are disabled by society's reaction to physical, intellectual and sensory impairment and to emotional distress have the right to assert control over their lives
- Disabled people have the right to participate fully in society (Morris 1993: 21).

When independent living remains the goal, a discourse of personalisation becomes meaningful and relevant to the process. In this context, service commissioning, management and planning can be approached confidently, based on a shared understanding of independent living as the end product. This shared aim, to minimise the distance between ideas about independent living and personalisation, is what will drive changes towards best practice in independent living for both service providers and disabled people.

To live an independent life, to have choice and control over one's life, is something wanted by most people, including disabled people.

For Discussion

- Can you think of ways in which service provision would be changed if independent living was the core aim of all care and support systems?
- What are the challenges of making independent living a reality for governments and service managers?
- What are the challenges faced by disabled people seeking to make independent living a reality and how can these be circumvented?

Further Reading

Dodd, S. (2013) 'Personalisation, individualism and the politics of disablement', *Disability & Society*, 28 (2): 260–73.

Goble, C. (2014) 'Dependence, independence and normality', in J. Swain, S. French, C. Barnes and C. Thomas (eds), *Disabling Barriers – Enabling Environments*, 3rd edn. London: Sage, pp. 31–36.

Independent Living in Scotland (2012) *What is Independent Living?*, www.ilis.co.uk/independent-living.

References

Dodd, S (2013) 'Personalisation, individualism and the politics of disablement', *Disability & Society*, 28 (2): 260–73.

Elder-Woodward, J. (2012) *Independent Living: The Frontier of Communication Welfare?* Lancaster: ESRC Seminar Series, Lancaster University.

Glasby, J. and Littlechild, R. (2009) *Direct Payments and Personal Budgets: Putting Personalisation into Practice*. Bristol: Policy Press.

Independent Living in Scotland (2012) *What is Independent Living?*, www.ilis.co.uk/independent-living, accessed 23 February 2013.

Lothian Centre for Inclusive Living (2010) *Survey 2009–10*. Edinburgh: LciL.

Morris, J. (1993) *Independent Lives? Community Care and Disabled People*. Basingstoke: Macmillan.

27

International Perspectives

Michele Moore

Papers in the world-leading journal *Disability & Society* present a range of international perspectives concerning disabled people in different cultures and locations across the world, providing a vivid resource for understanding the relationship between disability and society in the context of global changes faced by disabled people in the twenty-first century. Students who are serious about engaging with human rights, discrimination, definitions, policy and practices and other determinants of the experience of people with impairments across the world will find the journal an important source of international perspectives on disability (*Disability & Society* Special Issue 2013; Moore 2012). Key writing on international perspectives in Disability Studies focuses on social issues and human rights, frequently contending with policy intentions and practical outcomes that block realisation of the entitlements of disabled people. At the heart of the most powerful work seeking to enrich cross-national understandings of disabled people's lives lies a commitment to raising the voices of disabled people themselves, holding self-expression and self-determination as central to the process of advancing entitlement and inclusion.

At the start of the twenty-first century constantly changing challenges and forms of resistance associated with global conflicts and crises face disabled people, their allies and representative organisations in different parts of the world. These conflicts and crises are many and varied, concerning, for example, economic challenges which threaten to widen inequality and deepen poverty; changing demographics; social revolutions and transformations including conflict-led change and cultural upheaval in the wake of turmoil; environmental challenges; new approaches to health and medicine and so on, all of which demand new approaches to theorising and engaging with disability in diverse contexts. Highlighting and sharing different international perspectives concerning disability issues has the potential to expose and reconcile complex agendas of social justice and exclusion at local, national and global levels.

Upholding the central importance of placing disabled people's voices at the heart of cross-cultural activity, as part of a process of building new international communities of knowledge, policy and practice, requires constant reimagining of the boundaries of our thinking. In my own international work I constantly struggle for a modus operandi that incorporates the aims and aspirations of all of those involved, including my own, without unintentionally reproducing imbalances in power relationships that are contrary to those aims. When working to understand international perspectives in Disability Studies we cannot work in an academic vacuum; our efforts are always located within a complex set of relational, situational, cultural and political conditions (Lavia and Moore 2010). Never doubt that cross-cultural work to expand international perspectives on disability issues will be intensely problematic; we must expect it to be fraught with the inevitable challenges of politics, power and history.

As a UK scholar invited to help drive forward an agenda for inclusive education or services in many countries around the world I inevitably find some voices more dominant than others. Despite an assumption of equity, engaging with international perspectives can easily be set up in ways in which the voices of some participants find their voice matters less than those of others. People whose voices are most seldom heard are individuals who have been historically marginalised, so that the voices of disabled people are routinely difficult to access. In some parts of Asia or the Middle East for example, insider perspectives of disabled women and girls are more difficult to raise; in East Caribbean countries I found perspectives of poor disabled people hard to garner; in Syria and Iraq the voices of disabled people caught up in war or living in exile are hardest to access and so on. A tangible difficulty in operationalising international studies of disability involves making sense of which groups have their issues and perspectives privileged in contrast to others. In my own work this reflects a legacy of colonialism, exclusion and oppression of disabled people by dominant voices and practices which must always be acknowledged.

As is true across the field of Disability Studies, there is invidious potential in international work for disabled people's own aspirations to be colonised by groups with particular interests, impeded by competing and contradictory policy developments and diluted within academic discourse and practice. There is often a set of tacit assumptions about the kind of approach to be taken to Disability Studies in international contexts. It is important to recognise that contemporary discourses familiar within one's own world, of 'empowering' or 'capacity-building' in mine, for example, can operate to induct disabled people and their representative agencies into normalising practices of Western thinking before anyone has worked out whether these are even appropriate to local disabled people themselves (Brunskell-Evans and Moore 2012). The transformative role of non-Western perspectives is yet to be adequately realised in contemporary Disability Studies.

Nonetheless in order to learn about, and through international perspectives on disability, it is necessary to seek to find a modus operandi. Tuhiwai Smith (2005) places emphasis on the critical importance of always being *reflective* in engagements with communities. She promotes awareness of *'lines of relating'* to offer a way of articulating the nature of insider–outsider distance in our cross-cultural studies and relationships. While I am not an indigenous member of the international communities in which I am working, I *may* claim some meaningful *'lines of relating'* that help enhance the utility of an outsider gaze. Through my status as the mother of two children with impairments, for example, the consequences of my engagements in schools, whether at home in the UK or the deserts of Oman, do impact on my own children's destinies. So although it is simply not possible for me to claim robust insight into perspectives on disability in the Arab world, careful reflection on my own *lines of relating* can help to scrutinise the meaning I am making with some measure of integrity. An element of muddle has to be recognised as embodied in the multiple – and confused – dimensions of insider/outsider perspectives in comparative international Disability Studies. In my own work I hold on to values of openness and honesty, trust and *'a politics of grace'* described by Darder and Yiamouyiannis (2010) as embodying principles of reciprocity, redemption and revolution. Even though such dimensions may not be concretely realised, I feel they are useful as part of a general approach to understanding international perspectives which will have practical, methodological, ethical or theoretical merit. Through working in many international settings I have learned that the basis for respectful and transformative engagement is trust. It is the most powerful resource we can offer and its power lies in the extent to which we can invoke it. Trust is only generated through serious commitment to the voices of others.

Opening up wider international perspectives in Disability Studies cannot be an easy or comfortable process because it compels willingness to continually alter one's own view of the world and of how disabled people are positioned within it. But through expansion of international perspectives there does emerge a critical space for fresh thinking on globally informed new possibilities for enabling the lives of people with impairments. Specifically, the transnational power of the voices of disabled people for forming new global activism and alliances will reshape disabled people's lives, identities and futures, making international perspectives a critical arena of enquiry.

For Discussion

- Critically reflect on your own *'lines of relating'* to people that you work with. What are the differences, and what is similar between you? How do these *'lines of relating'* influence your perspective?
- How do you think your personal experiences, power and choices shape your perceptions, relations and actions in cross-cultural studies of disability?

Further Reading

Disability & Society (2013) Special Issue: Disability, Global Conflicts and Crises.
Matsui, A., Nagase, O., Sheldon, A., Goodley, D., Sawada, Y. and Kawashima, S. (eds) (2012) *Creating a Society for All: Disability and Economy*. Leeds: The Disability Press.
Moore, M. (ed.) (2012) *Moving Beyond Boundaries in Disability Studies: Rights, Spaces and Innovation*. London: Routledge.

References

Darder, A. and Yiamouyiannis, Z. (2010) 'Political grace and the struggle to decolonize community practice', in J. Lavia and M. Moore (eds), *Cross-cultural Perspectives on Policy and Practice: Decolonizing Community Contexts*. London: Routledge, pp. 10–27.
Disability & Society (2013) Special Issue: Disability, Global Conflicts and Crises.
Brunskell-Evans, H. and Moore, M. (eds) (2012) *Reimagining Research for Reclaiming the Academy in Iraq: Identities and Participation in Post-conflict Enquiry*. Rotterdam, The Netherlands: Sense Publishers.
Lavia, J. and Moore, M. (eds) (2010) *Decolonizing Community Contexts: Cross-Cultural Perspectives on Policy and Practice*. London: Routledge.
Moore, M. (ed.) (2012) *Moving Beyond Boundaries in Disability Studies: Rights, Spaces and Innovation*. London: Routledge.
Tuhiwai Smith, L. (2005) *Decolonizing Methodologies. Research and Indigenous Peoples*. London: Zed Books.

28 Intersectionality

Sarah Woodin

In 2008, Jane Campbell, then Chair of the Equality and Human Rights Disability Committee in England, argued in favour of an end to single-identity politics of the disabled people's movement, which had long been defended on the basis of commonality of oppression (Finkelstein 1993). Instead, Campbell spoke about diversity of disabled people and their common interests with other disadvantaged groups in overcoming societal barriers and seeking redress for injustice. Her speech unsurprisingly led to considerable debate in the UK disabled people's movement. It also reflected the progress that disabled people had made in the past two decades and a confidence in the future. Six months later the financial crisis began and with it a period of retrenchment and welfare spending cuts. In this new climate the entitlement of disabled people to welfare payments was brought into question, once more forcing disabled people to defend themselves as worthy and 'really disabled'. The way that personal experiences, identities, structures and politics interact in terms of commonality and difference is therefore complex, historically contingent and contested.

Social groups, divisions, and classifications (gender, disability, 'race', age, etc.) are a feature of all societies and are central to identity and sense of belonging (Young 1990; Yuval Davis 2011). Groups may be more or less enduring regarding membership, composition and the way they are perceived. One group is frequently privileged as the taken-for-granted norm in relation to the one it is compared with (disabled/non-disabled, men/women, old/young); the marginalised group is seen as 'Other' (de Beauvoir 1997: 81). Conversely, marginalised groups may also use group membership as a source of strength in resisting oppression (Driediger 1989).

The term intersectionality was first used by Crenshaw (1989) to explain aspects of black and minority ethnic (BME) women's experiences of discrimination in relation to the law. The law, for example, uses identity categories to describe discrimination (e.g. disability, 'race', gender), and unless it could be shown that an instance of discrimination related to one or the other, there was no recourse to justice. However, for people with more than one negatively valued characteristic, e.g. black women, the basis for discrimination is not always clear.

Originating in Gender Studies, the concept of intersectionality has been used to describe relationships between social groups, with an emphasis on boundaries and perceptions of difference. However, the concept is complex and is deployed in several ways. It has been used to describe locations of oppression and marginalisation, the processes through which oppression happens, and the methods for researching it. McCall (2005) has developed an influential typology regarding methods. An anti-categorical approach involves the deconstruction of categories; an intercategorical method the comparison of existing categories, and the intracategorical method entails a focus on boundaries and people at the margins of groups. Although there have been important contributions to the discussion of intersectionality in regard to disability and gender (Garland-Thomson 2005; Meekosha 2007) within Disability Studies, the discussion has mainly remained at the levels of experience and identity. The rest of this chapter will discuss intersectionality in relation to Disability Studies and disabled people.

A continuing question concerns whether the discrimination faced by disabled people who have more than one marginalised status is additive (where one devalued status adds to another) or mutually constitutive (qualitatively different as a result). Using an additive approach, Hanna and Rogovsky (1991: 49) describe 'double discrimination' against disabled women, resulting in 'two handicaps plus'. This description is still often used, for example in several key documents of the United Nations Convention on the Rights of Disabled People (UNCRPD) regarding disabled women. However, it has been criticised on the basis that the resulting discrimination is qualitatively different rather than simply the sum of two oppressions (Stuart 1996).

Begum (1994) and Stuart (1996) prefer the term simultaneous oppression to describe the situation of black disabled people, denoting the presence of racism and disablism at the same time. Stuart (2012), for example, describes how the exclusion of BME disabled people from political participation on direct payments resulted from a Department of Health decision to work with user-led organisations, which have been poor at involving BME service users. Black disabled people may be marginalised by both the disabled people's movement due to racism and the anti-racist movement due to disablism, a point that has been made in relation to other identities such as women and lesbian, gay, bisexual and transgendered (LGBT) disabled people, where disablism and homophobia result in exclusion from both groups (Rainbow Ripples and Butler 2006). Despite common experiences of oppression therefore, not all oppressed groups identify with one another (Priestley 1995).

Vernon (1999) goes further by arguing for the specificity and changing nature of oppression according to context. Pointing out that different kinds of oppression may be to the fore at different times, she uses the term 'multiple Other' (Vernon 1999: 389), reflecting also that the status of being Other applies to the majority of the population in one way or another – most people not being white, privileged, heterosexual men. Begum (1994) and Vernon (1999) recognise that disabled people are not simply passive victims. As noted above, marginalised people also participate in oppression when they form alliances with some groups against others and the form of this is linked to the social context of the time.

Erevelles' (2011) materialist analysis of difference takes an intercategorical approach (McCall 2005), while also locating the experiences of class, disability, race and gender in specific social contexts of history and structure. She documents the extreme violence experienced by some disabled people who are located at the margins, and her account makes distinctions between levels of analysis. Distinctions between intersections at the levels of experience, identity, structure and politics may be identified in relation to material and cultural aspects (Yuval-Davis 2006). Work on intersectional relations at each of these levels is just beginning in Disability Studies and, as was recognised at the start of this chapter, it has to take into account the material realities of disablism and the need for concerted effort to challenge it.

For Discussion

- What disadvantages do you think are faced by black disabled women today? Are these additive or qualitatively different?
- What might be some of the difficulties of researching intersectionality?
- What might be the advantages and disadvantages for political elites of separate single identity groups?

Further Reading

Erevelles, N. (2011) *Disability and Difference in Global Contexts: Enabling a Transformative Body Politic*. Basingstoke: Palgrave Macmillan.

Meekosha, H. (2007) 'What the hell are you? An intercategorical analysis of race, ethnicity, gender and disability in the Australian body politic', *Scandinavian Journal of Disability Research*, 8 (2–3): 161–76.

Vernon, A. (1999) 'The dialectics of multiple identities and the disabled people's movement', *Disability & Society*, 14 (3): 385–98.

References

Begum, N. (1994) *Reflections: The Views of Black Disabled People on their Lives and Community Care*. London: Central Council for Education and Training in Social Work.

Campbell, J. (2008) 'Fighting for a slice or for a bigger cake?' Sixth Annual Disability Lecture at St John's College, Cambridge, 29 April, University of Cambridge.

Crenshaw, K. (1989) 'Demarginalizing the intersection of race and sex: a black feminist critique of antidiscrimination doctrine, feminist theory and antiracist politics', *University of Chicago Legal Forum*, 139–67.

de Beauvoir, S. (1997) *The Second Sex*. London: Picador.

Driediger, D. (1989) *The Last Civil Rights Movement: Disabled People's International*. London: Hurst.

Erevelles, N. (2011) *Disability and Difference in Global Contexts: Enabling a Transformative Body Politic*. Basingstoke: Palgrave Macmillan.

Finkelstein, V. (1993) 'The commonality of disability', in J. Swain, V. Finkelstein, S. French and M. Oliver (eds), *Disabling Barriers – Enabling Environments*. London: Sage, pp. 13–16.

Garland-Thomson, R. (2005) 'Feminist disability studies', *Signs*, 30 (2): 1557–87.

Hanna, W.J. and Rogovsky, B. (1991) 'Two handicaps plus, women with disabilities', *Disability, Handicap and Society*, 6 (1): 49–63.

McCall, L. (2005) 'The complexity of intersectionality', *Signs*, 30 (3): 1771–99.

Meekosha, H. (2007) 'What the hell are you? An intercategorical analysis of race, ethnicity, gender and disability in the Australian body politic', *Scandinavian Journal of Disability Research*, 8 (2–3): 161–76.

Priestley, M. (1995) 'Commonality and difference in the movement: an association of blind Asians in Leeds', *Disability & Society*, 10 (2): 157–69.

Rainbow Ripples and Butler, R. (2006) *The Rainbow Ripples Report: Lesbian, Gay and Bisexual Disabled People's Experiences of Service Provision in Leeds*. Leeds: Leeds Involvement Project.

Stuart, O. (1996) 'Double oppression: an appropriate starting point?', in J. Swain, V. Finkelstein, S. French and M. Oliver (eds), *Disabling Barriers – Enabling Environments*. Buckingham: Open University Press, pp. 93–100.

Stuart, O. (2012) 'Not invited to the party? Black and minority ethnic adults and the personalisation of social care', in G. Craig, K. Atkin, S. Chattoo and R. Flynn (eds), *Understanding Race and Ethnicity*. Bristol: The Policy Press, pp. 133–50.

Vernon, A. (1999) 'The dialectics of multiple identities and the disabled people's movement', *Disability & Society*, 14 (3): 385–98.

Young, I.M. (1990) *Justice and the Politics of Difference*. Princeton, NJ: Princeton University Press.

Yuval-Davis, N. (2006) 'Intersectionality and feminist politics', *European Journal of Women's Studies*, 13 (3): 193–209.

Yuval-Davis, N. (ed.) (2011) *The Politics of Belonging: Intersectional Contestations*. London: Sage.

29   Language

Rebecca Mallett and Jenny Slater

Language matters for our understanding of disability because it is through the words we use that our expectations and assumptions are shaped. These, in turn, impact upon the extent to which people are valued. The language we use has material impact upon the ways and the extent to which people are treated and valued. The language we use is not a trivial question about what is, or is not, 'politically correct'; the language we use has material impact upon the lives we all lead (Titchkosky 2008).

There are global differences in what language is preferred around disability. One of the great debates is the choice between 'disabled people' and 'people with disabilities' (Swain et al 2003). In the UK the preferred term, used by those influenced by disabled people's movements, is 'disabled people'. The emergence of a social model approach led to the separation of disability from impairment, shifting the focus from the individual to the oppressive structures of society (Oliver 1990). This was a radical step in disability politics. The social model gave disabled people language to shift disability from a medicalised 'problem' residing *within* an individual, to a 'problem' of social inequality. To be a disabled person, therefore, refers to a person with an impairment who is disabled by society (Slater 2013). At this point, 'disabled' emerges as an identity category and becomes part of identity politics (Davis 2002) alongside gender, race and sexuality. For Barnes (1992) this shift of emphasis makes the choice of terminology simpler as 'disabled person' accurately highlights the oppression a person with impairment faces. Aubrecht (2012: 34) agrees, stating 'my description of myself as a disabled person reflects an interest in reclaiming the living significance of disability in how I understand what it means to be recognized as a person within ablest social and cultural environments'.

At a global level, language choice is even more complicated. Disability scholars from North America often use the term 'people with disabilities' Some say this is preferable because it stresses the person (or 'personhood') before disability. In Titchkosky's (2008) fascinating sociological consideration of 'person-first' language in Canada, she argues that the phrase has been in circulation since 'at least the 1970s' and is now hegemonic in its use. Many international organisations also adopt this approach, for instance, The World Health Organization (WHO) use the term 'people with disabilities' and stress that:

> Disabilities is an umbrella term, covering impairments, activity limitations, and participation restrictions. An impairment is a problem in body function or structure; an activity limitation is a difficulty encountered by an individual in executing a task or action; while a participation restriction is a problem experienced by an individual in involvement in life situations.

(WHO 2012)

Here the term 'disabilities' is used to cover both 'impairment' and 'disability' and is in contrast to, what has been called, the *British* social model distinction (Thomas, 2004) where 'impairment' and 'disability' is separated out to enable 'disability' to be acknowledged and addressed as a social consequence. By not explicitly separating them out, disability remains an individual matter and it is this individualisation that worries scholars such as Titchkosky (2008).

Global differences in language are also apparent when we consider those labelled with 'learning difficulties'. People First, a British self-advocacy organisation of people with labels of 'learning difficulty', explain their commitment to the British social model of disability through their use of terminology:

> we believe that people labelled as having a learning difficulty are disabled by society. We choose to use the term 'learning difficulty' instead of 'learning disability' to get across the idea that our support needs change over time as we learn new skills and gain experience

(People First 2012)

Furthermore, they go on, 'when we talk about people with learning difficulties, we mean "people labelled as having a learning difficulty"' (People First 2012). You may come across similar clauses in the writing of Disability Studies scholars who explain that that although they omit the use of inverted commas, and do not continually use the phrase 'with the label of' for sake of ease or aesthetics, they recognise labels as problematic, and ask the reader to read them as such. Here, we again meet global discrepancies. The term more widely recognised globally being 'people (with the label of) intellectual impairment'.

It should also be remembered that so far we have discussed conceptualisations of 'disability' which have been developed in English-speaking arenas and these do not always translate across other languages or vice versa. A good example of this is the use of the word 'handicap'. Ville and Ravaud (2007: 142–3) explain that:

> whilst the term has more or less the same meaning in English and in French, it is not at all used in the same way in the two cultures [...] the traditional use of the word 'handicap' in French is far closer to that of the English term 'disability', i.e. a generic meaning which covers all the lesional, functional and social consequences of impairment or the consequences of environmental barriers, depending on whether one adopts the medical model or the social model.

Language considered 'acceptable' also changes over time. Although the use of once commonplace terms such as 'retard' are now recognised as overtly offensive, phrases such as 'the handicapped' or 'the disabled', dismissed by disabled people for their tendency to objectify, are less widely thought of as offensive, and thus continue to crop up in conversation (Goodley, 2010). Even when such use is metaphoric it remains significant as Ben-Moshe (2005 cited in Haller et al, 2006: 65) states 'when we use terms like 'retarded,' 'lame,' or 'blind' – even if we are referring to acts or ideas and not to people at all – we perpetuate the stigma associated with disability'.

Conversely, however, rather than merely dismissing language as 'disablist', some disabled people have chosen to reclaim the stigmatising labels conventionally used as tools of the oppressors and instead wear them with pride (Swain et al, 2003). McRuer (2006) for example, draws upon LGBT movement's reclamation of the word 'queer', and the later emergence of queer theory, to provocatively pose the potential of a 'crip theory'. Thomson (1996) has enacted a similar move to reappropriate academic interest in 'freak' while disabled British comedian and disability activist Laurence Clark's act of entitling his 2008 show 'Spastic Fantastic' should also been seen within the realm of resignification. The act of gaining control over definitions and language has been at the heart of the disabled people's movement from the very beginning (Hasler 1993), indeed the move to redefine disability as social rather than medical was itself a move of resignification.

Whether it is the use of disability in television comedy (Mallett, 2010), the positioning of 'disabled people' in the debates over economic austerity (Garthwaite 2011) or the cultural meanings made out of particular impairment categories, such as autism (McGuire 2011), the language used around disability continues to be contentious. There are no simple answers and to look for them might be missing the point. As Titchkosky (2008: 138) concludes:

> Alternative phraseology is not the main issue here, although I would suggest that an openness to a diversity of terms and expressions of disability would be beneficial to all ... the point is not 'say it this way ...' The point is, instead, *to examine what our current articulations of disability are saying* in the here and now.

Paying attention to language in 'the here and the now' is the important move, not only which term where and when but also the need for terms at all. Postmodern discussions around disability have questioned the usefulness of defining what we mean by disability. Shildrick (2009) argues that to define is to normalise rather than destabilise the categories we separate human beings into (Slater 2013). However, jettisoning the category of 'disabled people' has implications for the focus and clarity of disabled people's movements (Davis 2002) and brings us back to the idea that language use not only manifests and symbolises power but is also a site around and through which power is challenged, contested and subverted.

For Discussion

- Do you think Disability Studies should work towards a global agreement on the preferred terminology around disability?
- If all labels were removed what impact do you think this would have on 'disabled people'?
- If words such as 'crip' and 'freak' are being reappropriated by disabled people, is it now acceptable for anybody to use them?

Further Reading

Aubrecht, K. (2012) 'Disability studies and the language of mental illness', *Review of Disability Studies*, 8 (2): 31–44.

Garthwaite, K. (2011) 'The language of shirkers and scroungers? Talking about illness, disability and coalition welfare reform', *Disability & Society*, 26(3): 369–72.

Swain, J., French, S. and Cameron, C. (2003) 'What's in a name?', in *Controversial Issues in a Disabling Society*. Buckingham: Open University Press, pp. 11–20.

Titchkosky, T. (2008) 'Disability: a rose by any other name? "People-first" language in Canadian society', *Canadian Review of Sociology*, 38 (2): 125–40.

References

Aubrecht, K. (2012) 'Disability studies and the language of mental illness', *Review of Disability Studies*, 8 (2): 31–44.

Barnes, C. (1992) *Disabling Imagery and the Media: An Exploration of the Principles for Media Representations of Disabled People*. Halifax: BCODP/Ryburn Publishing.

Davis, L.J. (2002) *Bending Over Backwards: Disability, Dismodernism and Other Difficult Positions*. New York and London: New York University Press.

Garthwaite, K. (2011) 'The language of shirkers and scroungers? Talking about illness, disability and coalition welfare reform', *Disability & Society*, 26(3): 369–72.

Goodley, D. (2010) *Disability Studies: An Interdisciplinary Introduction*. London: Sage.

Haller, B., Dorries, B. and Rahn, J. (2006) 'Media labeling versus the US disability community identity: a study of shifting cultural language', *Disability & Society*, 21 (1): 61–75.

Hasler, F. (1993) 'Developments in the disabled people's movement', in J. Swain, V. Finkelstein, S. French and M. Oliver (eds), *Disabling Barriers – Enabling Environments*. London: Sage, in association with the Open University Press, pp. 278–84.

McGuire, A. (2011) 'Representing autism: a sociological examination of autism advocacy', *Atlantis: Critical Studies in Gender, Culture and Social Justice*, 35: 2.

McRuer, R. (2006) *Crip Theory: Cultural Signs of Queerness and Disability*. New York and London: New York University Press.

Mallett, R. (2010) 'Claiming comedic immunity: or, what do you get when you cross contemporary British comedy with disability', *Review of Disability Studies*, 6 (3): 5–14.

Oliver, M. (1990). *The Politics of Disablement*. Basingstoke: Macmillan.

People First (2012) *Info and FAQ*. http://peoplefirstltd.com/about-us/info-faq (accessed 20 December 2012).

Shildrick, M. (2009) *Dangerous Discourses of Disability, Subjectivity and Sexuality*. New York: Palgrave Macmillan.

Slater, J. (2013) 'Constructions, perceptions and expectations of being young and disabled: a critical disability perspective'. Unpublished PhD thesis: Department of Psychology, Manchester Metropolitan University.

Swain, J., French, S. and Cameron, C. (2003) *Controversial Issues in a Disabling Society*. Buckingham: Open University Press.

Thomas, C. (2004) 'How is disability understood? An examination of sociological approaches', *Disability and Society*, 19(6): 569–83.

Thomson, R.G. (ed.) (1996) *Freakery: Cultural Spectacles of the Extraordinary Body*. New York: New York University Press.

Titchkosky, T. (2008) 'Disability: a rose by any other name? "People-first" language in Canadian society', *Canadian Review of Sociology*, 38 (2): 125–40.

Ville, I. and Ravaud, J. F. (2007) 'French disability studies: differences and similarities', *Scandinavian Journal of Disability Research*, 9 (3–4): 138–45.

World Health Organization (WHO) (2012) *Disabilities*, www.who.int/topics/disabilities/en/, accessed 20 December 2012.

30

Media Representations

Colin Cameron

In the sense that the term is used in Disability Studies, *discourse* refers to a kind of intertextual 'conversation' that texts have with each other (Bowman 2008). By texts are meant any forms of representation of a subject. In a discussion of media representations we might describe as texts, for example, television or radio programmes, photographs, films, YouTube clips, newspaper stories or magazine articles. Media discourse is a conversation carried out between different media texts, a conversation in which conventional meanings are shared.

In framing our ways of knowing about and relating to a subject, and in suggesting ways we might act upon or experience it, discourse simultaneously opens up certain possibilities and shuts down others (Abberley 2002). As Titchkosky (2007) puts it, texts are always oriented social action, producing meanings: they act on us and help constitute our social contexts. Attempting to change the course of a conversation is difficult if those with the loudest voices only let you join in on their terms. As the media persist in holding a conversation which represents disability as individual limitation or tragedy, it has proved hard for disabled people to shift this.

My question here is not so much about whether representations of disabled people in the media have increased, as numerous disabled commentators (e.g. Barnes 1994; Darke 1998; Klobas 1988; Riley 2005) have shown that disability has rarely been far from the screen – as pathos, as comedy, as horror, as inspiration. Rather I want to ask whether any progress has been made during recent years in the *types* of representations of disabled people seen in the media.

Klobas (1988) made a number of observations about disability representation in television and film, including that:

- stories are bound to a confining formula treatment where disability is a personal problem one must overcome;
- viewers seldom see disabled characters as multifaceted human beings for whom physical limitations are a fact of nature;
- disability is rarely depicted as being integrated into a busy and full life.

Klobas argued that disability has been typically represented by the media as a private trouble to be dealt with at a private level. Disabled people are not 'real' people who get on with life's ordinary challenges. Instead they find their lives beset by one single challenge – that of disability. They are not blended into the ordinariness of community life but are only seen when foregrounded for effect. For every piece which tries to shift the focus to the social issues disabled people face, there are ten stories reminding us that their real problem is emotional (Klobas 1988).

Drawing on Cumberbatch and Negrine's 1992 study *Images of Disability on Television*, Barnes (1994: 44) commented that in television and film disabled people were rarely shown as integral and productive members of the community. They did not feature incidentally as students, as teachers, as parents or as part of the workforce. They seldom appeared in non-fiction programmes apart from those dealing solely with disability.

One issue is to decide whether media representations of disabled people have moved on since the 1990s. Bowler, writing in 2009, asserts that they have, and argues that there are numerous recent positive examples of TV's increased incidental inclusion of disabled people (Bowler 2009: unpaged). She cites the Channel 4 game show *Deal Or No Deal* as an example. Given that Cumberbatch and Negrine (1992) stated that not one of forty-four game shows they watched had contained a disabled contestant, it might be argued that it is good to see more disabled people on programmes like *Deal Or No Deal*. A closer examination of an episode, however, reveals a continuing attach-ment to the personal tragedy model. An episode first broadcast in December 2008 featured a star contestant named Rhys, a young wheelchair user. From the moment Rhys is called into the limelight, the show's presenter Noel Edmonds focuses on his impairment: 'Welcome ... Rhys Devereaux ... from Llanelli... tell me about Friedrich's ataxia ...' (Cameron 2010: 209).

It becomes clear during the programme that Rhys's aim is to win a maximum amount of prize money to pay for medical treatment to cure his impairment:

Noel: Would I be right in thinking that your ambition for this game ... the object of winning as much money as possible ... it is to be able to have more treatment ...

Rhys: Yeah ... this is going to take a long stretch of perseverance and just determination ...

Noel: Perseverance ... determination ... pure guts ... and regrettably, because of the world in which we live ... money ...

(Cameron 2010: 210)

Rhys is exhibited as a cripple with the right attitude, as somebody who will not just passively accept his lot. This is not just entertainment, but a learning experience in which the cultural message is reinforced that impairment is misfortune to be struggled with and overcome at an individual level. It is inevitable that during the course of the show Rhys is described as 'an inspiration' (Cameron 2010).

In Cameron (2010: 172), Roshni, a blind woman from Glasgow, described her experience of being filmed as a charity recipient at a special school during the 1990s:

We had a lot of visits from *Children in Need* and all these sort of charity-inspired telethons and game shows and all of that, and they all came and filmed us ... I remember that all of our family and different relatives and some close friends packed into the house to see these disabled kids on TV of which I was one ... I remember being struck by how much of an impact this was having, in terms of striking at people's emotions and everybody saying how amazing this was and these poor disabled children ... and it was so wonderful to see them on TV and that they were getting this money...

The BBC charity fund-raising telethon *Children in Need*, which has run annually since 1980, in common with many other media pseudo-events, directs its focus at the emotional aspects of social issues without any attempt to address these in a political context (Taylor and Harris 2008). Such pseudo-events actively undermine the identification of disability as an issue of discrimination and oppression by ensuring that the whole business of supporting disabled people is seen as a worthy cause requiring an individual response. Talking in Cameron (2010: 172) about *Children in Need*, Ben, a man with autism from Coventry, said:

> Within the disability community it's despised and hated, but when you're in the wider community ... if you happen to be in a pub and someone comes in raising money for it with a large bucket you just don't feel as if you can say anything about it for fear of the consequences ... it's self-policed by majority consensus.

The conversation being held between the celebrities involved in *Children in Need* and the public who are encouraged to donate excludes the possibility of questioning the common understanding that disability is a charity issue. Shifting the terms of that conversation remains a struggle.

While it is true that disabled people have long argued for better representation in mainstream media, it is also true that popular culture has a way of assimilating challenges to its flow by incorporating them and offering them back for public consumption in a form in which they are likely to cause little disruption or offence (Chambers 1993). It seems that recent representations of disabled people in the media, rather than signifying an enlightened acceptance of difference, continue to be about the recycling of stereotypes which reinforce dominant normalising discourses.

For Discussion

- In what ways do media and charities feed off each other in their representations of disabled people?
- Get hold of some copies of lifestyle/gossip/chat magazines from your local newsagent. Where do you see disabled people in these? What does this tell you about media portrayals of disabled people?
- Do you think TV documentaries about disabled people reinforce or challenge stereotyped assumptions?

Further Reading

Darke, P. (1998) 'Understanding cinematic representations of disability', in T. Shakespeare (ed.), *The Disability Reader: Social Science Perspectives*. London: Cassell, pp. 181–97.

Haller, B.A. (2010) *Representing Disability in an Ableist World: Essays on Mass Media*. Louisville, KY: Advocado Press.

Williams-Findlay, R. (2014) 'The representation of disabled people in the news media', in J. Swain, S. French, C. Barnes and S. Thomas (eds), *Disabling Barriers – Enabling Environments*, 3rd edn. London: Sage, pp. 107–13.

References

Abberley, P. (2002) 'Work, disability, disabled people and European social theory', in C. Barnes, M. Oliver and L. Barton (eds), *Disability Studies Today*. Cambridge: Polity, pp. 120–38.

Barnes, C. (1994) 'Images of disability', in S. French (ed.), *On Equal Terms: Working with Disabled People*. London: Butterworth-Heinemann, pp. 35–46.

Bowler, E. (2009) 'Disabled talent starts to break through', *Broadcast Now*, www.broadcastnow. co.uk/printPage.html?pageid=1961010, accessed 20 January 2009.

Bowman, P. (2008) *Deconstructing Popular Culture*. Basingstoke: Palgrave Macmillan.

Cameron, C. (2010) 'Does anybody like being disabled? A critical exploration of impairment, identity, media and everyday experience in a disabling society'. PhD thesis, Queen Margaret University, http://etheses.qmu.ac.uk/258/, accessed 22 January 2013.

Chambers, I. (1993) *Popular Culture: The Cosmopolitan Experience*. London: Routledge.

Cumberbatch, G. and Negrine, R. (1992) *Images of Disability on Television*. London: Routledge.

Darke, P. (1998) 'Understanding cinematic representations of disability', in T. Shakespeare (ed.), *The Disability Reader: Social Science Perspectives*. London: Cassell, pp. 181–97.

Klobas, L. (1988) *Disability Drama in Television and Film*. Jefferson, NC: McFarland and Co.

Riley, C.A. (2005) *Disability and the Media: Prescriptions for Change*. Hanover, NE: University Press of New England.

Taylor, P. and Harris, J.L. (2008) *Critical Theories of Mass Media: Then and Now*. Maidenhead: Open University Press.

Titchkosky, T. (2007) *Reading and Writing Disability Differently: The Textured Life of Embodiment*. Toronto: University of Toronto Press.

31   The Medical Model

Colin Cameron

In the sense that the word is used here, a *model* is a framework of ideas used to make sense of phenomena and experience in the social worlds we inhabit. A model represents a particular way of ordering and structuring knowledge and, indeed, shapes what can be known. There is little about how we come to understand either ourselves or anybody else around us that is not determined by the way we are individually situated within a complex network of institutional patterns and arrangements. These structure our perceptions of, for example, gender, race, age, class, impairment and disability (Burr 2003), each reflecting certain assumptions embedded within explanatory and predictive models. What we know is learned and what we learn is moulded by the places and times we find ourselves and by how these are explained to us. At the same time, it needs to be recognised that the explanations that are most loudly and frequently heard, which seem to carry authority and appear uncontroversial, are those which reflect the interests of powerful groups in society, e.g. professionals and the media. The medical model of disability is one such representation.

While the origins of the individualisation of disability are explored more fully else-where in this book, the medical model involves a gaze which establishes disability as an individual problem. Disability is conceived as personal limitation arising from the func-tional impairments that are part of a person's physical constitution, whether these impairments are congenital or acquired. This view is expressed most clearly in the World Health Organization's 1980 International Classification of Impairments, Disabilities and Handicaps (ICIDH):

> Impairment: any loss or abnormality of psychological, physiological or anatomical structure or function.
>
> Disability: any restriction or lack (resulting from impairment) of ability to perform an activity in the manner or within the range considered normal for a human being.
>
> (WHO 1980, in Barnes and Mercer 2010: 20)

The terms *loss, abnormality, restriction* or *lack of ability* are heavily laden with cultural meaning and indicate a perception of impairment and disability as characteristics of individual deficit or personal tragedy. Disability is regarded as emerging as a consequence of impairment. The ICIDH identified lack of ability to climb the stairs or to walk to the shops as examples of 'disabilities' (WHO 1980, in Barnes and Mercer 2010).

When disability is understood in this way, appropriate social responses to disabi-lity are regarded in terms of treatment and care by medical/technological means; prevention through biological/genetic intervention or screening; treatment through rehabilitation services; and prevention through early diagnosis and treatment (Rioux 1997). Resources are targeted at individuals in order to fix them for participation in the world around them, while the environment in which they live is regarded as unproblematic. The responsibility is upon the impaired individual, with what is con-sidered appropriate professional support, to make the effort to adjust and fit in. To be disabled is to have 'something wrong with you' (Oliver 1996: 30) which must be put right.

> If we define situations as real, they are real in their consequences ... As far as disability is concerned, if it is seen as a tragedy, then disabled people will be treated as if they are the victims of some tragic happening or circumstance.
>
> (Oliver and Barnes 2012: 14)

The medical model is experienced by disabled people as problematic in that it is materialised in everyday practice through the myriad of behaviours, decisions and interactions taking place in the contexts in which they experience their lives. It is put into practice in hopes and expectations held, in thoughts unspoken and words spoken, in gestures and assumptions made, and through the processes by which services are planned and delivered. Because it is a dominant model of disability, reflecting the view of the world of the non-disabled, its character as a model, as a way of looking at things, is almost always overlooked. Medical model thinking does not appear as just 'one way of looking' but as established fact. It is considered common sense to regard impairment as misfortune. This impacts upon disabled people's lives not just in terms of professional judgements and assumptions about what are appropriate services, but also in terms of the restriction of life opportunities, experiences and roles.

In that it distorts our perceptions of humanity and relationships between human individuals, Mason identifies the influence of the medical model of disability as having a role in the oppression of *all* people, both disabled and non-disabled. The removal of people identified as having significant impairments from the mainstream of social life, as well as being oppressive to people with impairments themselves, has rendered impairment a subject of fear and embarrassment that non-disabled people feel unsure about and uncomfortable dealing with (in Rieser and Mason 1992: 78). Through a process involving the medicalisation of society (Zola 2005), forms of social knowledge have been imposed which suggest that aberration from socially valued norms of physical embodiment is exceptional, rather than an ordinary part of human experience, and is best addressed by professionals. A message is communicated to those identified as unimpaired that disability is an individual problem, but not *their* problem. When impairment is removed from sight, it becomes an object of pity, of comedy, of charity, of fear or hostility, to be dealt with by others elsewhere.

Disabled critics, however, argue that the medical model represents an ideological position and is a particular manifestation of what Oliver has termed 'the ideology of normality' (Oliver 1996: 104). This is to use the term *ideology* in the sense proposed by Gramsci, as having a material existence embodied in the social practices of individuals and in the institutions and organisations within which these social practices take place (Gramsci 1996). While there have been more recent attempts by the WHO to move on from the ICIDH and to develop a 'biopsychosocial' approach through the International Classification of Functioning, Disability and Health (ICFDH), 'this is not that far removed from its original formulation in that it retains the individual as the starting point for the analysis of "bodily functioning and activity"' (Oliver and Barnes 2012: 25). In attempting to draw together insights of the medical and social models, the ICFDH overlooks the point made by Robert Drake (1999: 14) that these are 'fundamentally opposed ways of understanding disability' and are irreconcilable.

For Discussion

- What impact do you think the medical model has on the way the non-disabled people regard disabled people?
- What impact do you think the medical model has on the way disabled people see themselves?
- Why do you think disabled people have rejected the medical model?

Further Reading

Barnes, C. and Mercer, G. (2010) *Exploring Disability*, 2nd Edn. Cambridge: Polity.

Gosling, J. (2011) *Abnormal: How Britain Became Dysphoric and the Key to a Cure*. London: Bettany Press.

Thomas, C. (2007) *Sociologies of Disability and Illness: Contested Ideas in Disability Studies and Medical Sociology*. Basingstoke: Palgrave Macmillan.

References

Barnes, C. and Mercer, G. (2010) *Exploring Disability*, 2nd edn. Cambridge: Polity.

Burr, V. (2003) *Social Constructionism*. London: Routledge.

Drake, R. (1999) *Understanding Disability Policies*. Basingstoke: Macmillan.

Gramsci, A. (1996) *Selections from the Prison Notebooks*. London: Lawrence and Wishart Ltd.

Oliver, M. (1996) *Understanding Disability: From Theory to Practice*. Basingstoke: Macmillan.

Oliver, M. and Barnes, C. (2012) *The New Politics of Disablement*. Basingstoke: Palgrave Macmillan.

Rieser, R. and Mason, M. (1992) *Disability Equality in the Classroom*. London: Disability Equality in Education.

Rioux, M.H. (1997) 'When myths masquerade as science', in L. Barton and M. Oliver (eds), *Disability Studies: Past, Present and Future*. Leeds: Disability Press, pp. 99–112.

Zola, I.K. (2005) 'Healthism and disabling medicalization', in I. Illich, I.K. Zola, J. McKnight, J. Caplan and H. Shaiken (eds), *Disabling Professions*. London: Marion Boyars, pp. 41–68.

32 Narrative

Tanya Titchkosky and Rod Michalko

Most importantly, disability is a life that is lived. It is lived in the midst of the meanings given to it. The meaning of disability is given whenever we speak of it, act upon it, or even think of it. To say anything about disability is to *tell* something of the life of disability – its meaning – and 'to tell' is the Latin root-meaning of 'narrative'. Disability, then, always has a narrative form; insofar as we say, do, or imagine something about disability, it is a storied life.

Sometimes, people are aware that they are presenting disability in a narrative form, as in disability arts and culture (Cameron 2007). More often, though, the life of disability is told in such a way that does not recognise its narrative structure. This is typically the case in narratives titled 'diagnosis' or 'prognosis', or in research that narrates disability as an objective problem. Whether we recognise it or not the life of disability is both a story that we live and a story we tell, and it is surrounds us. As King (2003: 2), native storyteller, says, 'The truth about stories is that that's all we are.' We may judge a story about disability to be fictional or factual, realistic or mythological, medical or social but, still, the truth about any of these stories is that they are ways that the life of disability is narrated and lived.

We forge our lives in the midst of different disability stories, including religious, social and political, educational, as well as the ever-present medical stories. And people may subscribe to one particular story of disability. An important story today says that *disability is a social phenomenon produced by a society's failure to respond adequately to impairment* – this story is titled the 'social model of disability' (Oliver 1996: 30–42). This story, however we judge it, does not eliminate other dominant storytellers, such as medicine, that tell the story of disability as something unwanted that lurks in an individual and must be rooted out or managed. King (2003: 10) also tells us that once a narrative is told, it 'cannot be called back. Once told, it is loose in the world', and this is why no story of disability can eliminate any other story. Thus, stories compete with one another for the right to tell the definitive story of disability. Like any other competition, power is at play. Some stories of disability prevail while others are shoved to the side. Whether a story captures us depends upon many factors, including the power of the story teller and, in contemporary times, 'science' powerfully tells many definitive stories.

With the understanding that disability is always a storied life, we are now faced with a perplexing question: how best to live with these disability-stories and with their power and competing meanings? One answer to this question is 'narrative inquiry'. Such inquiry is both a way to live with the stories told about disability while simultaneously engaging with these stories by telling yet another story. This means we can live in the midst of disability-stories by telling our own story.

Narrative inquiry can focus on those stories that arise when people are directly asked to narrate their experience with disability, as in narrative life-writings or interviews (Clough et al. 2004). Another form of narrative inquiry attends to how a culture's storytellers, for example, those involved in literature and the arts, have already narrated disability. As Mitchell and Snyder (2000) have shown, literature in the Western cannon is provoked and propped-up by a version of disability as a disruption to the normative order. Still another form of inquiry addresses those stories within daily life that are not necessarily oriented to the fact that they are narrating the life of disability (Michalko 1998; Titchkosky 2007). Hidden narratives of disability abound. They are found in all aspects of life, from policy to the mass media; from bureaucracy to intimate relations; from social issues to life on the street. Whatever form narrative takes, it both draws out and gives meaning to disability; narrative inquiry can uncover these meanings so that we have an opportunity to reflect on how we *are* living disability.

Regardless of the kind of story investigated, narrative inquiry is grounded on the basic premise that any disability story reflects the symbolic social order from which it arises and into which the story returns. This is so, according to Schutz (1970: 96–7), insofar as every utterance *is* composed from a 'treasure house of ready-made pre-constituted types', and since the 'whole history of the linguistic group is mirrored in its way of saying things'. Thus, any telling of disability can be examined for the history of the linguistic group that it reflects.

The history of disability as an umbrella term for a host of human variations is not a long one. The term, generated during the Enlightenment, tells the story of the growing belief in rationality where humans and their productive relations were believed to be knowable. The term 'the disabled' became a way to know and manage the pre-constituted type 'the deserving poor'. The rise of capitalism intensified the need to know people according to their production power, mirrored today in the numerous processes for judging whether a person qualifies (or not) as disabled. Disability, narrated as such, reflects the myriad ways that disability has a history of being little else than an administrative category. While the administrative story is part of how we live with disability, Stiker (1999: 51) also tells us that 'We are always other than society made us and believes us to be.' After all, it is nearly impossible to live any life as a single story, especially if it is an administrative one; we invest in some other meanings while excluding yet other ones (and narrative inquiry investigates this too).

Many disability-narratives today tell us that disability is really no life at all – as though it is only a problem that we would all be better off without. While it is fascinating that people are able to narrate human life *as if* it is lifeless, as a 'limit without possibility' (Titchkosky 2012) or as a 'use-less difference' (Michalko 2002: 93–103, 146), it is also dangerous to contain the meaning of disability as such. Plotted as a problem, the notion of life in disability is limited to elimination, cure, or overcoming. But who is telling this story? Is it told by disability or by normalcy? Darke (1998: 184) suggests that while it may seem that disability is being narrated, in reality such stories only reproduce a 'nor-mality genre'. Still, there is hope in knowing that every utterance or action that is tied to disability *is* a narrative, since we can then attend to these disability-stories in new ways and, in so doing, forge stories that both reveal and affirm the life that is disability.

For Discussion

- Are disabled people the primary storytellers of disability?
- What story does your culture need to tell about disability and why?
- What story of disability do you tell?

Further Reading

Clough, P., Goodley, D., Lawthom, R. and Moore, M. (2004) *Researching Life Stories: Method, Theory and Analysis in a Biographical Age*. London: Routledge.
Michalko, R. (1998) *The Mystery of the Eye and the Shadow of Blindness*. Toronto: University of Toronto Press.
Titchkosky, T. (2007) *Reading and Writing Disability Differently: The Textured Life of Embodiment*. Toronto: University of Toronto Press.

References

Cameron, C. (2007) 'Whose problem? Disability narratives and available identities', *Community Development Journal*, 42 (4): 501–11.
Clough, P., Goodley, D., Lawthom, R. and Moore, M. (2004) *Researching Life Stories: Method, Theory and Analysis in a Biographical Age*. London: Routledge.
Darke, P. (1998) 'Understanding cinematic representations of disability', in T. Shakespeare (ed.), *The Disability Reader: Social Science Perspectives*. Cassell: London, pp. 181–200.
King, T. (2003) *The Truth About Stories: A Native Narrative*. Toronto: Anansi Press.
Michalko, R. (1998) *The Mystery of the Eye and the Shadow of Blindness*. Toronto: University of Toronto Press.
Michalko, R. (2002) *The Difference that Disability Makes*. Philadelphia, PA: Temple University Press.
Mitchell, D. and Snyder, S. (2000) *Narrative Prosthesis: Disability and the Dependencies of Discourse*. Michigan, MI: University of Michigan Press.

Oliver, M. (1996) 'The social model in context', in M. Oliver, *Understanding Disability: From Theory to Practice*. New York: St. Martin's Press, pp. 30–42.

Schutz, A. (1970) *On Phenomenology and Social Relations*. Chicago, IL: University of Chicago Press.

Stiker, H.-J. (1999) *A History of Disability*. Ann Arbor, MI: The University of Michigan Press.

Titchkosky, T. (2007) *Reading and Writing Disability Differently: The Textured Life of Embodiment*. Toronto: University of Toronto Press.

Titchkosky, T. (2012) 'The ends of the body as pedagogic possibility', *Review of Education, Pedagogy, and Cultural Studies*, 34 (3–4): 82–93.

33

Need

Larry Arnold

I describe myself as 'neurodiversive', which already means you will have to think hard about notions of 'need' as you read this chapter.

In the context of understanding the relationship between disability and impairment, it is necessary to examine the notion of whether people with impairments really do have additional needs. Are these needs conditioned by an impaired person's experience of embodiment, or by some psychological and cognitive difference that predisposes one to engage the negotiation of 'need' from a different perspective?

The way I think about it is that the individual is never divorced from society, even when shipwrecked and alone. For instance, the way in which Robinson Crusoe met his individual need for survival was absolutely conditioned by his prior experience of the social structures that brought him to experience shipwreck. His response to his circumstance was shaped by the proximity of that society's more readily available constructs in the form of goods to be salvaged. This all begs questions about 'dependence', for, looking objectively, is any individual, impaired or otherwise, actually 'independent' of need for others in order to have their most basic needs met? Picture this example, based on a familiar image from an English children's rhyme. Mother Hubbard goes to her empty cupboard only to discover it is a public holiday, the shops are shut. How does she prepare a meal? Well, she cannot manage this alone. She must be reliant upon a neighbour at least, without the usual access to a taken-for-granted infrastructure. It is thus apparent that the way in which one's essential needs are met is very much determined by the configuration and assets of the society one happens to be born into.

Taking this a step further and assuming an industrial rather than a feudal or hunter-gatherer society, one can begin to look at the social model of disability as exposing how something beyond the given environment one inhabits (roads, houses, shops etc.) is important for understanding need. In an exchange-based society, multiple categories of need are engendered. For instance, the need to work in order to earn those tokens of exchange one uses to ride the roads; purchase one's food; pay one's rent or mortgage.

These needs are not 'natural'. They are determined and regulated by the structures of the economy, for in the absence, for example, of capitalist structures one could simply grow one's own food and barter. However, at every level in every society there exists a set of rules that determine the limits of what one can do with one's own property and how one negotiates the system of exchange. That essentially is what is referred to by the principles of the social model of disability. Everything – including 'need' – is socially determined by the will of one group in relation to any other. When employment is scarce, there arises the question of how the need for money is met, whether it be dependence upon one's kin, charitable structures, insurance or state welfare. When money is abundant these 'needs' no longer exist in the same way.

It is here, as we try to understand particular levels of need, that the social model of disability offers a powerful counternarrative to the notion of a disabled person as an inadequate individual who cannot service their own need at the pre-industrial basic level. It is the structure of society which determines how such needs (in reality no different for an unimpaired person) are catered for, which groups are privileged and have their 'needs' prioritised and which have their 'needs' sidelined and thus find they live marginalised lives. It can easily be seen that what some communities will call a common need will be differently negotiated into a category of exceptional or special need by others. I want to argue that an understanding of need that derives from embodied experience is wrong because it is a perceived absence of normality that gives rise to the categorisation of some needs as 'ordinary' and positions others as 'exceptional'.

Bodies are all different, one can argue, but the average perfect body has two legs, two arms and is constrained within certain parameters. Therefore a pullover for a one-armed person becomes an exceptional need, or clothes that conform to the seated position of a wheelchair user become an exceptional need. Because the embodied situation of the person who has this need for particular clothing is deemed 'abnormal' (that is simply to say in statistical terms fewer people require such garments than others) it becomes more expensive to manufacture particular items and they become harder to find. Thus the need for such an item becomes a special need, and very often its rarity gives rise to rationing.

But wait a minute! Don't people come in all shapes and sizes anyway, from a toddler to a Sumo wrestler? It is only because we are accustomed to be able to purchase clothing that follows demand-led trends that anything outside of such demand-led norms becomes more expensive or impossible to manufacture. Following the demand-led model, a person such as myself who does not match the Vitruvian ideal of arms in proportion to his height is effectively disabled from finding a suit that is a good fit. Either the jacket is too broad in the chest or the arms too short. In a sense, what is required then becomes bespoke provision which is not 'normally' available and so becomes a privilege of the rich. This example serves to explain how many adaptations for disabled people, similarly from adapted door-to-door transport to individualised machinery to facilitate work, are pushed out of an ordinary domain to the domain of the wealthy, so that what might be called a 'need for a jacket' is now considered a luxury requirement. It is this equation of 'exceptional need' with privilege that has conditioned the reluctance of society to fund, and in some cases, even countenance, diverse provision to respond to the full range of people's entitlements. Economic considerations are still one of the exceptions a disabling service provider can cite as a defence for not providing access to one's premises, for instance.

It was mooted by Maslow (1943) that whether or not a need is met is decided by what a community sees as a priority, so that any idea of need is contingent upon the wishes and desires of a particular community. Disabled people have historically experienced marginalisation and discrimination, which means that value is not typically attached to their needs or even to their entitlements. In industrial societies there has been an assumption that people with impairments make a lesser contribution to communal labour and so response to their needs has been lessened because it is assumed they do not contribute as much as others to economic stability. It becomes self-fulfilling that there will be significantly unmet categories of need as depleted esteem diminishes the probability of self-actualisation, meaning that people with impairment are further oppressed.

In summary, making disabled peoples' needs exceptional is part of the disabling process that inevitably has repercussions, because unmet need is identified as need requiring an exceptional response. However, if impairment is seen not as exceptional but as an inevitable dimension of difference in the continuum of human experience, then questions about the extra-ordinariness of responses to be made to a disabled person's need do not arise. Herein perhaps lies a pathway to an enabling society. If disabled people from the outset can have an expectation that their entitlements too will be met through provision on the same terms that sophisticated societies build for their non-disabled peers, then need being seen as entitlement can be eliminated.

For Discussion

- I describe myself as 'neurodiversive'. What 'needs' do you think I have? How does thinking about my 'entitlements' influence your thinking about me?
- Find an article on a social issue affecting disabled people (using a newspaper or the web) in which needs are referred to. Can you think of ways of understanding the same issue if the notion of need is replaced with the notion of entitlement?

Further Reading

Hughes, B., Russell, R. and Paterson, K. (2005) 'Nothing to be had "off the peg": consumption, identity and the immobilisation of young disabled people', *Disability & Society*, 20 (1): 3–17.

Maslow, A.H. (1943) 'A theory of human motivation', *Psychological Review*, 50 (4): 370–96.

Swain, J., French, S. and Cameron, C. (2003) 'Who needs special needs?', in J. Swain, S. French and C. Cameron, *Controversial Issues in a Disabling Society*. Buckingham: Open University Press, pp. 122–30.

References

Maslow, A.H. (1943) 'A theory of human motivation', *Psychological Review*, 50 (4): 370–96.

34   Normalcy

Colin Cameron

Normalcy is a term used to describe ways in which people think about themselves in relation to others around them. It is assumed until it is disrupted and is, as Titchkosky puts it, an 'unmarked viewpoint' (Titchkosky 2003: 148). Far from being a natural quality or characteristic, however, normalcy is dependent on measuring itself against those it has excluded. Normalcy needs abnormalcy in order to recognise itself.

Davis has pointed out that 'just as conceptualisations of race, class and gender shape the lives of those who are not black, poor or female, so the concept of disability regulates the bodies of those who are "normal"' (Davis 1995: 12). Our sense of who we are as individuals is tied up to a large extent in measuring and evaluating ourselves against others we have decided we are unlike, or wouldn't want to be like (Stryker 2002). In this sense, in Davis' words, 'disability is not a minor issue that relates to a relatively small number of unfortunate people; it is part of a historically constructed discourse, an ideology of thinking about the body under certain historical circumstances' (Davis 1995: 2).

The appearance of normality as a principle underpinning social organisation coincided with the struggle of emerging modern societies during the nineteenth century to find ways of controlling the rapidly growing amounts of information, products, processes, and human movement that accompanied industrialisation (Garland-Thomson 2009). The word 'normal', as used to mean 'conforming to, not deviating or differing from, the common type, standard, regular, usual', only enters the English language around 1840 (Davis 1995: 24). Previously the body had been represented in terms of the 'ideal' and the 'grotesque'. As Davis has pointed out, by definition nobody could have the perfect body. Pre-industrialisation, there was no expectation that populations would have bodies that conformed to the ideal (1995: 25). In contrast, however, as McDonnell (2007: 154) suggests, a considerable part of the potency of normality as an instrument for interpreting conditions and behaviours came from its capacity to represent both what 'is' and what 'ought to be'. A mythical 'average man' became the model for 'normal' physical and intellectual constitution.

Normality carries social advantage which is why, in order to achieve validation from those with whom we come into contact, we learn to 'abide by the rules', 'play the game' and 'look the part'. Normality is an exacting requirement, working at an unconscious level to shape our decisions about how we appear to other people – in terms of the clothes we wear, the postures we adopt, the language we use, the gadgets we are seen with, and so on – and binding us to structures of commodity capitalism. 'Getting it right' is important. Standing out and experiencing disap-proval for 'getting it wrong' can be sensed as a demeaning experience which leads to ostracism.

It can be argued that the problem of disability is not caused by the aberrant bodies of individual disabled people, but that the real problem relates to the way normalcy requires impairment to be identified as abnormality. Disabled people are required to internalise the values of the society which has marked their bodies as abnormal and to do their best to cover impairment up. 'Getting as close as possible to "normal" stand-ards of bodily engagement ... is a cultural expectation of disabled persons and assures that normalcy maintains its status as a dominant but taken-for-granted phenomenon' (Titchkosky 2003: 76).

From an early age disabled people undergo training to experience their bodies as challenges to be struggled with in the pursuit of normality. This is expressed in two statements below by Charles and Mary, two disabled people I interviewed in Cameron (2010), recounting their experiences at segregated 'special' schools:

> Charles: I didn't use a wheelchair in school, I used, like, a walking frame ... and you're under pressure to not end up in a wheelchair, to keep walking ... (p. 86)

> Mary: I went there from when I was six to ... nearly fourteen ... and I left ... without, I think, the words disability, handicap ... certainly not impairment ... ever being mentioned ... all the time we were extolled to act like other children ... to be like other children ... it was a culture that really denied children any sense of themselves as being disabled ... (p.82)

Charles, an adult wheelchair user now and happy being so, describes the pressure he experienced at school to maintain a posture as close as possible to 'normal' standards of bodily engagement. To use a wheelchair was seen as a mark of having failed in the emulation of normalcy. Mary's account tells of how, throughout her school career, 'other children' ('normal' children) were held up as exemplars of physicality and behaviour. As she says, no opportunity was given for the possibility of learning to value herself as a disabled child.

As noted in Swain et al. (2003: 83), many disabled people are well into adulthood before they manage to abandon, or at least challenge, expectations of normality. For most this is a gradual process which comes with the confidence of age, but for some it can be a sudden realisation. A deaf woman cited in Campling (1981) is quoted recount-ing such an experience:

> They were laughing and talking and didn't give a damn that the whole place knew they were deaf ... My years of pretence seemed suddenly absurd. I had been making life 'normal' and easy for everyone except myself.

> (Swain et al. 2003: 83)

Morris believes the assumption that disabled people want to be 'normal', rather than just as they are, is one of the most oppressive experiences they are subjected to. She states that 'I do not want to have to try and emulate what a non-disabled woman looks like in order to assert positive things about myself. I want to be able to celebrate my difference, not hide from it' (Morris 1991: 184).

Human experience is characterised by variety, of which impairment is part. While the pursuit of normality involves a requirement to hide away and deny, rather than to acknowledge and include impairment on its own terms, this results in a significant distortion of our understanding of what being human is about.

For Discussion

- Are you normal? How do you know? How does the degree of normality you claim (or, conversely, you can't claim) impact on your life?
- Who do you know who is considered 'abnormal'? How does your view of their abnormality impact on their life?
- What's so good about being normal?

Further Reading

Corbett, J. (1991) 'So, who wants to be normal?', *Disability & Society*, 6 (3): 259–60.
Davis, L. (2010) 'Constructing normalcy', in L. Davis (ed.), *The Disability Studies Reader*. London: Routledge, pp. 9–28.
Wheeler, M. (2011) 'Syndrome or difference: a critical review of medical conceptualisations of Asperger's syndrome', *Disability & Society*, 26 (7): 839–51.

References

Cameron, C. (2010) 'Does anybody like being disabled? A critical exploration of impairment, identity, media and everyday experience in a disabling society'. PhD thesis, http://etheses.qmu.ac.uk/258/1/258.pdf, accessed 31 October 2012.
Campling, J. (ed.) (1981) *Images of Ourselves: Women with Disabilities Talking*. London: Routledge and Kegan Paul.
Davis, L.J. (1995) *Enforcing Normalcy: Disability, Deafness and the Body*. London: Verso.
Garland-Thomson, R. (2009) *Staring: The Way We Look*. Oxford: Oxford University Press.
McDonnell, P. (2007) *Disability & Society: Ideological and Historical Dimensions*. Dublin: Blackhall.
Morris, J. (1991) *Pride Against Prejudice: Transforming Attitudes to Disability*. London: The Women's Press.
Stryker, S. (2002) *Symbolic Interactionism: A Social Structural Version*. Caldwell, NJ: The Blackburn Press.
Swain, J., French, S. and Cameron, C. (2003) *Controversial Issues in a Disabling Society*. Maidenhead: Open University Press.
Titchkosky, T. (2003) *Disability, Self and Society*. Toronto: University of Toronto Press.

35

Oppression

Colin Cameron

In order to explain clearly what is meant when disability is named an *oppressive social relationship* (UPIAS 1976), it might be helpful to explore what is meant by 'oppression'. We may initially think of oppression as involving the subjugation of one group by another through, for example, the exercise of physical coercion. New social movements that developed in the second half of the twentieth century, including the feminist movement, the black civil rights movement and the disabled people's movement have, however, reframed the term to give it a structural meaning.

Young has described structural oppression as involving 'the disadvantage and injustice some people suffer not because a tyrannical power coerces them, but because of the everyday practices of a well-intentioned liberal society' (1990: 41).

In these terms oppression is not necessarily the outcome of intentional acts and behaviours deliberately calculated to hurt or demean. Oppression can be identified as being imposed, for example, in assumptions encountered in the midst of everyday life by disabled people in their interactions with the non-disabled. Morris (1991: 19ff.), citing Evans, identifies a long list of oppressive assumptions about disabled people. These include, for example:

- that we feel ugly, inadequate and ashamed of our impairments;
- that our lives are a burden to us, barely worth living;
- that we are aware of ourselves as disabled in the same way that non-disabled people are and have the same attitude towards it;
- that nothing can be gained from the experience;
- that we don't have, and never have had, any real or significant experiences in the way that non-disabled people do;
- that we can't ever really accept our condition, and if we appear to be leading a full and contented life, or are simply cheerful, we are 'just putting a good face on it';
- that we desire to emulate and achieve normal behaviour and appearance in all things;
- that we never 'give up hope' of a cure.

As Young notes, 'for every oppressed group there is a group that is privileged in relation to that group' (1990: 42). It is not that non-disabled people are conscious of their roles in the structural oppression of disabled people. Rather, the reverse might be said to be usually true: that non-disabled people generally feel sympathy towards people with impairments and seek their welfare. But it is precisely in this relationship, in which sympathy is regarded as an appropriate response to impairment, that oppression takes place. Being fixed in a role as an object of others' condescension can have a damaging impact on a disabled person's sense of self and often leads to internalised oppression. This is described by Reeve as something which happens

> when individuals in a marginalised group in society internalise the prejudices held by the dominant group ... This form of oppression is most effective when acting at the subconscious level, affecting the self-esteem of the individual in addition to shaping their thoughts and actions.

> (Reeve 2004: 87)

At the same time, in contexts where roles underlie the stability of social structure (Stryker 2002: 76) and are required to be played out by individuals, this way of relating to disabled people affirms non-disabled people's sense of their own worth.

Structural oppression is hard to identify because it involves taken-for-granted ways of doing and thinking which, in their repetition, reinforce and sustain conformist ways of acting and being. It closes off alternative ways and marks these as inferior or deviant. It limits and shuts down possibilities for people regarded as flawed, or as failing to achieve socially valued behaviours and attributes, because it regards doing things differently as evidence of inadequacy. It is difficult to recognise because it happens within the apparently insignificant details of everyday life, details not usually consciously brought into focus. Martin suggests that the difficulty in seizing hold of and recognising what goes on in the everyday arises

> because we are not trained to think of the repetitive activities and apparently banal objects that make up our everyday experience in an intellectual way. Instead, we tend to experience them as a kind of ubiquitous but unremarkable 'background' to the things in our life that we think 'really' matter.

> (Martin 2003: 1)

Yet it is in these details that the contexts and relationships which construct disabling barriers are experienced. When these are allowed to pass without critical reflection, they are experienced as parts of life individuals cannot really do very much about and as being just the way things are. In identifying disability as oppression, the social model gives us a critical tool with which to regard these details differently.

While disability is an oppressive social relationship because it involves inequality between disabled and non-disabled people, it is too simplistic to suggest that non-disabled people are always, only and inevitably oppressors of disabled people, or that disabled people are always, only and inevitably victims of oppression. Like everybody else, each disabled person is individually situated within structures of oppression according to the multiple social identities which root their sense of self. This means they are just as likely to be oppressive as anybody else, depending on how they are individually subjectively positioned in relation to other groups. Disabled men may act oppressively towards disabled or non-disabled women (Garland-Thomson 2001). White disabled people may act oppressively towards disabled or non-disabled black people (Swain and Vernon 2002). Where hierarchies of impairment are perceived, disabled people with certain impairments may act oppressively towards disabled people with other impairments (Deal 2003). Disabled people are no different from anybody else and can be

equally prejudiced, having been socialised within the same culture. In a society characterised by social division, disability is one oppressive social relationship among many.
People in possession of more than one group characteristic defined by dominant culture
as undesired difference, e.g. black disabled women, can experience simultaneous oppression, their experience being 'commonly characterised by multiple rejections, discrimina-
tions and fragmentations of their identity even in the equality movements, including the
disabled people's movement' (Vernon 1998: 208).

The oppression that disability involves leads many disabled people to accept the idea
that their impairments are the cause of their social disadvantage. The cultural imperial-
ism of the non-disabled permeates disabled people's experience so thoroughly that the
possibility of its contestation goes unnoticed or is denied. Disempowerment, isolation
and poverty, all of which have structural causes, rather than the need 'to come to terms
with' or overcome their impairments, are the real problems experienced by disabled
people. Identifying and addressing disability as oppression rather than as an individual
condition is a requirement for meaningful and lasting social change.

For Discussion

- Consider the variety of social identities that combine to give you your sense of self.
  Which of these give you a sense of privilege? Are there any that give you a sense of
  disadvantage?
- Look again at the examples of oppressive assumptions identified by Morris. Can you
  think of any more commonly held oppressive assumptions about disabled people?
- Why is it important to identify disabling assumptions as oppressive?

Further Reading

Deal, M. (2003) 'Disabled people's attitudes towards other impairment groups: a hierarchy of
    impairments', *Disability & Society*, 18 (7): 897–910.
Oliver, M. and Barnes, C. (2012) *The New Politics of Disablement*. Basingstoke: Palgrave
    Macmillan.
Young, I.M. (1990) *Justice and the Politics of Difference*. Princeton, NJ: Princeton University Press.

References

Deal, M. (2003) 'Disabled people's attitudes towards other impairment groups: a hierarchy of
    impairments', *Disability & Society*, 18 (7): 897–910.
Garland-Thomson, R. (2001) *Re-shaping, Re-thinking, Re-defining: Feminist Disability Studies*.
    Washington, DC: Center for Women Policy Studies.
Martin, F. (2003) *Interpreting Everyday Culture*. London: Arnold.
Morris, J. (1991) *Pride Against Prejudice: Transforming Attitudes to Disability*. London: The
    Women's Press.
Reeve, D. (2004) 'Psycho-emotional dimensions of disability and the social model', in C. Barnes
    and G. Mercer (eds), *Implementing the Social Model of Disability: Theory and Research*. Leeds:
    The Disability Press, pp. 92–98.

Stryker, S. (2002) *Symbolic Interactionism: a Social Structural Version*. Caldwell, NJ: Blackburn Press.

Swain, J. and Vernon, A. (2002) 'Theorising divisions and hierarchies: towards a commonality or diversity?', in C. Barnes, M. Oliver and L. Barton (eds), *Disability Studies Today*. Cambridge: Polity, pp. 77–97.

Union of the Physically Impaired Against Segregation (UPIAS) (1976) *Fundamental Principles of Disability*. London: UPIAS.

Vernon, A. (1998) 'Multiple oppression and the disabled people's movement', in T. Shakespeare (ed.), *The Disability Studies Reader: Social Science Perspectives*. London: Cassell, pp. 201–10.

Young, I.M. (1990) *Justice and the Politics of Difference*. Princeton, NJ: Princeton University Press.

36 Personalisation

Alan Roulstone

Personalisation has been manifested in a range of self-directed social polices including direct payments, individual budgets, personal budgets and person-centred planning. Personalisation as an idea has been interpreted variously to be a valued response to bureaucratised and professionally dominated services (Leadbeater 2008; Stainton and Boyce 2004), to be a mode of personal control over everyday decisions (Carr 2008; Duffy 2007) and as an aspect of a neo-liberal project of responsibilising all forms of social policy (Ferguson 2007). How then can personalised approaches be critiqued, as they are surely an unobjectionable 'apple pie' development in the social relations of support? Well, Beresford recently warned against the term personalisation being seen as a new, inherently progressive and irreversible development and language, especially where adequate funding might not be seen to underpin new ideas (Beresford 2008). So often newly minted terms in adult social care arise and are aggrandised by use and exchange to take on proportions and promise that cannot be delivered or at worst distort reality. Empowerment, citizen control, user-led services and emancipatory practice in their time all offered new visions while emanating from a traditional practice and policy context. Raymond Williams writing in 2004 noted that 'community' had suddenly become fetishised as a place of new possibilities and argued that the language being used could lull us into suspending cultural critique (Williams 1983: 76).

What makes personalisation different is the apparent borrowing of the language of the disabled people's movement and a perceived convergence of the UK Department of Health (DH) 'putting people first' agenda and the disabled people's movements' 'choices and rights' agenda (Roulstone and Morgan 2009). This apparent convergence could be the result of genuine listening and an attempt by the DH to deliver on the process of capturing the voices of the disabled people's movement more fully. Reappraising the role of professionals seems a key facet of this re-evaluation for both these organisations. Alternatively, personalisation and self-direction more generally can be seen as a cynical use of the term – a sort of Trojan Horse for obscuring cuts and the externalising risk to sick and disabled people longer term. For example, by simply changing the language slightly from personalisation to personalised solutions we can undertake a policy 'sleight of hand' that increasingly expects self-determination and self-provisioning to prevail in an era of chronic austerity. Personalisation has featured in a range of neo-liberal developments, most notably in the use of the term 'personalised conditionality' in welfare reform (Gregg 2008). The uncritical embracing of this term by the UK Department for Work and Pensions (DWP) reflects in an alarming way the prosyletising zeal with which the DH has embraced personalised solutions.

The truth is arguably somewhere between the above extremes. Beresford's concern that personalisation does not enter the established lexicon without health warnings is quite correct. However, there have undoubtedly been genuine attempts to listen to organisations of disabled people from the mid-1990s. There are many examples of personalised support working (Stainton and Boyce 2004), and personalisation is clearly a counter to paternalist Fordist principles where services are delivered according to professional needs and not those of service users. However, the term and its use seriously risks becoming post-Fordist in the sense that limited funding and the spending of meagre budget on essentials, rather than transforming social care, may simply be the equivalent of changing the outer appearance of disabled people's lives. Personalisation in this sense would revert to a consumerist interpretation – one where small-scale choices mask underlying immiseration of services and the reduction of substantive support. Such limited interpretations can be paralleled in consumerism more widely. While new products become fetishised – for example mobile phone casings – is this really choice in any meaningful sense? Strictly speaking we *are* making choices, but not under conditions of our own choosing. In this sense personalisation in its purest sense has to be seen as synonymous with wider personal determination and choice-making.

The substantiating of personalisation requires a broader shifting of the social relations of support to ensure choice and control, so that the term is seen to be meaningful only where social support systems are humane, equitable *and* personalised. Where these conditions are not met there is a risk that ideological and linguistic distortion will shift personalisation to a mere consumerist analogy – a position where personalisation is a shorthand for de-collectivised lives. The origins and ideological precursors of personalisation will continue to be hotly debated. It is important however not to dismiss personalisation outright, as another term will likely take its place – one suffused with the same levels of ambiguity and ideological fudge that bedevils much disability policy. Similarly any prophetic and uncritical use risks simply shifting many disabled people from an enforced collectivism to an enforced individualism. It is in the nature of power and ideology that the true nexus of power is not revealed until ideas, words and policy direction are fundamentally challenged.

It is axiomatic that to talk uncritically of personalised and responsive social care at a time that most disabled people cannot get access to support is a cruel irony. In this sense, it would be using one-dimensional language to talk of personalised adult social care when the 'Fair' Access to Care guidance has been inverted to only offer support to the highest category of need in the majority of local contexts. How can social support be personalised if the wider system operates in a very de-personalised way, denying many people access to any adult social care support? Academics and practitioners have to be aware of this particular 'language game'.

It is tempting to reject the term personalisation outright. Its associations with a neo-liberal era should be regarded as a warning. However, this is not sufficient grounds to reject the term as it emanated from a complex set of dynamics that would not unravel by a simple change of nomenclature. Despite this, a contestation of the term is crucially important, as is a similar challenging of practice tenets around personalised support. This is made especially piquant by the decline of the global economy. Some services will manage, largely via street-level creativity, to ensure small *islands of personalisation*. What we don't have is a system of *personalised social support*, and we need to guard against any linguistic and policy slippage towards a misuse of the latter term. Personalisation cannot be seen as an end in itself but as a means to independent living more generally. Arguably personalisation cannot be substantiated without decent packages of social support, accessible environments and a better understanding and acceptance of disabled people, as Carr and Robbins note:

> Ensuring universal access to public and community services; prevention and early intervention; promoting coproduction of services and the growth of social capital in communities and the social care sector; improving access to information and advice for all people who use social care services regardless of how they are funded; and recognising and supporting carers.

(Carr and Robbins 2009: 3)

For Discussion

- How can personalisation be seen to support the choices and rights agenda for disabled people?
- In what ways might personalisation have been hijacked by political 'top-down' agendas
- What are the prerequisites of meaningful personalisation?

Further Reading

Glasby, J. and Littlechild, R. (2009) *Direct Payments and Personal Budgets: Putting Personalisation into Practice*. Bristol: Policy Press.
Harris, J. and Roulstone, A. (2011) *Disability, Policy and Professional Practice*. London: Sage.
Roulstone, A. and Prideaux, S. (2012) *Understanding Disability Policy*. Bristol: Policy Press.

References

Beresford, P. (2008) 'Personalisation of social care can't be done on the cheap', *Community Care*, 22 October.
Carr, S. (2008) *Personalisation: A Rough Guide*. London: Social Care Institute for Excellence.
Carr, S. and Robbins, D. (2009) *SCIE Research Briefing 20: The Implementation of Individual Budget Schemes in Adult Social Care*. London: Social Care Institute for Excellence.
Duffy, S. (2007) 'Care management and self-directed support', *Journal of Integrated Care*, 15 (5): 3–14.
Ferguson, I. (2007) 'Increasing user choice or privatizing risk? The antinomies of personalization', *British Journal of Social Work*, 37 (3): 387–403.

Gregg, P. (2008) *Realising Potential: A Vision for Personalised Conditionality and Support*. London: Department for Work and Pensions.

Leadbeater, C. (2008) *Personalisation Through Participation*. London: Demos.

Roulstone, A. and Morgan, H. (2009) 'Neo-liberal individualism or self-directed support: are we all speaking the same language on modernising adult social care?', *Social Policy and Society*, 8 (3): 333–45.

Stainton and Boyce (2004) '"I have got my life back": users' experience of direct payments', *Disability & Society*, 19 (5): 443–54.

Williams, R. (1983) *Community-Keywords: A Vocabulary of Culture and Society*, revised edn. New York: Oxford University Press,

37

The Personal Tragedy Model

Colin Cameron

During the run-up to the 2012 London Olympics there was much media coverage of the journey of the Olympic torch and the torchbearers who carried it, many of whom were disabled people. There were plenty of news stories about 'inspirational' people who had 'overcome disability'. A number of torchbearers even struggled from their wheelchairs to walk the final yards of their parts of the route before handing the torch over. These people have been described in local and national media as 'sufferers' displaying 'tenacity', 'sheer courage and determination', and as 'defying the odds'; 'personifying the spirit and courage of an inspiring day', and 'winning the hearts of the thousands of people who lined the streets' (BBC 2012; *This is Leicestershire* 2012a, b).

Levin (1996) has used the term 'sociological snapshots' to describe the ways in which the details of everyday life can be read as texts revealing the unceasing reproduction, transformation and stabilisation of social structural relations. If we regard the scenes described above as snapshots we can ask questions of what we see. I would argue that what is going on is the reproduction and stabilisation of disabling social structural relations. These scenes involve a ritualistic endorsement of a personal tragedy narrative on disability, an acknowledgement by the torchbearers of the discredited subject position of people with impairments and an affirmation of the normative subject position. The crowds applaud because they are participating in a ceremony which validates their own sense of normalcy.

Oliver (1996) has talked about walkers, non-walkers and nearly walkers; about walking being rule-following behaviour and not-walking being rule-ignoring, rule-flouting or even rule-threatening behaviour. He suggests that not-walking is tolerated as long as individuals are prepared to undergo rehabilitation in order to nearly walk or to come to terms with their non-walking, and that not-walking or rejecting nearly-walking as a personal choice is regarded as confrontational. The actions of these torchbearers – struggling from their wheelchairs and enduring crippling pain (*This is Leicestershire* 2012b) to hear the cheers of those lining the streets – involve an acknowledgement of the superiority of walking, and a disavowal of non-walking. Through these actions the assumptions inherent in the personal tragedy model are validated.

The personal tragedy model is the cultural expression of the individual or medical model and is materialised through the recycling of disciplinary messages that 'able-bodiedness' is valued while impairment is a mark of misfortune: to be endured, struggled against and overcome. The endless reiteration of the view that impairment signifies personal tragedy reinforces assumptions about the normality of health and involves relentless pressure on disabled people to disown impairment. Implicit in the personal tragedy model is a confirmation of the largely unchallenged view that treats health as the normal condition most people enjoy, and departure from health as an inconvenient state of being to be endured and battled with temporarily until normal functioning is restored (Frank 1997; Parsons 1951). In describing 'the sick role', Parsons (1951) suggests that people are reprieved from ordinary social responsibilities so long as they keep to their side of the bargain and display a keenness to 'get better'. In struggling from their wheelchairs, the torchbearers are embodying and acting out this role. Frank has noted that people learn the restitution narrative through participation in 'institutional stories that model how illness is to be told' (Frank 1997: 78). The snapshot of the torchbearers is a particularly dramatic illustration of the re-telling of the institutional story of impairment as personal tragedy. Oliver and Barnes observe that 'the overwhelming majority of the population with and without impairments internalise the personal tragedy view of disability' (Oliver and Barnes 2012: 139). Participation in social rituals like this naturalises this view.

Disabled people often find themselves placed permanently in the sick role even when they are not sick and while this role has little relevance for them. Many disabled people will 'accept some level of illness as the permanent background and intermittent foreground of their lives' (Frank 1997: 82). Many other people with long-term impairments which do not constitute sickness live healthy lives on a day-to-day basis. Yet the sick role impacts on their lives by marking impairment as a condition to be dealt with privately and struggled with cheerfully. Cultural disapproval is reserved for those who see no point striving to attain the unattainable, who complain instead about access. These are regarded as people with chips on their shoulders, who have just not come to terms with their limitations.

French (1994) has described 'the disabled role' placed on people with impairments. This is given legitimacy within everyday interactions, practices and contexts in which assumptions equating impairment with tragedy go unchallenged, and is characterised by a number of features. Among these is the expectation that disabled people will always seek to be independent. While unequal relationships of care can create their own problems by developing mutual dependency, pressures placed on disabled people by professionals to carry out time-consuming physical tasks for themselves in order to demonstrate their independence can also be regarded as oppressive. The thinking underlying such requirements is that 'this is how normal people go about things' and that normality is something disabled people should aspire to. Many disabled people believe that spending hours completing tasks for themselves (putting on socks, for example) is a waste of time when they could get a personal assistant to do these instead, freeing them up to do more interesting things with their lives. Independence is about being in control of what happens rather than about being physically able to do things.

The expectation that disabled people will aspire to normality is another oppressive characteristic of the disabled role, leading to situations in which people cannot be open about their impairments or access requirements for fear of other people's responses. The disabled role imposes a requirement on disabled people to accept and adjust to the 'loss' that impairment involves, making it very difficult to think about or to experience impairment other than as personal tragedy. Finally, disabled people are expected to take responsibility for the feelings that non-disabled people have about impairment and disability:

> People with epilepsy may, for example, be expected to explain constantly their condition and offer reassurance, deaf people may struggle to lip-read, and visually-impaired people may endure boredom rather than 'spoiling other people's fun' ... In contrast, non-disabled people are not expected to understand deafness, blindness, epilepsy or paralysis, or to alter their behaviour in any substantial way.

> (French 1994: 56)

When the disabled role, imposed in countless daily interactions with professionals, family members and strangers, and encountered in media narratives that relentlessly reinforce personal tragedy stereotypes, is the only role apparently available to disabled people, it can be very hard to resist. As Kroger (2000: 20) has noted, people 'are largely ascribed identities according to their manner of embedding within a discourse – in their own, or in the discourse of others'. The imagination is given little positive to build on with which to make sense of the experience of living with impairment. Disabled people often find themselves caught up in playing a part, and receiving social approval for playing a part, which does nothing to challenge the disabling social relations they experience. While a sense of short-term personal gratification might be achieved, bringing about meaningful change requires 'conscientisation' (Freire 1976) and a commitment to the long haul.

For Discussion

- In what ways do assumptions about personal tragedy distort relationships between disabled and non-disabled people?
- How might ideas about personal tragedy impact on the way disabled people view themselves?
- In what ways does the affirmation model, which identifies impairment as difference to be expected and respected on its own terms, challenge the personal tragedy view of disability?

Further Reading

Cameron, C. (2012) *Nothing to do with me, Everything to do with me: Disability, Self and Identity*. Disability Arts Online, www.disabilityartsonline.org.uk/domains/disabilityarts.org/local/media/audio/Nothing_To_Do_With_Me_FINAL.pdf.

Michalko, R. (2002) *The Difference that Disability Makes*. Philadelphia, PA: Temple University Press.

Riddell, S. and Watson, N. (eds) (2003) *Disability, Culture and Identity*. Harlow: Pearson Education Ltd.

References

BBC (2012) 'Olympic torch relay: injured soldier walks with flame', www.bbc.co.uk/news/uk-18579631, accessed 30 October 2012.

Frank, A. (1997) *The Wounded Storyteller: Body, Illness and Ethics*. London: University of Chicago Press.

French, S. (1994) 'The disabled role', in S. French (ed.), *On Equal Terms: Working with Disabled People*. London: Butterworth-Heinemann, pp. 47–60.

Freire, P. (1976) *Pedagogy of the Oppressed*. London: Penguin.

Kroger, J. (2000) *Identity Development: Adolescence Through Adulthood*. London: Sage.

Levin, J. (1996) *Sociological Snapshots: Seeing Social Structure and Change in Everyday Life*. Thousand Oaks, CA: Pine Forge Press.

Oliver, M. (1996) *Understanding Disability: From Theory to Practice*. London: Macmillan.

Oliver, M. and Barnes, C. (2012) *The New Politics of Disability*. Basingstoke: Palgrave Macmillan.

Parsons, T. (1951) *The Social System*. London: Routledge and Kegan Paul.

This is Leicestershire (2012a) 'Olympic spirit personified by Leicester torchbearer Lucy Davies', www.thisisleicestershire.co.uk/OLYMPIC-SPIRIT/story-16477405-detail/story.html, accessed 6 March 2013.

This is Leicestershire (2012b) 'Pride and joy as the flame arrives in Leicester', www.thisisleicestershire.co.uk/Pride-joy-flame-arrives-Leicester/story-16477417-detail/story.html, accessed 6 March 2013.

38 Professionals

Toby Brandon

This chapter explores what it means to be a professional with reference to three models of the way professionals work and the implications that these may have for disabled people. Historically disabled people's contact with professionals has encompassed everything from empowering respect through to extreme abuse. Within our society at different points in our lives all of us come into contact with professionals, whether a GP, dentist, police officer, teacher or social worker. However, it can be argued that disabled peoples' frequency and intensity of contact with professionals is far greater. In addition these professionals often have increased control over the lives of disabled people in a number of appropriate and potentially inappropriate ways, for example health professionals giving social advice and social care professionals giving health advice.

The first of the three models is the 'trait' model (Abbott and Meerabeau 1998), which defines a profession in terms of the following distinct traits or characteristics:

- Conducting highly skilled work based upon theoretical knowledge.
- Having the power to make autonomous decisions.
- Being trustworthy.
- Focusing on a service-orientated philosophy.
- Following a professional code of conduct.
- Having a monopoly over a certain area of work, usually through specific legislation and registration.
- Adherence to a professional body which selects, safeguards and controls its members by, for example, disciplinary action and the accreditation of training.

To be a professional therefore involves extensive training with the acquisition of large amounts of knowledge. The nature of this knowledge is to develop and clearly demarcate experts or professionals from lay or ordinary people. To be a professional you do not necessarily have to have all the above traits, just a selection of them. Swain et al. (2003) and Koehn (1994) would argue that the only trait common across all professions is a pledge to the greater good, embodied in an ethical code. Banks (2003: 50) goes further, drawing a distinction between espoused professional ethics around the ideals, principles and rules of a profession and enacted professional ethics around the norms of behaviour actually accepted and followed by professionals in their every day work. Lipsky's (1980) analysis of street-level bureaucracies explains how policy can be structured by professionals through their systemic bias towards certain disabled people. Professionals use mechanisms for creating routines to cope with the pressures of their work. One such mechanism is to distance themselves from disabled people and create the potential for punitive action upon disabled people who do not behave in appropriate ways within the services they provide.

The second model is concerned with power as the key determinate in professionals' and disabled people's relationships. The exchange of professional information and knowledge is the expression of this power. Each profession can develop a hierarchy and this can extend between different professions, for example nursing and medics. The disabled person can be lost in these hierarchies. As a result power divides can develop, for example, one of the significant places that professions grew and substantiated powers were institutions. Institutions for doctors and ward managers became places of power based on the number of beds they had under their control. The physical isolation and size of institutions encouraged abuse and maltreatment. It is important to note that the power divide is not only one unique to disability but also relates to gender, ethnicity and sexuality. The power model can be used to challenge the claims of professionals as the only experts and frames them as self-interested and attempting to make disabled people dependent upon them. Illich et al. (2005) consider professions as disabling, as one of their goals is to diminish people's ability to look after themselves.

The third approach that criticises the professions is the social model of disability, which is primarily concerned with counteracting the oppression experienced by disabled people.

This oppression is expressed by professions seeking to maintain the status quo by individualising problems to the person, not to the society. For example, historically a health problem is regarded as the fault of the person, not the outcome of poor housing, limited transport or lack of opportunity for education. Social controls are the processes by which professionals regulate disabled people's behaviour and encourage them to conform to certain key norms. Foucault (1971) argues that in psychiatry social control had intensified in the twentieth century and moved from an enclosed system of incarceration in institutions to a more open one. This involved obvious physical restraints being replaced by less obvious medical ones such as drugs. Foucault sees the role of the doctor as primarily being one of social control of the masses. Historically professionals have often reinforced the view of disabled people as tragic and inferior. They have categorised them, removed and isolated them in institutions, attempted to cure them with sometimes bizarre treatments and on occasion rehabilitated them through painful surgeries and medication (Oliver 1990). Disabled peoples' lives have therefore often been medicalised by health and caring professionals beyond their obvious health issues to impinge on wider aspects of their lives. Professionals may be involved, for example, in decisions about their employment, education and social benefits. Albrecht (1999) argues that disability is exploited by what he terms the disability industry. Within this professionals acquire status from disabled people through, as Illich et al. put it, converting their need into deficiency; deficiency being within the disabled person, not the situation or environment they find themselves in. If a disabled person has a problem then the professional has the solution. McKnight (2005: 83) writes on this subject 'To be professional is to distance – to ensure that the relationship is defined in terms that allow the client to understand who is really being serviced.'

Labelling disabled people is the domain of the professional; it can be a tool to either reassure or distance them. Words are not neutral. As the self-advocacy group People First famously state, 'Label jars not people'. In a classic study members of Rosenhan's (1973) research team got themselves admitted to various psychiatric hospitals in the US and were instructed to only say they had a heard a voice and nothing else. All were diagnosed as having schizophrenia by professionals. Rosenhan describes how the behaviour of these pseudo patients was interpreted and reframed as continuing evidence of their illness.

The keys to understanding the relationship between professionals and disabled people are the values, ideology and sharing of power and control. Jones et al. (1978) wrote about the two faces of professionalism, one traditionally benevolent and the other greatly self-interested. Perhaps here it is helpful to distinguish between being a professional and acting professionally. It has not been my intention to portray professionals as the enemy of disabled people, but to critically explore how Disability Studies provides a framework to challenge their potentially oppressive structures and practices.

For Discussion

- Describe some institutions that disabled people have been held in during the past century.
- How are you socially controlled every day by professionals?
- What have your experiences of meeting professionals been like?

Further Reading

Illich, I., Zola, I., McKnight, J., Caplan, J. and Shaiken, H. (2005) *Disabling Professions*. London: Marion Boyars.

Finkelstein, V. (2014) 'Disability and the helped helper relationship', in J. Swain, S. French, C. Barnes and S. Thomas (eds), *Disabling Barriers – Enabling Environments*, 3rd edn. London: Sage, pp. 5–8.

Roulstone, A. and Prideaux, S. (2012) *Understanding Disability Policy*. Bristol: The Policy Press.

Swain, J. and French, S. (2008) *Understanding Disability: A Guide for Health Professionals*. London: Churchill Livingstone Elsevier.

References

Abbott, P. and Meerabeau, L. (1998) *The Sociology of the Caring Professions*. London: Routledge.

Albrecht, G. (1999) *Handbook of Disability Studies*. London: Sage.

Banks, S. (2003) *Ethics, Accountability and the Social Professions*. London: Palgrave.

Foucault, M. (1971) *Madness and Civilization: A History of Insanity in the Age of Reason*. London: Tavistock.

Illich, I., Zola, I., McKnight, J., Caplan, J. and Shaiken, H. (2005) *Disabling Professions*. London: Marion Boyars.

Jones, K., Brown, J. and Bradshaw, J. (1978) *Issues in Social Policy*. London: Routledge.

Koehn, D. (1994) *The Ground of Professional Ethics*. London: Routledge.

Lipsky, M. (1980) *Street-level Bureaucracy: Dilemmas of the Individual in Public Services*. New York: Russell Sage Foundation.

McKnight, J. (2005) 'Professionalized service and disabling help, in I. Illich, I. Zola, J. McKnight, J. Caplan and H. Shaiken (eds) *Disabling Professions*. London: Marion Boyars. pp. 69–92.

Oliver, M. (1990) *The Politics of Disablement*. London: Macmillan.

Rosenhan, D.L. (1973) 'On being sane in insane places', *Science*, 179: 250–8.

Swain, J., French, S. and Cameron, C. (2003) *Controversial Issues in a Disabling Society*. Buckingham: Open University Press.

39 Psycho-emotional Disablism

Donna Reeve

While the social model of disability has been very effective at campaigning for the full inclusion of disabled people as active citizens, some feminists within Disability Studies have argued that the focus on the public barriers 'out there' has neglected the impact of disabling barriers that operate at a more personal inner level. Drawing on the UPIAS statement which underpins the social model of disability, Thomas (2007) has produced an extended social relational definition of disablism which includes reference to both the public and private forms of social oppression: 'Disablism is a form of social oppression involving the social imposition of restrictions of activity on people with impairments and the *socially engendered undermining of their psycho-emotional well-being*' (Thomas 2007: 73, my emphasis).

Using the term *disablism*, rather than *disability*, makes explicit connections with other forms of social oppression such as racism and sexism. This definition of disablism recognises the impact of both structural disablism (barriers to *doing*) and psycho-emotional disablism (barriers to *being*) in the lives of people with impairments. While the social model has never denied the reality of disabling barriers operating at this inner, personal level, this extended social relational definition specifically includes reference to both structural *and* psycho-emotional forms of disablism, thereby offering a framework for a more nuanced understanding of the lived experience of disablism in contemporary society.

The most important form of psycho-emotional disablism emerges from the relationship that a disabled person has with other people or themselves – *direct psycho-emotional disablism*. The often unwitting agents of this form of disablism can be family members, friends, professionals or strangers on the street, and often take the form of acts of invalidation or disavowal. Examples of direct psycho-emotional disablism include:

- when a disabled child is not invited to a family wedding because they might be 'disruptive';
- being subject to jokes or stares from strangers because someone walks differently or uses a wheelchair;
- when assumptions about quality of life result in a 'Do Not Resuscitate' notice being put on the hospital notes of a disabled patient;
- being denied access to family planning services because of assumptions about disabled people as asexual and undesirable;
- the experience of disablist hate crime.

Direct psycho-emotional disablism undermines self-confidence and self-esteem because of the negative messages being received about self-worth and value. These messages are reinforced by cultural myths and prejudices about the inherent undesirable status of disability, particularly in the Western world where the demands of capitalism require a stable, reliable, autonomous body and mind. Although disability discrimination law is slowly removing many of the structural barriers to inclusion, such as inaccessible buildings and public transport, it is far more difficult to challenge prejudices and assumptions which lurk at the level of the unconscious. So it is not surprising that government studies into attitudes reveal that disabled people are still seen as less capable than non-disabled people, as well as being in need of care and dependent on others (Staniland 2011). Additionally, the likelihood of experiencing prejudice from other people is much higher for those with learning difficulties or mental health difficulties than for those people with physical or sensory impairments.

These negative messages circulating within society can also lead to *internalised oppression*, which is a form of direct psycho-emotional disablism arising from the relationship a disabled person has with themselves. Negative messages about the value and ability of disabled people can become internalised and therefore impact on self-worth and self-esteem. Because this form of social oppression is often unconscious it can be difficult to challenge, especially when a disabled person is not exposed to more positive counter-representations of disabled people. This is particularly problematic for disabled children who are often the only ones in their family who are disabled, and whose weaker position in society means that they are more influenced by the behaviours and beliefs of adults, such as parents, teachers and health professionals. In the case of people who acquire their impairments as adults it can be emotionally difficult to confront a lifetime of internalised messages about disability; now they are no longer part of the non-disabled majority and instead are one of 'them', a group of people they may have actively avoided in the past.

Finally *indirect psycho-emotional disablism* can arise from the experience of structural disablism. This allows for recognition of the emotional impact of being faced with an inaccessible building or being denied information in accessible formats (structural disablism) – of being reminded that one is 'out of place' (Kitchin 1998). Indirect psycho-emotional disablism can also happen when the 'reasonable adjustments' made to meet the requirements of disability discrimination legislation are undignified or humiliating to use, such as being forced to access a building through a back entrance. Such adjustments may remain unused because the emotional costs of this legalised form of spatial apartheid are too high for the individual to bear – ironically the removal of a structural barrier has resulted in a psycho-emotional barrier with the identical outcome of excluding the disabled person.

It is important to note that psycho-emotional disablism is not inevitable; whereas a flight of steps disables all wheelchair users, disabled people will have different emotional reactions to a patronising comment or invalidating action, and these will vary according to time, place and personal history. Psycho-emotional disablism may be interconnected with structural disablism, and can be influenced by impairment/impairment effects as well as any other aspect of identity such as class, gender, sexuality, age or ethnicity. Like any other form of emotional abuse, the effects of psycho-emotional disablism can be cumulative, with past experiences reinforcing the negative impact of current psycho-emotional disablism. If psycho-emotional disablism is viewed as a form of invalidation and disrespect, then relationships with others that are validating and respectful can be very healing. It is vital that professionals who work with disabled people, some of whom will be socially isolated, ensure that they are aware of psycho-emotional disablism so that they do not behave in ways that are disabling rather than enabling.

Many disabled people actively resist psycho-emotional disablism, particularly those in disability arts and the disabled people's movement, which promote more positive images and messages about disability and validate different ways of being-in-the-world. These images of disability as diversity rather than lack help many disabled people reject the disabling stereotypes foisted on them by strangers and others. Disabled people may also undertake emotion work to manage the reactions of others, for example by educating the other person that they will not 'catch' anything by sitting next to them in a class. Finally, people who have invisible impairments may choose to 'pass' as normal, which will reduce the likelihood of psycho-emotional disablism, particularly from strangers; however they are always at risk that their disability status will be revealed if they fail to maintain this performative act.

For Discussion

- How might the experience of psycho-emotional disablism impact on self-identity as disabled (or not)?
- What role can organisations of disabled people play in helping disabled people challenge psycho-emotional disablism?
- How can professionals avoid psycho-emotional disablism within their relationships with the disabled person they are supporting?

Further Reading

Reeve, D. (2014) 'Psycho-emotional disablism and internalised oppression', in J. Swain, S. French, C. Barnes and C. Thomas (eds), *Disabling Barriers – Enabling Environments*, 3rd edn. London: Sage, pp. 92–8.

Reeve, D. (2012) 'Psycho-emotional disablism: the missing link?', in N. Watson, A. Roulstone and C. Thomas (eds), *Routledge Handbook of Disability Studies*. London: Routledge, pp. 92–8.

Thomas, C. (2007) *Sociologies of Disability and Illness: Contested Ideas in Disability Studies and Medical Sociology*. Basingstoke: Palgrave Macmillan (see chapter 3).

References

Kitchin, R. (1998) '"Out of place", "knowing one's place": space, power and the exclusion of disabled people', *Disability & Society*, 13 (3): 343–56.

Staniland, L. (2011) *Public Perceptions of Disabled People: Evidence from the British Social Attitudes Survey 2009*. London: ODI.

Thomas, C. (2007) *Sociologies of Disability and Illness: Contested Ideas in Disability Studies and Medical Sociology*. Basingstoke: Palgrave Macmillan.

40 Resilience

Katherine Runswick-Cole and Dan Goodley

How can we understand resilience in the lives of disabled people? Is the concept of resilience a useful one for disabled people and for Disability Studies as a discipline? This chapter explores two stories about resilience. The assumptions on which these stories rest are identified and held up to scrutiny so that an alternative, enabling view of resilience in the lives of disabled people is developed. The chapter draws on material from a recently completed research project, *Resilience in the Lives of Disabled People Across the Life Course* (Runswick-Cole and Goodley 2012, see http://disability-resilience.posterous.com).

> Christa Brelsford lost her right leg when she was caught under falling debris during the earthquake in Haiti in January … Now, with the help of a prosthetic leg, she continues to pursue her passion for rock climbing and has seen the top of steep cliffs all over New Mexico. Unstoppable, Brelsford hopes to run a half-marathon in December, and would like to return to Haiti to continue helping people.

(Kong 2010)

> By the time she turned 18, Khadijah Williams … had lived in shelters, in parks and in motels, never in a permanent residence for more than a few months … But in 2009, at age 18, Khadijah had also been accepted at Harvard University. Homeless since early childhood, Khadijah struggled all her life to hide her circumstances from teachers and fellow students. At age 9 she was placed in the 99th percentile on a state exam, and her teacher told her she was 'gifted.' From that moment forward, Khadijah decided to do whatever it took to keep herself in that category. 'I was so proud of being smart I never wanted people to say, "You got the easy way out because you're homeless,"' she told The LA Times. 'I never saw it as an excuse.

(Degree Scout, n.d.)

In the first story, disability is clearly present. Indeed, it is the presence of disability and the 'triumph over its tragedy' that allows resilience to emerge. Disabled people are often described as resilient when they achieve in spite of their disability. It seems that in public discourse, to be a resilient disabled person you must overcome the tragedy of your disability, live the life of a non-disabled person (as far as you possibly can), and bravely bide your time while you wait for a cure. In other words, you must be a 'super-crip' (Goggin and Newall 2004).

In the second story, disability is absent. Indeed here, paradoxically, it is the absence of disability that allows resilience to emerge. Khadijah is gifted, she is bright, she goes to Harvard.

The understandings of resilience evident in the stories above rest on psychological models that see resilience as 'good outcomes in spite of serious threats to adaptation of development' (Masten 2001: 228).

Social psychologists have shown the dangers of conceptualising resilience in individualised ways. Those judged to lack resilience may be blamed for 'failing to overcome' or may be deemed to have used their exposure to adversity as 'an excuse'. Disabled people who fail to embrace the 'triumph over tragedy' narrative, or fail to 'seek a cure', also risk being accused of lacking resilience.

Behaviours viewed as resilient differ between cultures. For Ungar (2007) resilience is 'the outcome from negotiations between individuals and their environments for the resources to define themselves as healthy amidst conditions collectively viewed as adverse' (Ungar 2004: 242).

Disability Studies scholars have demonstrated how the body and disability are, like behaviours, also socially constructed (Goodley 2011; Tremain 2005). The stories we are exploring reveal a discourse of 'ableism' inherent in conventional approaches to resilience in which 'ableism' is viewed as

> a network of beliefs, processes and practices that produces a particular kind of self and body (the corporeal standard) that is projected as perfect, species-typical and therefore essential and fully human. Disability … is cast as a diminished state of being human.

(Campbell 2001: 44)

Using these ideas, we suggest that resilience is not simply an individual matter; it is constantly made and re-made in relationships with other people and in access to resources as described below:

1. Material resources: availability of financial, educational, medical, and employment opportunities or assistance, as well as access to food, clothing, and shelter to meet basic needs.
2. Relationships: relationships with significant others, peers, adults and children/young people within one's family and community.
3. Identity: personal and collective sense of self and purpose, self-appraisal of strengths and weaknesses, aspirations, beliefs and values, including spiritual and religious identification.
4. Bodies: the influence of one's body – including impairment – in relationships with others.
5. Power and control: experiences of caring for oneself and others; the ability to affect change in one's social and physical environment in order to access health, educational and community resources.
6. Community participation: taking part in one's community through a host of activities and engagements.
7. Social justice: experiences related to finding a meaningful role in community and a sense of social equality.
8. Community cohesion: balancing one's personal interests with a sense of responsibility to the greater good; feeling a part of something larger than one's self socially and spiritually.

(Runswick-Cole and Goodley 2012)

A network of resilience implies interconnections and interdependence in people's lives. 'Non-disabled' people also require access to the resources we have identified in order to be able to identify themselves as resilient. However, non-disabled people are rarely required to reveal explicitly the resources upon which they rely and the interdependent relationships they engage with in the ways that disabled people are (Shildrick and Price 2006). Disabled people are often required to make their interdependencies explicit, particularly when they are required to provide evidence of their entitlements to accessing welfare and support. We conclude that resilience is not something that emerges only in the context of exceptional achievement. You don't have to be a 'super-crip' to be resilient.

For Discussion

- What forms of community participation have enabled Khadijah and Christa to live the lives they have and to achieve what they have achieved?
- Which resources did they draw on to develop a positive identity?
- What kinds of interdependencies can enhance resilience in a disabling society?

Further Reading

Burke, P. (2008) *Disability and Impairment: Working with Children and Families*. London: Jessica Kingsley.

Goodley, D. (2005) 'Empowerment, self-advocacy and resilience', *Journal of Intellectual Disabilities*, 9: 333–43.

Runswick-Cole, K. and Goodley, D. (2013) 'Resilience: a disability studies and community psychology approach', *Social and Personality Psychology Compass*, 7 (2): 67–78.

References

Campbell, F.K. (2001) 'Inciting legal fictions: disability's date with ontology and the ableist body of the law', *Griffith Law Review*, 10: 42–62.

Degree Scout (n.d.) *Khadijah Williams: 10 Students Who Overcame Massive Obstacles to Achieve their Dream in Education*, www.degreescout.com/business-degrees/10-students-who-overcame-massive-obstacles-to-achieve-their-dream-of-an-education, accessed 17 June 2013.

Goggin, G. and Newell, C. (2004) 'Fame and disability: Christopher Reeve, super crips and infamous celebrity', *M/C Journal*, 7 (5): 48–78.

Goodley, D. (2011) *Disability Studies: An Inter-disciplinary Introduction*. London: Sage.

Kong, V. (2010) 'Beating the odds', *Alberquerque Journal*, www.abqjournal.com/north/22231725north08-22-10.htm, accessed 17 June 2013.

Masten, A.S. (2001) 'Ordinary magic: resilience processes in development', *American Psychologist*, 56 (3): 227–38.

Runswick-Cole, K. and Goodley, D. (2012) *Resilience in the Lives of Disabled People Across the Life Course: A Literature Review*, http://disability-resilience.posterous.com/pages/findings, accessed 28 July 2012.

Shildrick, M. and Price, M. (2006) 'Deleuzian connections and queer corporealities: shrinking global disability', *Rhizomes*, 11/12, www.rhizomes.net/issue11/shildrickprice/index.html, accessed 28 February 2007.

Tremain, S. (ed.) (2005) *Foucault and the Government of Disability*. Ann Arbor, MI: University of Michigan Press.

Ungar, M. (2004) 'Constructionist discourse on resilience: multiple contexts, multiple realities among at-risk children and youth', *Youth & Society*, 35 (3): 341–65.

Ungar, M. (2007) 'Contextual and cultural aspects of resilience in child welfare settings', in I. Brown, F. Chaze, D. Fuchs, J. Lafrance, S. McKay and S. Thomas Prokop (eds), *Putting a Human Face on Child Welfare*. Toronto: Centre of Excellence for Child Welfare, pp. 1–24.

41

Rights and Legislation

Joanne Brown

This chapter provides an overview of the development of the legislation and fundamental rights that affect disabled people in everyday life. It explores the interdependency of rights and legislation, and considers the institutional practices that maintain societal inequality. Finally, it evaluates the current legislation and considers what still needs to be done in order to promote equal rights and treatment for all.

To understand the oppressive forces affecting disabled people, it is essential to consider not only personal prejudices, but also the practices of society (Oliver 1996).

Bynoe states 'laws can provide the means to define civil and political relationships in society, and, where these are unequal or are non-existent, to modify or to create them' (1995: 123).

As this statement suggests, rights and legislation are interdependent. It is therefore fundamental to protect via legislation the rights of individuals potentially at risk of discrimination. Anti-discrimination legislation governs the provision of services and access to such areas as employment and education. The Equality and Human Rights Commission (2012) identifies those at risk of discrimination as individuals or groups of people who are perceived by society to have particular characteristics. These 'protected characteristics' include race, gender, age and disability.

Minority groups have campaigned successfully for anti-discrimination legislation, as evidenced by The Sex Discrimination Act (1975) and The Race Relations Act (1976). Legislation combating disability discrimination has, however, taken much longer to reach the statute books. Cameron states that 'the Conservative Government under Margaret Thatcher argued that, while gender and race were legitimate rights issues, disabled people had charity instead' (2007: 92, translated).

This ran counter to the wishes of the disabled people's movement. Care and charity carry connotations of need and dependency, which can often shift the government's focus away from an individual's rights. The Conservative government's insistence that only charity was required to safeguard disabled people overlooked the real barriers to full equality with their non-disabled counterparts.

The Disability Discrimination Act (DDA) was the outcome of a lengthy political campaign by the disabled people's movement. Prior to this, discrimination on the basis of impairment was lawful. The DDA did not become law until 1995 and numerous sections failed to come into force immediately, due in part to the Conservative government's belief that there was minimal discrimination against disabled people (Barnes 1992).

While the DDA was represented widely as a step forward in that it recognised disability discrimination, it nevertheless received much criticism (Barnes et al. 1999; Swain et al. 2003): 'Many within the Disability Movement have denounced it as a sham: a "bigot's charter", without any teeth or real understanding of the operation of disability discrimination' (Gooding 1996: 1).

It was based on 'the orthodox individualistic view of disability' (Barton 2001: 18) as opposed to being rooted in the social model of disability. Additionally, the DDA failed to take into account both education (which was not included until 2001 with The Special Educational Needs and Disability Act (SENDA)) and the requirement for local authorities to actively promote disability equality (which was later included in a DDA amendment in 2005). A further problem with the legislation was the notion of 'reasonable adjustments', in particular the lack of a definition of 'reasonableness'. This left the area somewhat vague and up to interpretation by employers, service providers and disabled individuals. It can also be argued that the cost of taking individual cases to court under the Act frequently proved prohibitive.

A major criticism of the Act was the absence of an effective enforcement system to oversee its implementation. It wasn't until 1999, after intense lobbying, that The Disability Rights Commission came into place in order to support the DDA (Barnes 2000). However, legislation has continued to develop.

The Equality Act (2010) is the most recent piece of UK anti-discrimination legislation. It replaces and repeals the DDA, and has been designed to offer legal protection not solely to disabled people, but to all those in possession of the 'protected characteristics' mentioned above. It covers various types of discrimination, including ones not mentioned by the DDA. It covers both direct and indirect discrimination, failure to make reasonable adjustments, harassment and victimisation. However, the Act is still potentially problematic: it has been argued that it may dilute the rights of disabled people by grouping all 'at-risk' individuals within one piece of legislation (Barnes and Mercer 2010). A further issue of contention lies within the Act's definition of disability. The Equality Act (2010, Chapter 15) states that

A person has a disability if –

(a) the person has a physical or mental impairment, and

(b) the impairment has a substantial and long-term adverse effect on the person's ability to carry out normal day-to-day activities.

This definition still provides an individualised perception of disability. It focuses on the individual's impairment, and on that individual's ability to carry out 'normal' activities. In order for this legislation to fully address discrimination it must recognise the societal, environmental and institutional factors that affect the degree to which people can access 'normal day-to-day activities'.

As stated with regards to the DDA, '[it] is, in a sense, a direct expression of the politics of disability founded within a social model of disability, but remains grounded in the dominant/individual/medical/tragedy model of disability' (Swain et al. 2003: 159).

This statement still holds true with regards to The Equality Act (2010, Chapter 15). This individualised grounding will continue to weaken the rights of disabled people, which anti-discrimination legislation is intended to protect. In conclusion, it is important to consider that although anti-discrimination legislation is a significant tool in promoting individuals' rights and equality, inequality cannot solely be tackled by implementing legislation, but through the everyday practices of society.

For Discussion

- How are oppressive attitudes towards disability reflected in legislation?
- Does the Equality Act 2010 strengthen or weaken the rights of disabled individuals?
- How does the social oppression and discrimination of disabled people relate to other forms of discrimination based upon gender, age, race or religion?

Further Reading

Gooding, C. (1996) *Blackstone's Guide to the Disability Discrimination Act 1995*. London: Blackstone Press Limited.

Swain, J., French, S. and Cameron, C. (2003) 'Politics: where does change come from?', in *Controversial Issues in a Disabling Society*. Buckingham: Open University Press, pp. 151–60.

Wadham, J. (2010) *Blackstone's Guide to the Equality Act 2010*. London: Blackstone Press Limited.

References

Barnes, C. (1992) 'Institutional discrimination against disabled people and the campaign for anti-discrimination legislation', *Critical Social Policy*, 12 (5): 5–22.

Barnes, C. (2000) 'A working social model? Disability, work and disability politics in the 21st century', *Critical Social Policy*, 20 (4): 441–57.

Barnes, C. and Mercer, G. (2010) *Exploring Disability*, 2nd edn. Cambridge: Polity Press.

Barnes, C., Mercer, G. and Shakespeare, T. (1999) *Exploring Disability: A Sociological Introduction*. Cambridge: Polity Press.

Barton, L (ed.) (2001) *Disability, Politics and The Struggle for Change*. London: David Fulton Publishers Ltd.

Bynoe, I. (1995) 'Discrimination and the law: what can legislation achieve?', in G. Zarb (ed.), *Removing Disabling Barriers*. London: Policy Studies Institute, pp. 123–30.

Cameron, C. (2007) 'Breve storia del movimento delle persone disabili nel Regno Unito', *Rivista Sperimentale di Freniatria*, cxxxi (2): 83–99.

Equality Act 2010. London: HMSO. Available at: homeoffice.gov.uk/equalities/equality-act/, accessed 24 June 2013.

Equality and Human Rights Commission (2012) *Protected Characteristics: Definitions*, www.equalityhumanrights.com/advice-and-guidance/new-equality-act-guidance/protected-characteristics-definitions/.

Gooding, C. (1996) *Blackstone's Guide to the Disability Discrimination Act 1995*. London: Blackstone Press Limited.

Oliver, M. (1996) *Understanding Disability from Theory to Practice*. London: Macmillan Press Ltd.

Swain, J., French, S. and Cameron, C. (2003) 'Politics: where does change come from?', in *Controversial Issues in a Disabling Society*. Buckingham: Open University Press, pp. 151–60.

42 Service Users' Organisations

Peter Beresford

Service user- (or disabled people-) led organisations (ULOs and DPULOs) represent a radical innovation in public policy, pressure group politics and disability action. They have their origins in the organisations of disabled people that began to emerge in the 1980s with the advent of the disabled people's movement. These drew a sharp distinction between themselves, where control lay with disabled people, and the traditional disability charities where control lay with non-disabled people. Since then, such user-led organisations have extended to a wider range of groups as they too have developed social movements, including mental health service users/survivors, people with learning difficulties, young people living in care, older people and others.

Some of these 'self-organisations' involve one particular group of people, for example, people with visual impairments or mental health service users/survivors. Others seek to involve a wider range of service users. Nonetheless, while all groups of service users may be seen as having common concerns, for example, discrimination, marginalisation and exclusion, each also tends to identify its own particular history, traditions, culture and concerns. In some cases, local service user organisations have also formed coalitions, gaining strength and solidarity and encouraging inclusion by developing formal links with other groups of service users.

These ULOs represent the crucial bridge between individual service users and disabled people and their broader political movements. They provide an effective base both for responding to formal opportunities to get involved in democratic structures and processes and to campaign from without for change. There are now local, national and international ULOs and DPULOs. Organisations established at local level can be seen as providing the life blood for such a development and are probably where it is strongest and most firmly rooted. These user organisations, which have largely been rights-based, have exerted a major influence on policy and practice over a relatively short period. While this should not be over-estimated, it has led to fundamental changes in public perceptions of disabled people and other long-term health and social care service users, new approaches to support and services and the introduction of new legislation, including disability discrimination legislation. In the case of disabled people, these developments have been based particularly on the social model of disability and the philosophy of independent living, but for all people, these groups have advanced a more social approach to understanding disabled people's situation, difficulties and identities which has challenged traditionally dominant medicalised individual interpretations of them and their lives. Service user organisations are also the repositories and formulators of service user cultures, values, ideas and theories for change.

Such service user organisations have not only been the vehicle for the development of collective social and political action. They have also been identified repeatedly as the most effective means of supporting people's personal empowerment, through a process of collective 'conscientisation', so that they can then be in a position both to live a fuller more equal life, making better use of the opportunities available to them, and also be equipped with the confidence and skills to get involved collectively to work for social change.

The sharp distinction that was originally drawn between organisations 'of' and 'for' service users has in recent years become more difficult to discern. Some large traditional charities have rebadged themselves as ULOs. In some cases, disabled people and service users remain unconvinced that they have really changed their orientation. There is no agreement about what 'user-controlled' actually means. An official definition has been that 75 per cent of the management board or trustees of such organisations should be service users or disabled people. Some organisations, however, require 100 per cent representation of service users/disabled people on their board and even then raise concerns about user boards being manipulated by non-service user staff or subject to pressures to be 'funding' rather than values-led.

These organisations have also been a key part of a process of service users developing different more inclusive ways of doing things together. Many service users have traditionally been excluded from mainstream life and activities. This has included being excluded from public transport and education, employment, political and recreational activities. Service user organisations have both modelled different inclusive and accessible ways of doing things and worked to open them up to service users for the future. As part of this, service user organisations have been the focus for developing new forms of support for service users, from developing the idea of personal assistants and direct payments, to developing peer, complementary and user-led approaches to support. They have been at the heart of developing user-controlled research, to develop the knowledge base of service users; the involvement of service users in professional education and training to change its culture, and in developing user-defined quality measurement and standard setting.

While governments internationally have increasingly acknowledged the importance of service users' own organisations, in countries like the UK these have historically been financially insecure and under-resourced. As a result such organisations have often been short-lived. Traditionally they have been funded by central and local government grants and related financial support, but this has been an inadequate and increasingly unreliable source of funding.

Service users organisations still feel overshadowed by the traditional large disability and other charities. These tend to have much greater visibility, credibility and funding support and it is very difficult for most service user organisations to compete with them. Service user organisations often also find themselves competing with each other for limited financial resources. Their limited resources means that it is often difficult for service user organisations to be able to network with each other as much as they would like to, and often there are not service user organisations in particular areas or organisations available for particular groups of service users.

In the past service user organisations largely relied on subsidies or grants from the local and central state. This has long left them financially vulnerable, but in times of neo-liberal politics and the reduction of public expenditure as a proportion of the gross domestic product, this has become less and less tenable. To begin with, some disabled people's and service user organisations sought to develop alternative income streams through providing services to support direct payment schemes, but they have faced increasing competition from non-service user organisations which have been more successful in securing contracts because they have put less emphasis on quality than on low price.

Service user organisations are now seeking to develop funding alternatives to ensure their sustainability in line with their founding values and principles. They are increasingly having to be 'business-like' while still true to their principles. This means capacity-building and skill development for the service users involved. This is resulting in some of the most innovative of those organisations working to develop both a wider range of services to meet the needs of service users and also to ensure that mainstream markets take account of requirements to safeguard the rights and needs of disabled people and other service users. This is still largely unknown territory, which is giving rise to new and complex relationships between such third-sector service user organisations, market ideology, the provision of services and the maintenance of campaigning and self-advocacy roles.

I would like to acknowledge the insights I have gained from Steve Carey of Anglia Ruskin University, who is currently completing his PhD on 'Towards professionalisation in disabled people's user-led organisations'.

For Discussion

- What are the defining features of service user organisations?
- What do you see as the particular importance of user-led or user-controlled organisations?
- What are the key contributions that they have made since they first emerged?
- What barriers and problems do service user organisations face?
- What do you think will most help ensure their sustainability for the future?

Further Reading

Barnes, C. and Mercer, G. (2006) *Independent Futures: Creating User-led Disability Services in a Disabling Society*. Bristol: Policy Press in association with the British Association of Social Workers.

Beresford, P. and Carr, S. (eds) (2012) *Social Care, Service Users and User Involvement*. London: Jessica Kingsley.

Branfield, F., Beresford, P. with Andrews, E. J., Chambers, P., Staddon, P., Wise, G. and Williams Findlay, B. (2006) *Making User Involvement Work: Supporting Service User Networking and Knowledge*. York: Joseph Rowntree.

43   Sexuality

Margrit Shildrick

The issue of sexuality within disability circles – whether academic or activist – has not historically been at the forefront of the agenda. Put simply, sexuality was considered an area undeserving of disabled people's intellectual and campaigning energy because it did not appear to be one where substantive advances in law or policy could be achieved. Given the dominance of the social model of disability, in the UK in particular, questions of the body, of affect and of desire seemed too nebulous for broadly rights-based approaches. Recently, however, priorities have changed and disabled people are now producing both demands for changed policy and a range of cutting-edge theorisations rethinking the meaning of 'sexuality' in the context of disability.

For many people, the term simply suggests a range of sexual practices that occur within the wider categories of heterosexuality, homosexuality and bisexuality. On consideration, this is an inadequate approach and sexuality should be understood to include not only questions of practice and sexual orientation (itself expanded to include a more complex set of possibilities), but issues of identity, emotion, intimacy, self-esteem and general flourishing. For people with disabilities, both physical and cognitive, the new approach has opened up the importance of recognising the sexuality of all of those who are unable to unable to fit their own bodies and practices into normative forms. Where once the conjunction of disability and sexuality was seen as either unthinkable or at best a problem to be managed, it is now widely accepted that the attempt to silence discussion or to subject the sexual lives of people with disabilities to high levels of surveillance and control damages the very self-hood of those involved.

In *The History of Sexuality* (1979), Foucault famously deconstructs the Western notion of sexuality as the *truth* of the self, outlining its fluid discursive construction, while at the same time revealing it as the focus of the disciplinary and regulatory practices directed towards the body. That such constraints are especially marked in the case of people with disabilities indicates a widespread anxiety that the conjunction of disability and sexuality is potentially a point of disruption, a matter so disturbing that it must be closed down – disavowed even – as far as possible. But why should this be? One explanation that delves into the nature of the sociocultural imagination sees *both* disability and sexuality as points at which the comfort and familiarity of normative expectations are overturned (Shildrick 2009). Given an imaginary body that is always whole, impermeable, self-contained and under the subject's own rational control, it is clear that sexuality represents not simply the potential of pleasure but the threat of a dangerous merging of self and other, an exchange of fluids, and a lack of control. Similarly the person embodied as disabled may be perceived as having misplaced bodily parts, compromised rationality and forms of dependency that confuse the distinctions between self and other. The breaching of any normative boundary always causes anxiety, so when sexuality and disability come together the effect is greatly heightened to an extent that severely limits possibilities for people with disabilities.

There are many different ways in which the sexuality of disabled people can be thwarted, ranging from the limiting or absence of sex education in school, a dearth of disabled role models in the popular media, rigid attributes of masculine and feminine attractiveness, social policy initiatives that address everything but sexuality, a failure to ensure areas of privacy for disabled people, and a wide public belief that disabled people do not experience desire. Add to that the surveillance and management strategies that both family and professional carers exert – often with the best intentions – over those whose disability may necessitate assistance from others (Shakespeare et al. 1996), and it's clear that disabled sexuality is little discussed except as a problem. In the UK, *The Sexual Politics of Disability* (Shakespeare et al. 1996) represented a real breakthrough by enabling a range of disabled people, who understood their own sexualities in many different ways, to talk about their experiences. Further empirical research followed that consistently indicates that disabled people are no less engaged with issues of sexuality than the general population. Nosek's large empirical study of both disabled and non-disabled women noted a lower level of sexual *activity* for the former but concluded: 'There were no differences, however, between the groups on sexual desire' (2001: 20).

At the present time, much energy is devoted to the issue of sexual citizenship for people with disabilities, which would guarantee rights and recognition across a range of sexual matters, including that of expressing the sexuality of choice (Shakespeare 2000; Siebers 2008). The idea works best for those with physical disabilities, but despite growing acknowledgment that people with intellectual disabilities have sexual needs and desires, support there remains constrained and conspicuously heterosexist. In short, the sexuality LGBTQ people with intellectual disabilities remains 'a taboo within a taboo'. In any case, the notion of sexual citizenship should be treated with caution, in that it both tends towards the establishment of new exclusionary normativities and gets caught up in an inappropriate neo-liberal agenda. In encouraging people with disabilities to willingly self-regulate within prevalent civic norms, neo-liberalism sees disability not in terms of the discrimination that partially creates it, but as a malleable state that can be turned around through personal endeavour. The disabled person is trapped into developing their own coping mechanisms which operate at the level of individual inadequacy, rather than challenging the inherent ableism that marks their sexual otherness as problematic. Their pleasures and desires *may* be accommodated within the social/civic body, but only insofar as they will cause no disruption.

My point is that the irreducible needs and desires of people with disabilities cannot be simply addressed by a more equitable social justice, nor by sexual citizenship. Different forms of corporeality inevitably figure new dimensions of sexuality and self-identity that resist assimilation to normative standards. Not surprisingly, critics of the appeal to sexual citizenship tend to align themselves with a queer politics developed through both Deleuzian and cripqueer thinking (Goodley and Lawthom 2011; McRuer 2006). Both emphasise the process of desiring production – rather than desire as an individual affective state – as it arises in the unpredictable flows and intensities of hybrid associations and practices, in the acceptance of ambiguity, and in an ever-expansive connectivity between all the differential elements of human becomings. In stark contrast to the image of the neo-liberal citizen – the epitome of stable self-regulated well-being – queer theory opens up radical new possibilities that can engage with disability and sexuality as an unexplored positivity.

For Discussion

- How is the sexuality of people with disabilities regulated through existing social policy?
- What makes disability and sexuality such a general point of anxiety?
- Does queer politics offer a better way forward than sexual citizenship?

Further Reading

Earle, S. (1999) 'Facilitated sex and the concept of sexual need: disabled students and their personal assistants', *Disability & Society* 14: 309–23.

Shildrick, M. (2013) 'Sexual citizenship, governance and disability', in S. Roseneil (ed.) *Beyond Citizenship: Feminism and the Transformation of Belonging*. Basingstoke: Palgrave Macmillan, pp. 138–60.

Tremain, S. (2000) 'Queering disabled sexuality studies', *Sexuality and Disability*, 18 (4): 291–9.

References

Foucault, M. (1979) *History of Sexuality, Vol. 1*. London: Allen Lane.

Goodley, D. and Lawthom, R. (2011) 'Disability, Deleuze and sex', in Frida Beckman (ed.), *Deleuze and Sex*. Edinburgh: Edinburgh University Press, pp. 89–105.

McRuer, R. (2006) *Crip Theory: Cultural Signs of Queerness and Disability*. New York: New York University Press.

Nosek, M. Howland, C., Rintala, D.H., Young, M.E. and Chanpong, G.F. (2001) 'National study of women with physical disabilities: final report', *Sexuality and Disability*, 19 (1): 5–39.

Shakespeare, T. (2000) 'Disabled sexuality: toward rights and recognition', *Sexuality and Disability*, 18 (3): 159–66.

Shakespeare, T., Gillespie-Sells, K. and Davies, D. (1996) *The Sexual Politics of Disability: Untold Desires*. London: Cassell.

Shildrick, M. (2009) *Dangerous Discourses of Disability, Subjectivity and Sexuality*. Basingstoke: Palgrave Macmillan.

Siebers, T. (2008) *Disability Theory*. Ann Arbor, MI: University of Michigan Press.

44   The Social Model

Colin Cameron

While the medical model establishes a view which identifies disability as physical incapacity or abnormality, an alternative framework emerged as a result of the self-organised activity of disabled people during the 1970s. The definitions which would become known as the social model first appeared in *Fundamental Principles of Disability*, published by the Union of the Physically Impaired Against Segregation (UPIAS) in 1976 (Barnes 2004; Oliver 1990). Disability was reconceptualised here not as an individual problem or as a personal trouble but as a social structural issue. The social model made the following distinctions:

> Impairment: lacking part of or all of a limb, or having a defective limb, organ or mechanism of the body.

> Disability: the disadvantage or restriction of activity caused by a contemporary social organisation which takes little or no account of people who have physical impairments and thus excludes them from the mainstream of social activities.

> (UPIAS 1976: 14)

In these terms, while impairment was recognised as a physical condition or as an individual attribute, disability became identified as a matter of how society responded to, or failed to respond to, the needs of people with impairments. It was considered that not only had society omitted to include people with impairments, but that through its provision of segregated environments and institutions, such as residential homes, day centres and 'special' schools, it had consciously organised itself to exclude people with physical impairments from ordinary life. From a social model view, then, disability ceases to be something that people 'have' and is understood instead as an oppressive relationship, as something 'done to' people with impairments. People have impairments but are not 'people with disabilities'. They are disabled by poor or non-existent access to the public places where ordinary life happens and by the condescending and unwelcoming responses of those who occupy these spaces: 'In our view, it is society which disables physically impaired people. Disability is something imposed on top of our impairments by the way we are unnecessarily isolated and excluded from full participation in society' (UPIAS 1976: 14).

Extended by the Disabled People's International in 1981 to include people with sensory, emotional and cognitive impairments (Barnes 1994), the social model was the founding principle which united the collective consciousness of those who were instrumental in developing the disabled people's movement. It provided a new framework for analysis and a narrative through which feelings of self-blame and personal inadequacy could be challenged. It made clear that what was necessary in order to improve the lives of disabled people was not more treatment, better care or nicer attitudes, but the recognition and removal of the physical and social barriers and practices by which people with impairments are excluded from the mainstream (Swain and Lawrence 1994). Addressing the problem of disability required political action rather than therapeutic intervention.

Oliver has observed that dependency is not the inevitable outcome of impairment, but is created by the social, economic and political system in which disabled people live (Oliver 1996).Whereas a medical model understanding would regard impairment as the underlying reason for the disadvantage and disempowerment experienced by disabled people – and suggest the resolution of these could be achieved by changing the individual – the social model made possible a different gaze. It allowed disabled people to recognise that what was required in order to address disabling barriers were legislative changes so that access became a legal requirement, effective means of ensuring that new laws are complied with, and changes in the thinking underpinning public service planning and delivery at local authority level (Swain et al. 2003). The social model established the possibility for a new discourse on disability.

Criticism of the social model has, however, long been a focus for Disability Studies academics. Oliver (2004: 8) has identified five main criticisms of the social model from within Disability Studies itself. These include suggestions that the social model:

ignores or is unable to deal adequately with the realities of impairment;

ignores our subjective experiences of the 'pains' of both impairment and disability;

is unable to incorporate other social divisions such as race, gender, ageing and sexuality;

ignores the way that cultural values position disabled people as 'other';

is inadequate as a social theory of disability.

Oliver has responded to these criticisms by pointing out that:

the social model is not about the personal experience of impairment but the collective experience of disablement. Of course disabled people are aware of the limitations their impairments impose, and of course they struggle with that, and of course these create personal difficulties, but this is not what disability is about;

the social model emerged out of the lived experiences of disabled people;

the problem isn't that it cannot cope with other differences, but that people just haven't tried forging the social model in action in dealing with issues of race, gender, sexuality and age, preferring instead to criticise;

there is nothing in the social model that can be described, in principle, as ignoring cultural values. While so many disabled people continue to live in deprivation, though, to try to move disability politics exclusively into the realm of the politics of representation would be an error;

the social model was never premised as a grand theory intended to explain all questions relating to disability in all contexts.

(Oliver 2004: 8, 9)

The social model is 'a simplified representation of a complex social reality' and 'a practical guide to action' (Oliver and Barnes 2012: 22). As a tool it has provided disabled people with a robust foundation in which to ground their claims for equality. Pragmatic reasons have meant that the politics of the disabled people's movement has largely focused on what needs to be changed and can be changed – 'to identify and address issues that can be changed through collective action' (Oliver 1996: 38) – rather than those things which don't necessarily need to be changed or can't be changed, in other words, the reality of living with impairment. This may have led to a lack of focus on impairment, but this does not mean impairment is not central to the social model, or that the social model does not acknowledge that living with impairment can be painful and messy. To argue that the social model does not include impairment is to miss the point, for it is a tool for making sense of the experience of impairment in a disabling society. As Oliver and Barnes have stated recently, the strength of the social model lies in the fact that it offers a fundamental alternative to the individual model and poses a very different set of questions (Oliver and Barnes 2012).

For Discussion

- In what ways does the social model allow us to challenge traditional ways of thinking about disability?
- The social model is an idea that has been developed by disabled people rather than by professionals or 'carers'. Why is this important?
- What implications does the social model have for the way local services are planned and delivered?

Further Reading

Goodley, D. (2014) 'Who is disabled? Exploring the scope of the social model of disability', in J. Swain, S. French, C. Barnes and C. Thomas (eds), *Disabling Barriers – Enabling Environments*, 3rd edn. London: Sage, pp. 130–37.

Morgan, H. (2012) 'The social model of disability as a threshold concept: troublesome knowledge and liminal spaces in social work education', *Social Work Education*, 31 (2): 215–26.

Oliver, M. and Barnes, C. (2012) *The New Politics of Disablement*. Basingstoke: Palgrave Macmillan.

References

Barnes, C. (1994) *Disabled People in Britain and Discrimination: A Case for Anti-Discrimination Legislation*. London: Hurst and Co. in association with BCODP.

Barnes, C. (2004) 'Reflections on doing emancipatory research', in J. Swain, S. French, C. Barnes and C. Thomas (eds), *Disabling Barriers – Enabling Environments*. London: Sage, pp. 47–53.

Oliver, M. (1990) *The Politics of Disablement*. Basingstoke: Macmillan.

Oliver, M. (1996) *Understanding Disability: From Theory to Practice*. Basingstoke: Macmillan.

Oliver, M. (2004) 'If I had a hammer: the social model in action', in J. Swain, S. French, C. Barnes and C. Thomas (eds), *Disabling Barriers – Enabling Environments*. London: Sage, pp. 7–12.

Oliver, M. and Barnes, C. (2012) *The New Politics of Disablement*. Basingstoke: Palgrave Macmillan.

Swain, J. and Lawrence, P. (1994) 'Learning about disability: changing attitudes or challenging understanding?', in S. French (ed.), *On Equal Terms: Working With Disabled People*. Oxford: Butterworth-Heinemann, pp. 87–102.

Swain, J. French, S. and Cameron, C. (2003) *Controversial Issues in a Disabling Society*. Buckingham: Open University Press

Union of the Physically Impaired Against Segregation (UPIAS) (1976) *Fundamental Principles of Disability*. London: UPIAS.

45 Sport

Colin Cameron

It might at first seem unreasonable to take issue with the aspirations of the International Paralympic Committee (IPC) expressed here:

> Athletes and the Paralympic Games are at the heart of our Movement. Their performances and incredible stories teach the values of acceptance and appreciation for people with a disability. The Paralympic Movement builds a bridge which links sport with social awareness thus contributing to the development of a more equitable society with respect and equal opportunities for all individuals.

> (International Paralympics Committee 2012)

Aims of the IPC involve the 'enablement' and 'empowerment' of disabled athletes from beginner to elite level in order to 'inspire and delight' and 'touch the heart of all people for a more equitable society' (International Paralympics Committee 2012). Paralympic values include 'courage', 'determination', 'inspiration' and 'equality'. Paralympian athletes, the IPC tells us, demonstrate 'unique spirit' by pushing 'their physical ability to the absolute limit' and seek 'to accomplish what the general public deems unexpected' (International Paralympics Committee 2012). The IPC sees Paralympic Sport 'as an agent for change to break down social barriers of discrimination for people with a disability' (International Paralympics Committee 2012).

Critical examination of these statements, however, gives rise to concern. As Peers (2009), a former Paralympic champion has pointed out, the 'enablement' and 'empowerment' spoken about here is something to be *done to* Paralympic athletes *by* the IPC and the Paralympic movement which are mostly made up of non-disabled professionals and volunteers. Descriptions of 'courage' 'determination' and 'inspiration' draw us worryingly back to narratives which portray disability as tragic limitation to be overcome. References to 'incredible stories' sentimentalise disability. Rather than accomplishing what 'the general public deems unexpected', it might be argued that Paralympic athletes are, on the contrary, obliged to conform precisely to stereotyped expectations in their quest to push their bodies 'to the absolute limits'. What is revealed through this critique of IPC rhetoric is a deep attachment to detrimental medical model understandings of disability. The question needs to be asked whether there is a contradiction between this approach and the aspiration to breaking down disabling barriers through sport that is also expressed.

Peers (2009: 654) talks of

> the necessary, mutually dependent elements of Paralympic discourses, which include progressive, empowering and benevolent able-bodied experts; heroic, empowered and grateful Paralympians; tragic, passive and anonymous disabled.

She draws attention to the Paralympic Movement's roots within practices of therapy and rehabilitation most often associated with Guttmann's post-war work with paralysed war veterans at Stoke Mandeville Hospital in England. Guttmann is credited as 'primarily responsible for igniting hope, through sport, in a population [represented] as unequivocally tragic, hopeless, passive and as good as dead' (Peers 2009: 656).

The Paralympic Movement grew through a paternalistic ethos which envisaged sport not as an end in itself but as a means to recovery. 'Empowerment' in Paralympic terms is viewed in terms of overcoming personal limitations, and involves athletes in giving assent to, and complying with, a dominant view which regards impairment as deficit. Those who will overcome are hailed as inspirational role models. All of this has damaging implications, however, for other disabled people: 'the heroic Paralympian relies on discourses of the pitiful cripple who can't overcome and the burdensome gimp who won't' (Peers 2009: 654).

The Paralympic champion inadvertently reinforces narrow expectations about what disabled people should aspire to. In a 2012 interview in *The Guardian* Jerome Singleton, a Paralympic sprinter, announced 'We all know somebody with a disability and now we can point to the Games and ask them: "Why aren't you seeking to become a Paralympian?"' (Bagchi 2012).

Such a statement shows disabled athletes caught up in proselytising the IPC view. The implied suggestion, that there is something remiss if disabled people do not aspire to Paralympian status, is clearly oppressive. Its absurdity is revealed through the suggestion that likewise, all non-disabled people should seek to become Olympians. Hardin and Hardin (2008: 27) observed that the 'supercrip' image reinforces the idea that disabled people should be able to accomplish at heroic levels and provokes a requirement for all disabled people to be judged against this standard: 'What makes the supercrip stereotype most egregious ... is the manner in which it emphasise[s] individual effort as a way to overcome barriers erected by an able-bodied culture.'

Clearly there are different possible meanings behind the use of the word 'barriers'. Padraig, a Paralympic swimmer, refers to challenges elite athletes are always setting themselves, explaining:

> When you're training as an elite athlete you come across barriers all the time, but if you've got enough belief and confidence to do what you set yourself to do, be that winning or being active in general then you can do it.

(Purdue and Howe 2012: 8)

Disabled activists view barriers as structural and embedded within disabling discourses, practices and environments. The use of the word in the first sense here is likely to reinforce public perceptions that all disabled people need to do is to try harder.

Media coverage plays a major role in sentimentalising stories of Paralympians, and not solely because non-disabled journalists exploit disabling stereotypes. Arguably the recycling of disabling stories is something Paralympians are complicit in. Ade Adepitan, a British wheelchair basketball champion, for example, asserted that the Paralympic Games would 'change the way we view each other' (Adepitan 2012: unpaged). He described 'remarkable people, who have gone to amazing lengths and often overcome great adversity' promising 'inspirational human feats' from 'some of the most extraordinary human beings':

> the equestrian rider whose limbs were contorted at birth, a mass of scar tissue, has gone on to become majesty itself on his horse … the American archery ace who has no arms but uses his feet to fire his bow…
>
> an American wheelchair athlete, dedicated, powerful … she was born in Russia just over 20 years ago with a hole in her spine and was left to die …
>
> British single amputee … who had meningitis as a child and faced death, but came through it to be 19 and challenging for the 100m title in the blue riband event.
>
> (Adepitan 2012: unpaged)

Descriptions of impairments are contrived to add pathos and encourage emotional engagement with the lives of disabled athletes. The discourse of 'triumph over tragedy' is recycled through these stories so that the likelihood of Paralympic representation creating positive change in the way disabled people are viewed seems miniscule.

Confusingly perhaps, Sir Philip Craven, president of the IPC, is reported as calling for the word 'disability' to be dropped: 'This is sport. It's not disability anything. I come from sport' (Gibson 2012: unpaged). While these words seem to contradict and disregard not only the IPC's values but also the emphasis placed by Adepitan on impairment, some sense can be made of the reasoning. Craven adds 'You know what the word "disabled" means. It means something that doesn't work, doesn't function' (Gibson 2012: unpaged). In consideration of sport and disability it seems we are never far away from the medical model insistence that disability is associated with loss, limitation, or deficit.

Downes, a disabled blogger, noted comments of partygoers watching athletes taking part in the televised opening ceremony of the 2012 Paralympics:

> What's that one going to do? They certainly won't be doing the hop, skip and jump without legs!
>
> Look at that!
>
> What a shame!
>
> What a mong!
>
> (Downes 2012: unpaged)

Such offensive and disabling talk gives little confidence that Paralympics play any meaningful role in changing attitudes towards disability for the better.

While many disabled people value the fact that Paralympics enable disabled people to be on TV at all, scepticism about how much real change is promoted has to be retained. The removal of physical and social barriers is the only way to ensure real attitude change; not wall-to-wall media coverage of segregated sports events that regurgitate disabling stereotypes.

For Discussion

- Do you think that public attitudes towards disabled people have changed as a result of media coverage of the 2012 London Paralympics? Do you think they will change as a result of media coverage of the 2016 Paralympics in Brazil?
- Is it any better for disabled people to be represented by the media as 'inspirations' than as, for example, 'scroungers'?
- Do you think it is possible, given current representations of disability, for disabled people to participate in sports without being drawn into triumph over tragedy narratives?

Further Reading

Howe, P.D. (2008) *The Cultural Politics of the Paralympic Movement: Through an Anthropological Lens*. Abingdon: Routledge.

Purdue, D. and Howe, P.D. (2012) 'Empower, inspire, achieve: (dis) empowerment and the Paralympic Games', *Disability & Society*, 27 (7): 903–16.

Schantz, O.J. and Gilbert, K. (eds) (2012) *Heroes or Zeros? The Media's Perceptions of Paralympic Sport*. Champaign, IL: Common Ground Publishing.

References

Adepitan, A. (2012) 'Paralympics 2012: prepare to be amazed by the superhumans', www.telegraph.co.uk/sport/olympics/paralympic-sport/9507205/Paralympics-2012-prepare-to-be-amazed-by-the-superhumans-says-Ade-Adepitan.html, accessed 31 August 2012.

Bagchi, R. (2012) 'Paralympics 2012: Jerome Singleton is on a crusade', *The Guardian*, 21 July.

Downes, R. (2012) 'The Paralympics – reinforcing attitudes towards disability', www.disabilityartsonline.org.uk/?location_id=1588&item=1444, accessed 30 August 2012.

Gibson, O. (2012) 'Drop the word "disabled" from Games coverage, demands Paralympics committee president', www.guardian.co.uk/sport/2012/aug/26/paralympics-philip-craven-disabled-disability, accessed 5 September 2012.

Hardin, M. and Hardin, B. (2008) 'Elite wheelchair athletes relate to sports media', in K. Gilbert and O.J. Schantz (eds), *The Paralympic Games: Empowerment or Side Show*. Maidenhead: Meyer and Meyer, pp. 25–33.

International Paralympics Committee (2012) *The IPC: Who We Are*, www.paralympic.org/TheIPC/HWA/AboutUs, accessed 30 November 2012.

Peers, D. (2009) '(Dis)empowering Paralympic histories: absent athletes and disabling discourses'. *Disability & Society*, 24(5): 653–65.

Purdue, D. and Howe, P.D. (2012) 'Empower, inspire, achieve: (dis) empowerment and the Paralympic Games', *Disability & Society*, 27 (7): 903–16.

46   Stereotypes

Colin Cameron

In everyday human interactions, people make sense of unexpected information presented to the senses by relating it to similar, already internalised, perceptions. Shoham explains:

> Related to our tendency to categorise is our desire to group together people who we define as having identical or similar attributes … We apparently feel happy and secure when we are able to classify people into groupings by some common denominators. Mostly, however, we classify groups of people … in order to attach to them value-laden labels.

(Shoham 2006: 44)

Classifying this way involves stereotyping. Stereotypes are 'vivid but simple representations that reduce persons to a set of exaggerated, usually negative characteristics' (Barker 2004: 263). Stereotyping involves the operation of power, because it is powerful social groups, like the media, who get to shape popular perceptions of the supposed characteristics of members of marginalised or devalued groups: old people are clumsy and forgetful; women should be passive and nurturing, etc. Narratives circulated by the media are transmitted into institutional cultures and practices which may be, for example, sexist, racist or ageist. Stereotypes shape the way marginalised social groups are perceived by others, and simultaneously limit the range of narratives available for members of those groups to make sense of their own experience.

Young (1991: 59) suggests that 'the culturally dominated undergo a paradoxical oppression, in that they are both marked out by stereotypes and at the same time rendered invisible'. Group members' individuality is erased and they are recognised only in terms of the groups they belong to. Stereotypes reduce people to one defining characteristic, often associated with their physicality, and therefore hard to deny. Young continues: 'These stereotypes so permeate the society that they are not easily noticed as contestable.' Because stereotypes reflect the view of the powerful, they carry the weight of authority and are widely accepted as valid representations. It is unsurprising that many people get caught up in the stereotyped roles and expectations set before them.

Disabled writers, e.g. Rieser and Mason (1992); Barnes (1994); Cameron (2011) and Gosling (2011), have identified a number of widely circulated stereotypes of disabled people. These include the pitiable, pathetic victim; the tragic but brave supercrip who triumphs over adversity; the bitter and twisted crip with a chip. It is easy and unsurprising to find these stereotypes in Victorian classics, e.g. poor, tragic Tiny Tim in Dickens' *A Christmas Carol* (1843 [2003]); the plucky, determined cripple, struggling against adversity, Clara in Spyri's *Heidi* (1880 [1995]); and the dreadful, 'eyeless creature' Blind Pew in Stevenson's *Treasure Island* (1883 [1998]). What is revealing is to discover how little distance has been travelled since these were written. In contemporary cultural texts the same stereotypes circulate, barely changed. Disabled people are regarded widely either as charity cases, 'superhuman' inspirations or fraudulent burdens on society. We think of media events such as the BBC's *Children in Need* or the 2012 London Paralympics, or of newspaper coverage identifying disabled people as benefit cheats. Disabled people are rarely portrayed as ordinary people looking to get on with their lives.

Stereotypes are pernicious because the dominant culture's 'inferiorised images of the group must be internalised by group members at least to the extent that they are forced to react to behaviour of others influenced by those images' (Young 1991: 60). For the disabled person who experiences life as complex, interesting and absorbing, to be constantly objectified as a one-dimensional problem can be humiliating and undermining. As McBryde Johnson has expressed it:

> I used to try to explain that I enjoy my life ... But it gets tedious ... They don't want to know. They think they know everything there is to know, just by looking at me. That's how stereotypes work.
>
> (in Garland-Thomson 2009: 191)

Young refers to a phenomena first named by Du Bois as 'double consciousness' – 'this sense of always looking at oneself through the eyes of others, of measuring one's soul by the tape of a world that looks on in amused contempt and pity' (in Young 1991: 61). Double consciousness, Young (1991: 60) says, 'arises when the oppressed subject refuses to coincide with these devalued, objectified, stereotyped visions of herself or himself'.

One common, and understandable, response to double consciousness among disabled people is to distance oneself from association with disability identity and from other disabled people. In my own experience, for example, as an adolescent I recognised myself as somebody who had been involved in a serious road traffic accident, who had experienced brain injuries, talked slowly and had a bit of a limp, but I responded with anger to any suggestion that I was disabled. The artist Eddie Hardy tells of how, as a teenager, he was still in denial about being disabled: 'If I saw anyone who was disabled I didn't want to talk to them, and if I did talk to them it was as if I was able-bodied, doing the old patronising bit' (Shakespeare et al. 1996: 51). Disavowing disability does not mean, however, that one escapes being either stereotyped or disabled.

An alternative response is to embrace a collective identity as disabled. Young (1991: 60) suggests that members of subordinated groups

> express their specific group experiences and interpretations of the world to one another, developing and perpetuating their own culture ... Because they can affirm and recognise one another as sharing similar experiences and perspectives on social life, people in culturally imperialised groups can often maintain a sense of positive subjectivity.

Through the development of a subjectivity of resistance a new understanding of disability emerges. Stereotypes can become less hurtful because they are recognised as absurd and as part of oppression. Through collective action, new narratives are developed and new disability discourses emerge (Swain and Cameron 1999).

In Cameron (2010) I described having been met, during my research, at Chalk Farm Tube Station in London by a blind man, Donald. I was going for a meal with Donald and his partner Mary, and Donald had been waiting for me so he could show me to their flat. He told me that a few minutes earlier, while he had been smoking a cigarette, a stranger, presumably passing in or out of the station, had stopped and told him 'You're at Chalk Farm tube station.' Donald contends that disabled people see the world 'at its most stupid'. How, he wondered, did this man presume he manages the rest of the time, without people there to point out the obvious? Presumably the man had thought he was doing a kindness, but his assumption was based on a stereotyped judgement about Donald and his capabilities. He had seen a blind man and presumed that he needed help. Recounting this story, there were a number of ways Donald could have responded. As it was, he just laughed.

For Discussion

- Beyond the three identified in this chapter (pitiable and pathetic; tragic but brave; bitter and twisted), can you think of any other common stereotypes of disabled people?
- Describe the long-term impact on self-identity of having to deal with stereotyped judgements in everyday encounters.
- What kinds of responses are available to disabled people for dealing with the experience of being stereotyped?

Further Reading

Briant, E., Watson, N. and Philo, G. (2011) *Bad News for Disabled People: How the Newspapers are Reporting Disability*. Glasgow: Stratchclyde Centre for Disability Research and Glasgow Media Unit.

Cameron, C. (2011) 'Whose problem? Disability narratives and available identities', in G. Craig, M. Mayo, K. Popple, M. Shaw and M. Taylor (eds), *The Community Development Reader: History, Themes and Issues*. Bristol: Policy, pp. 259–66.

Gosling, J. (2011) *Abnormal*. London: Bettany Press.

References

Barker, C. (2004) *Cultural Studies: Theory and Practice*. London: Sage.

Barnes, C. (1994) 'Images of disability', in S. French (ed.), *On Equal Terms: Working with Disabled People*. London: Butterworth-Heinemann, pp. 35–46.

Cameron, C. (2010) 'Does anybody like being disabled? A critical exploration of impairment, identity, media and everyday experience in a disabling society'. PhD thesis, Queen Margaret University, http://etheses.qmu.ac.uk/258/1/258.pdf, accessed 1 November 2012.

Cameron, C. (2011) 'Whose problem? Disability narratives and available identities', in G. Craig, M. Mayo, K. Popple, M. Shaw and M. Taylor (eds), *The Community Development Reader: History, Themes and Issues*. Bristol: Policy, pp. 259–66.

Dickens, C. (2003) *A Christmas Carol*. London: Penguin.

Garland-Thomson, R. (2009) *Staring: How We Look*. Oxford: Oxford University Press.

Gosling, J. (2011) *Abnormal*. London: Bettany Press.

Rieser, R. and Mason, M. (1992) *Disability Equality in the Classroom: A Human Rights Issue*. London: Disability Equality in Education.

Shakespeare, T., Gillespie-Sells, K. and Davies, D. (1996) *The Sexual Politics of Disability*. London: Cassell.

Shoham, S.G. (2006) *Sociology and the Absurd: A Sociology of Conflictual Encounters*. Brighton: Sussex Academic Press.

Spyri, J. (1995) *Heidi*. London: Penguin.

Stevenson, R.L. (1998) *Treasure Island*. Oxford: Oxford World Classics.

Swain, J. and Cameron, C. (1999) 'Unless otherwise stated: discourses of labelling and identity in coming out', in M. Corker and S. French (eds), *Disability Discourse*. Buckingham: Open University Press, pp. 68–78.

Young, I.M. (1991) *Justice and the Politics of Difference*. Princeton, NJ: Princeton University Press.

47 Stigma

Colin Cameron

In his 1963 work on the subject (Goffman [1963] 1990), Goffman describes stigma in a number of ways. Stigma is an attribute which reduces a person in others' minds from a whole and usual person to a tainted and discounted one (Goffman [1963] 1990: 12); an undesired difference from what had been anticipated by 'normals' (Goffman [1963] 1990: 15); the situation of the individual who is disqualified from full social acceptance (Goffman [1963] 1990: 9); and a special kind of relationship between attribute and stereotype (Goffman [1963] 1990: 14). If there is uncertainty about whether we are meant to regard stigma as referring to an attribute itself or to the way an attribute is perceived, Goffman explains that in modern contexts the term is 'applied more to the disgrace itself than to the bodily evidence of it' ([1963] 1990: 11). Disgrace is not a quality of an attribute but of the way the attribute is regarded by others. Stigma does not reside in 'discredited' or 'discreditable' bodies, but in the social relations which mark some bodies as superior and others as inferior (Garland-Thomson 2009).

The main focus of Goffman's *Stigma* was the accomplishment of interpersonal interactions between stigmatised people and 'normals', and the responses of the stigmatised to the social awkwardness and discomfort they provoke in normals (Thomas 2007). In Goffman's view the stigmatised were required to 'manage' their encounters with normals and to be always sensitive about and aware of their own undesired difference; ready to apologise for and to feel the need to justify this. This is implied in the book's subtitle, *Notes on the Management of Spoiled Identity*. It was for the stigmatised, the bearers of spoiled identities, to take responsibility for people's reactions to their difference. While Goffman discussed other 'discrediting' attributes, disabled people featured most prominently in his

book, and in this chapter I will be relating the idea of stigma to the experience of impairment and disability.

There are many social situations where, until recently, it has been very uncommon to find
disabled people because of physical and institutional barriers. There are plenty of situations
where this is still relatively uncommon. Higher education is a good (or bad) example (Harvey
2011). People with impairments are often considered among those unlikely to be encountered in higher education settings. Encounters with people with impairments in higher education is regarded by normals as disrupting the ordinary flow of life, as requiring having to
think twice about what is usual (Goffman [1963] 1990). Where stigma breaks the claims for
recognition that an individual might expect on the basis of other personal characteristics
(Goffman [1963] 1990: 15), impairment is regarded as making a person less than they could
be, as a blemish which spoils the other parts of who they could have been. Impairment is
commonly regarded as a person's most significant defining characteristic. While higher education involves students encountering people and experiences from beyond their previous
horizons, disabled students frequently find themselves stigmatised on the basis of stereotypes.

In Goffman's terms, the stigmatised individual usually holds the same beliefs about
identity as normals: 'Shame becomes a central possibility, arising from the individual's
perception of one of his own attributes as being a defiling thing to possess, and one he
can readily see himself as not possessing' (Goffman [1963] 1990: 18).

A common strategy adopted by disabled people for dealing with stigma is to downplay the significance of their impairment or to attempt to distance themselves from their
impairment. Charles, a man with cerebral palsy I talked with in Cameron (2010: 87),
recalling his first days at college, said:

> What I wasn't used to was people asking me about being disabled, because at special school
> it wasn't something that was talked about ... to start off with you just say oh, you know, I just
> get on with it ... it's not really part of my life.

Another strategy, identified by Goffman, is that of 'passing'. Passing as non-disabled, or
as normal, involves non-disclosure of information about impairment and is a tactic most
usually employed by those with hidden impairments. It involves the 'discreditable'
individual managing information about his 'failing': 'To display or not to display; to tell
or not to tell; to let on or not to let on; to lie or not to lie; and in each case, to whom,
how, when and where' (Goffman [1963] 1990: 57).

Passing involves people with hidden impairments denying themselves an identity as
disabled and having anxiety about being found out. If somebody with epilepsy, for
example, has established relationships with non-disabled others on the understanding
that he too is a normal, the possibility of exposure creates tension.

A third strategy involves denial of impairment itself. Rousso (2013: 4) states:

> I grew up denying I had cerebral palsy or any kind of disability. I did not want to be seen as different
> or, more to the point, defective ... I was afraid that if I said I had a disability, I'd be rejected and
> excluded; whereas, if I kept my mouth shut and pretended I was 'normal', no one would notice.

The issue is that, while these types of response perhaps make sense in situations where
a disabled person has internalised a dominant medical or personal tragedy view of
the experience of living with impairment, it is this view itself which is problematic.
While Goffman may have identified stigma as a social relational issue, we are left with
the expectation that impairment will inevitably lead to stigma. Barnes and Mercer
(2011:50) argue that Goffman's 'representation of stigmatised individuals accentuates

the notion of helpless victims consumed by defensive and anxiety-ridden manoeuvrings'. Oliver and Barnes (2012:46) observe that Goffman

> asserts that the central feature of the stigmatised individual's existence is the quest for 'acceptance'. In this way, disabled people are placed permanently in a dependency role, constantly seeking acceptance from the rest of society.

Goffman's concept of stigma rests on an uncritical acceptance of a perspective which identifies impairment as something 'wrong' with people. His work, Oliver and Barnes conclude, is 'entirely reductionist – there can be no stigmatising process without a stigma or discrediting feature ... It confirms the inevitable: disability is a personal tragedy' (Oliver and Barnes 2012: 46).

An alternative to the passive acceptance of stigma is suggested in the idea of 'coming out' as disabled (Swain and Cameron 1999). This involves rejecting the stigmatising assumption that impairment signifies undesirable difference, and instead owning impairment and affirming self. Where each narrative is a claim to see what is going on (Carson 2009), coming out as disabled involves making a shift from a medical model narrative to a social model narrative. It involves, first, recognising that the personal is political. This involves a shift from a view which understands disability as personal limitation to a view which recognises the disabling barriers faced by people with impairments. Second, a shift is made from the dominant narrative which identifies disability as abnormality and dependence to one which takes pride in difference and collective disability identity. While coming out does not eliminate the likelihood of encountering discrimination in interactions with normals, it allows for a different way of responding to and challenging this.

For Discussion

- Goffman characterises those who don't experience stigma as 'normals'. Why does being a normal involve power in encounters with members of stigmatised groups?
- Identify reasons why distancing oneself from impairment, 'passing' or denying impairment might seem a natural response to the experience of stigma?
- How does 'coming out' as disabled allow for different ways of responding to the experience of discrimination?

Further Reading

Barnes, C. and Mercer, G. (2011) *Exploring Disability*. Cambridge: Polity Press.
Goffman, E. ([1963] 1990) *Stigma: Notes on the Management of Spoiled Identity*, revised edn. London: Penguin.
Green, G. (2009) *The End of Stigma? Changes in the Social Experience of Long-term Illness*. London: Routledge.

References

Barnes, C. and Mercer, G. (2011) *Exploring Disability*. Cambridge: Polity Press.
Cameron, C. (2010) 'Does anybody like being disabled? A critical exploration of impairment, identity, media and everyday life in a disabling society'. PhD thesis, Queen Margaret University, http://etheses.qmu.ac.uk/258/1/258.pdf, accessed 27 January 2013.

Carson, A. (2009) 'The narrative practitioner: theory and practice', *The International Journal of Narrative Practice*, 1 (1): 5–8.

Garland-Thomson, R. (2009) *Staring: The Way We Look*. Oxford: Oxford University Press.

Goffman, E. ([1963] 1990) *Stigma: Notes on the Management of Spoiled Identity*, revised edn. London: Penguin.

Harvey, J. (2011) '"Universities and colleges are increasingly aware of the needs of disabled students" (Direct.Gov 2010) Are they? ... My experience of support through university', *The Journal of Inclusive Practice in Further and Higher Education*, 3 (2): 52–9.

Oliver, M. and Barnes, C. (2012) *The New Politics of Disablement*. Basingstoke: Palgrave Macmillan.

Rousso, H. (2013) *Don't Call me Inspirational: A Disabled Feminist Talks Back*. Philadelphia, PA: Temple University Press.

Swain, J. and Cameron, C. (1999) 'Unless otherwise stated: discourses of labelling and identity', in M. Corker and S. French (eds), *Disability Discourse*. Buckingham: Open University Press, pp. 68–78.

Thomas, C. (2007) *Sociologies of Illness and Disability: Contested Ideas in Disability Studies and Medical Sociology*. Basingstoke: Palgrave Macmillan.

48   Traveller Identity

Rosaleen McDonagh

This chapter attempts to raise awareness of the experiences, culture and identity of disabled people who are members of the Traveller community. In exploring the particular issues and concerns for disabled Travellers, the focus will be on racism, ableism and access to culturally appropriate service provision. The definition of Traveller culture includes nomadism, the importance of the extended family, Traveller language (Cant), music and the Traveller economy. For the purpose of this chapter, Traveller identity and disability will be explored partly through my own experience as a disabled Traveller. While sharing my ethnicity with the general Irish population, I am also part of an indigenous separate ethnic minority group.

To begin with, a story in the news at the time of writing gives a glimpse of how Travellers in Ireland are treated. Racism and discrimination towards Travellers is endemic. Prejudice is experienced at many levels of Irish society, including institutional, environmental, attitudinal, legislative and individual responses to Traveller identity, as the story shows:

Early February 2013, in the North-West of Ireland, a house that was bought by the local authority for a family of 13 was burned to the ground. Gutted, believed to be fire-bombed because a Traveller family was due to move in the following week. The story made it into local and regional newspapers. There was no outcry of shame from local or national public representatives. The fact that the family were Travellers meant that the story was very slow in getting into the national media. When it did, there was still no public outcry. They were Travellers, nobody wants a Traveller family or Traveller-specific accommodation in their vicinity.

(*Irish Times* 2013, personal notes on a reported story)

The settled disabled community in Ireland has also oppressed Travellers, displaying ethnocentric positions with regard to identity politics. For example, Irish Sign Language (ISL) had a sign for Travellers which meant 'dirt'.

Although Travellers are named in the Census as a group with our own culture and heritage in Ireland, the concept of ethnic identifiers is relatively new in the Irish context. In the UK the Traveller population is recognised as the most marginalised ethnic minority (Stephenson et al. 2011) and Danaher (2000) has suggested that prejudice against Traveller communities is common worldwide.

An example of racism regarding service provision culminates in ableism and disablism. When first assessed for a powered wheelchair, service providers made pejorative remarks that my family might melt the power chair down to sell as scrap. Such prejudicial attitudes clearly restrict access to, and engagement with, community services and resources for disabled Travellers. Like settled disabled people, Travellers with impairments want to have accessible, safe environments and access to whatever service provision we need. While many members of the Traveller community travel for extended periods for business and economic reasons, and although nomadism is part of our heritage, fewer families nowadays are involved in such practice. Most Travellers live in sites or local authority accommodation.

Typically I have found the preference of service providers is to encourage disabled Travellers and their families to move into standard accommodation. This experience is oppressive, as moving away from your own community should not be a requirement in order to access services. Where disabled Travellers have no choice but to move into standard housing or residential services to meet their access needs this puts them in an extremely vulnerable position with severed connections from close family, friends, supports and social networks, leading to isolation. This phenomena of removing individuals from their community can also fracture rather than affirm their Traveller identity.

In some sites in 2013 in Ireland, toilets and running water, refuse collection and postal delivery services are not guaranteed. Stephenson et al. (2011) talked to disabled people in Gypsy, Roma and Traveller communities in England who reported restricted access to essential services: 'When the water freezes, we can't shower and therefore no toilet either. This affects our health with it being too cold and frequent lack of water' (2011: 6). Difficulty in accessing warm, appropriate and accessible facilities both compounds and creates disability within Traveller communities. As Stephenson et al. also describe, 'There aren't any wheelchair ramps in sites.' Often essential amenities are difficult to access for the whole community. Extra specific services for disabled people are almost non-existent. Adaptations that would be considered standard good practice in houses are often refused for trailers or caravans. Service providers don't see a caravan as someone's home.

Problems getting permission for stopping sites often come with threats, including fear of prosecution, causing stress, distress and mental health difficulties for Travellers. Traveller accommodation is a contentious issue. Local authorities need to provide good-quality sites with amenities, while ensuring access needs for disabled Travellers are included.

There has been a long history of mutual suspicion, hostility and prejudice between Traveller and settled communities. Racism makes access to services difficult for disabled Travellers. The engagement, if any, can be difficult for both parties. Service providers may refuse to enter a site. Experience of prejudice can often mean services are not easily trusted and providers need to be sensitive to attitudinal barriers towards Traveller families in their area. In Ireland Traveller-led Primary Healthcare projects have proved valuable for promoting disability support because someone from the Traveller community can offer culturally informed support and training to service providers. The added value of peer support and advocacy has had a positive effect within the community.

Within the Disability Rights Movement the term 'cared for' can be regarded as infantilising, but within the Irish Traveller community it is a term that indicates the cherishing and valuing of a person. Requirements for 'caring' are assumed as part of ordinary community life. The work of Travellers who have trained as service providers supports involvement with services because people from Traveller communities themselves recognise what needs to be done in terms of dismantling social and economic barriers and are not primarily focused on encouraging disabled people to change their Traveller identity.

In Ireland, education levels are very low with only about half of Traveller adults having completed at least primary school education (Pavee Point 2010). Racism and poor practice by educational service providers has made it very difficult for Travellers to participate and attain academic achievement. While education is highly valued and sought after within the community, Traveller youngsters with impairments, regardless of their academic capacity, will invariably be sent to special schools. This low expectation of the child is internal and external – internal within the family and the community and external from state educators and service providers who don't acknowledge Traveller ethnicity. In addition, Traveller parents find it difficult to engage with service provision and therefore do not make demands on mainstream educational services for their child.

In conclusion, the experience of disabled Travellers is one of marginalisation and often isolation. Having to make a choice to assimilate into the larger dominant settled culture in order to access services would seem racist and outdated. There are very few opportunities for members of the Traveller community to work in service provision so the gap between knowledge and capacity deepens. Cultural diversity is about celebrating who you are, and what you are. Traveller pride or esteem is not often put on a par with concepts of power and privilege in the gamut of identity politics. Responses to disability within these communities require systemic forms of positive affirmation. It is essential to develop projects which enable Travellers to take on roles which enable access to disability support without erasing Traveller identity, values and norms.

For Discussion

- If Travellers arrived in your community how would your neighbours respond? Why does your response matter?
- How can disability issues be considered within your own thoughts on Traveller communities?
- How can the voices of disabled Travellers be raised to enhance access to services of their own choosing?

Further Reading

Pavee Point (2010) *All Ireland Traveller Health Study: Our Geels*. Dublin: Pavee Point Traveller Centre and School of Public Health, Physiotherapy and Population Science, University College Dublin.

Pierce, M. (2003) *Minority Ethnic People with Disabilities in Ireland: Situation, Identity and Experience*. Dublin: The Equality Authority.

Stephenson, J., Hodgkins, S.L. and Close, M. (2011) *Lancashire's Hidden Stories: Experience of Disability among Gypsy, Roma and Travellers, Lesbian, Gay, Bisexual, Transgender and Black and Minority Ethnic Communities*. Norfolk, UK: Disability Listen, Include, Build for Disability Equality: Catton Print Limited.

References

Danaher, P. (2000) 'Guest editor's introduction', *International Journal for Education Research*, 33 (3): 221–30.

Irish Times (2013) www.irishtimes.com/newspaper/ireland/2013/0212/1224329951009.htm, accessed 8 March 2013.

Pavee Point (2010) *All Ireland Traveller Health Study Team*. Dublin: Pavee Point Traveller Centre and School of Public Health, Physiotherapy and Population Science, University College Dublin.

Stephenson, J., Hodgkins, S.L. and Close, M. (2011) *Lancashire's Hidden Stories: Experience of Disability among Gypsy, Roma and Travellers, Lesbian, Gay, Bisexual, Transgender and Black and Minority Ethnic Communities*. Norfolk, UK: Disability Listen, Include, Build for Disability Equality: Catton Print Limited.

49 Vulnerability

Colin Cameron

Among those it defines as 'adults at risk', the Adult Support and Protection (Scotland) Act 2007 includes those who 'because they are affected by disability, mental disorder, illness or physical or mental infirmity, are more vulnerable to being harmed than adults who are not so affected' (legislation.gov.uk 2007).

Within this definition vulnerability is identified as the direct outcome of impairment. Dominant assumptions about disability are reproduced and passed into Scottish legislation. Legislation intended to protect adults considered at risk locates the cause of that risk within the physicality of individuals rather than within the social contexts in which they live. The English Department of Health's 'No Secrets' report of 2000 similarly defines a 'vulnerable adult' as a person 'aged 18 years or over who is or may be in need of community care services by reason of mental or other disability and is or may be unable to protect him or herself against significant harm or exploitation' (cited in DH 2010: 14). The medical model is evident here, and vulnerability is regarded as an intrinsic characteristic of disabled people.

Hasler (2004: 229) has described vulnerability as 'a concept that owes nothing to disabled people and everything to professional concerns'. She explains that the word started to appear in social care jargon in the late 1990s as the then new Labour government sought to balance commitments to low spending with commitments to social justice:

> [T]hey focused on services to 'vulnerable' people; this both put disabled people into the category of the deserving poor (as opposed to undeserving dole scroungers, for example) and also put them firmly in the 'not like us' category.
>
> (Hasler 2004: 229)

Oliver and Barnes (1998: 14) have drawn attention to the importance of language in defining and classifying social groups, stating that 'We use words to ascribe meaning to situations and objects and orient our behaviour accordingly.' Legislation and social policy which defines disabled people as vulnerable has an impact on public perceptions. At a political demonstration in 2011, as part of the Hardest Hit campaign against cuts to disability benefits imposed by the UK Coalition government, I was surprised at how often the description of disabled people as 'the most vulnerable' was used. It is a term which implies victimhood rather than agency. This seems an instance where, once a word has been used often enough to describe disabled people, it becomes accepted as uncontroversial and passes into common use.

There is a very real sense, of course, in which as human beings we are all vulnerable. This is a point I will return to later in this chapter. My argument for the moment concerns the specific way in which impairment is identified as the cause of vulnerability. Thinking this way enables policy-makers and professionals to avoid recognising vulnerability as an outcome of disabling barriers and restricted opportunities and to evade responsibility for taking measures to effect real change. Almost three decades ago, the British Council of Organisations of Disabled People drew attention to the link between segregated 'special' education and the fact that many disabled school leavers find themselves unprepared for adult life:

> The special education system, then, is one of the main channels for disseminating the dominant able-bodied/minded perception of the world and ensuring that disabled school leavers are socially immature and isolated. This isolation results in passive acceptance of social discrimination, lack of skills in facing the tasks of adulthood and ignorance about the main social issues of our time. All this reinforces the 'eternal children' myth and ensures at the same time disabled school leavers lack the skills for overcoming the myth.
>
> (BCODP 1986 cited in Oliver and Barnes 2012: 139)

Rather than being an inevitable outcome of impairment, the specific vulnerability of disabled people is the result of having been socially marginalised; through, for example, the separation and segregation of disabled children and young people from their non-disabled peers. Adolescence is a time when personal, emotional and sexual identities are formed and talked about and boundaries tested in the context of peer relationships (Kroger 2000). Segregation means that disabled young people find themselves excluded from this process. Talking about her own experience as a teenager in special education, Roshni, a blind woman from Glasgow, said:

> Girls were becoming aware of boys and vice versa, and there ain't any of that going on ... and there's also this subtext within a lot of special schools that if you have a disability, you're not going to be interested in boyfriends, or alcohol, or any of that ... basically, it's way out of your league, you know.

(Cameron 2010: 134)

It is the exclusion from ordinary life as a result of segregation that leaves disabled people inexperienced and vulnerable. Social processes which involve their being made 'other', including segregated education, over-protective and risk-averse professional 'care', inaccessible environments and stereotyping media representations, create the opportunities and contexts within which abuse can happen.

Tollifson (1997: 106) suggests that imperfection and vulnerability should be recognised as an important part of what being human is about. 'If we need anything in this world, it's honest seeing and speaking, and the ability to be with the actual truth (including flawed bodies and responses).' She asks that we learn to value *what actually is* instead of being caught up in and entranced by *what we think would be better*' (1997: 106). This would require an openness to impairment: 'Imperfection is the essence of being organic and alive. Organic life is vulnerable; it inevitably ends up in disintegration. This is part of its beauty' (Tollifson 1997: 106).

Finkelstein (1998: 28) has drawn attention to the defining human characteristics of frailty and the ability to turn vulnerability into strength. He suggests, however, that a limit of this strength lies in the quickness with which our vulnerability is forgotten and that this forgetting is accomplished 'by imagining that vulnerability belongs only to certain types of people'. Where the 'normal' individual is required to experience themselves as self-sufficient, this involves a projection of attributes considered signs of weakness and inadequacy onto others. It is required that disabled people are considered vulnerable in order that non-disabled people are able to keep their own vulnerability out of mind. The cultural constitution of disability as deficit involves a relationship in which 'the 'non-disabled' points to 'the disabled' as if to say: 'You are in lack, not I' (Goodley 2011: 13).

Shildrick (2002: 73) has asked whether society's desire to keep disabled people at a distance 'through limiting access, through isolation and silencing' may be regarded as representing an attempt to deal with its own apprehension and denial of vulnerability. This would suggest that segregation of disabled people from the mainstream has involved a deliberate punitive exclusion in order to spare those with normative bodies the unwelcome reminder of their own finitude. When disabled people's impaired bodies, senses and minds present too uncomfortable a reminder of the ontological insecurity that exists within the human soul, it has been determined that they be shut out. As Markell has noted:

> We might say that social structures pay an ontological wage: they organise the human world in ways that make it possible for certain people to enjoy an imperfect simulation of the

invulnerability they desire, leaving others to bear a disproportionate share of the costs and burdens involved in social life.

(Markell 2003: 22)

Rather than being the outcome of impairment, vulnerability experienced by many disabled people is the outcome of poverty and social exclusion, itself the outcome of social policies and service provision rooted within medical model thinking. If vulnerability is to be addressed meaningfully, it is roots and causes its which need to be addressed in order to promote transformation of experience. Tinkering with existing care arrangements reproduces vulnerability when what is required is resistance.

For Discussion

- What are the causes and the consequences of vulnerability? Who is vulnerable that you know and what are the implications of this?
- What discussion, research and action is needed to raise awareness of the potential offence caused by assumptions that disabled people are vulnerable?
- What action can you take to widen the debate about *'the trouble with ideas on vulnerability and disability'* ?

Further Reading

Hasler, F. (2004) 'Disability, care and controlling services', in J. Swain, S. French, C. Barnes and C. Thomas (eds), *Disabling Barriers – Enabling Environments*. London: Sage, pp. 226–32.
Oliver, M. and Barnes, C. (2012) *The New Politics of Disablement*. Basingstoke: Palgrave Macmillan.
Oliver, M., Sapey, B. and Thomas, C. (2012) *Social Work with Disabled People*, 4th edn. Basingstoke: Palgrave Macmillan.

References

Cameron, C. (2010) 'Does anybody like being disabled? A critical exploration of impairment, identity, media and everyday experience in a disabling society'. PhD thesis, http://etheses.qmu. ac.uk/258/1/258.pdf, accessed 17 November 2012.
Department of Health (DH) (2010) *Clinical Governance and Adult Safeguarding: An Integrated Process*, www.dh.gov.uk/prod_consum_dh/groups/dh_digitalassets/@dh/@en/@ps/documents/digitalasset/dh_112341.pdf, accessed 14 November 2012.
Finkelstein, V. (1998) 'Emancipating disability studies', in T. Shakespeare (ed.), *The Disability Studies Reader*. London: Cassell, pp. 28–49.
Goodley, D. (2011) *Disability Studies: An Interdisciplinary Introduction*. London: Sage.
Hasler, F. (2004) 'Disability, care and controlling services', in J. Swain, S. French, C. Barnes and C. Thomas (eds), *Disabling Barriers – Enabling Environments*. London: Sage, pp. 226–32.
Kroger, J. (2000) *Identity Development: Adolescence Through Childhood*. London: Sage.

legislation.gov.uk (2007) The Adult Support and Protection (Scotland) Act 2007, www.legislation. gov.uk/asp/2007/10/part/1, accessed 16 November 2012.

Markell, P. (2003) *Bound by Recognition*. Princeton, NJ: Princeton University Press.

Oliver, M. and Barnes, C. (1998) *Disabled People and Social Policy: From Exclusion to Inclusion*. Harlow: Longman.

Oliver, M. and Barnes, C. (2012) *The New Politics of Disablement*. Basingstoke: Palgrave Macmillan.

Shildrick, M. (2002) *Embodying the Monster: Encounters with the Vulnerable Self*. London: Sage.

Tollifson, J. (1997) 'Imperfection is a beautiful thing: on disability and meditation', in K. Fries (ed.), *Staring Back: The Disability Experience from the Inside Out*. New York: Plume, pp. 105–12.

50   Welfare Reform

Bill Scott

There is a real sense in which, as Harlan Hahn (in Oliver and Barnes 1998: 36) has argued, 'Fundamentally disability is defined by public policy. In other words, disability is whatever policy says it is.' We can see this in the way that large numbers of people 'became' disabled during the 1980s when the Conservative government decided to move them from unemployment to Invalidity Benefit (later Incapacity Benefit and Employment Support Allowance) to mask their failure to reduce unemployment figures (Roulstone and Prideaux 2012: 16). Approximately half of the cuts (£4.87 billion) currently being made to disabled people's living standards are being achieved through moving disabled people off Incapacity Benefit/Employment Support Allowance onto Job Seekers Allowance. They are being redefined as non-disabled even though there has been no change to their impairment or condition.

Policy fluctuates and statements made in a chapter on welfare reform could quickly become dated. Since writing the first draft of this chapter in late 2012, disabled people have won the right to an urgent judicial review of the Bedroom Tax rules (referred to below) which require cutting housing benefit for those judged to be 'over-occupying' social housing (UKDPC 2013). The UK government's own equality impact assessment has indicated that the regulations would have a disproportionate impact upon disabled people, and it is argued that the regulations breach the Equality Act, the Human Rights Act and the UN Convention on the Rights of Persons with Disabilities (UKDPC 2013). The review will take place in May 2013, so even by the time this book is published things may well have moved on. Nevertheless, because welfare reform is such an important issue and has such a big impact on the quality of disabled people's lives, a chapter like this has its place.

The policy of welfare 'reform' may represent the single greatest threat in over a generation to disabled people's right and ability to live independently. The scale of the cuts is staggering – households containing a disabled person are estimated to lose £9.2 billion (Wood and Grant 2010) in benefits between 2011 and 2015. That represents over half of the total of £18 billion of benefit cuts already announced. It also means that over half of the cuts are falling on roughly 3 per cent of the population (the cuts are falling predominantly on disabled people of working age and families with disabled children).

Benefits paid solely to disabled people have also been singled out for cuts. Over £1.2 billion is being saved through time limiting contributory Employment Support Allowance (ESA); the budget for Disability Living Allowance is being slashed by 20 per cent; and the Independent Living Fund is being closed.

Moreover the introduction of the new Universal Credit is being used as an opportunity to cut the Disabled Child's Premium in half (from £57 to £28 a week); to abolish the Severe Disability Premium (worth £58 a week); and to cut the support available to disabled people in work. Up to 450,000 disabled people and their families could eventually lose out due to the introduction of Universal Credit (Children's Society 2012).

Because disabled people are much less likely than non-disabled people to be in employment, cuts to other benefits also affect them disproportionately. The freeze on Child Benefit and reductions to Housing Benefit are felt most strongly in households containing a disabled person.

The Under-Occupancy Rule, otherwise known as the 'Bedroom Tax', has a disproportionate impact on disabled people and their families. Households who are deemed to have one or more bedrooms than they 'need' have their Housing Benefit slashed by 14 per cent (one 'extra' room) or 25 per cent (two or more 'extra' rooms).

The Department of Work and Pensions' Equality Impact Assessment (DWP 2012a) identified that two-thirds of the households affected by this (420,000 out of 660,000) would contain a disabled person. The Scottish Government estimates that 11 per cent of the households affected by this measure will be evicted as they fall into rent arrears. Across the UK, over 45,000 households containing a disabled person face eviction.

The previous government introduced the Work Capability Assessment, currently administered by the private firm ATOS on behalf of the DWP. The new test is designed to reduce the number of sick and disabled people entitled to Incapacity Benefit/Employment and Support Allowance. It has far exceeded government expectations, with 36 per cent of previous Incapacity Benefit (DWP 2012b) recipients initially (before appeals) being found fully fit for work.

Many contend that the assessment system is both unjust and flawed: 40 per cent of the tens of thousands of disabled people who have appealed have successfully overturned their initial assessment. With representation by a CAB advisor or Welfare Rights worker this rises to nearly 70 per cent.

Sheffield Hallam University (Beatty and Fothergill 2011) has estimated that a combination of the Work Capability Assessments and time-limiting contributory ESA to 12 months will cut incapacity claimant numbers by nearly one million by 2014, of which more than 800,000 will be existing incapacity claimants who will lose their entitlement.

Nearly 600,000 of those claimants will lose all benefit entitlement, either because of the time-limiting of their non-means-tested benefits, or because they fail to qualify for other means-tested benefits. They face a minimum loss of £91.40 a week (£4,750 a year).

Disability Living Allowance is being replaced by a new benefit – the Personal Independence Payment (PIP). All existing DLA claimants of working age will gradually be transferred to the new benefit. All those transferred and all new claimants to PIP will be subjected to a new assessment regime which has been designed with a view to restricting entitlement to fewer, more severely impaired, disabled people. For example, there will be no Lower Rate Care element of the new benefit. DWP projections estimate that over 500,000 people currently entitled to DLA will lose entitlement when transferred to PIP.

However, this masks the overall true number of losers, as many will only lose part of their entitlement or have their entitlement to care or mobility reduced. Thus 280,000 claimants will lose entitlement to Enhanced/Higher Rate Mobility, and 370,000 claimants will lose Standard/Lower Rate Mobility.

These people will also lose entitlement to benefits such as the Blue Badge and concessionary fares. As one in three disabled people currently entitled to DLA Higher Rate Mobility lease a Motability vehicle, this means that up to 90,000 disabled people will lose their cars and scooters. Based on survey evidence, Disability Rights UK estimates that between 25,000 and 50,000 disabled people who lose their DLA will also be forced to give up their employment (Disability Rights UK 2012).

Space restricts us from examining all of the proposed reforms and their total cumulative impact. The DWP have been extraordinarily resistant to the idea of carrying out a cumulative impact assessment of the various reforms' impact on disabled people – perhaps because the scale of disabled people's impoverishment will become apparent.

We do know that the cuts will lead to the poorest fifth of the 2.7 million households currently receiving disability benefits losing on average 18 per cent of their cash income plus other benefits-in-kind (care services, passport benefits, etc.) over the period 2011–2015 (Edwards 2012).

Follow-up research to the original Demos report *Destination Unknown* (Wood 2012) also shows that disabled people and their families are already:

- Becoming more socially isolated and reducing their social and civil activities – from essentials such as work and medical appointments to 'luxuries' such as volunteering.
- Suffering from increased anxiety, depression and fear for the future, with some relying on increased medication.
- Increasingly reliant on informal carers taking the strain as they lose the financial support and services they once relied on.

Yet only 20 per cent of the planned £9.2 billion worth of cuts had taken place when the updated report was compiled. Much worse is to follow with many thousands of disabled people facing reduced incomes, impoverishment and homelessness.

For Discussion

- How might welfare reform impact on disabled people's ability, and right, to live independently?
- Why do you think the government seems to have targeted benefits paid to disabled people for cuts in expenditure?
- What are the short- and medium-term implications for disabled people of the current political rhetoric about 'scroungers' and 'benefit cheats'?

Further Reading

Disability Rights UK (2012) *Holes in the Safety Net: The Impact of Universal Credit on Disabled People*, www.disabilityrightsuk.org/holesinthesafetynet.pdf, accessed 4 February 2013.

Roulstone, A. and Prideaux, S. (2012) *Understanding Disability Policy*. Policy Press.

Wood, C. and Grant, E. (2010) *Destination Unknown*, www.demos.co.uk/files/Destination_ unknown_-_web.pdf, accessed 4 February 2013.

References

Beatty, C. and Fothergill, S. (2011) *Incapacity Benefit Reform: The Local, Regional and National Impact*. Sheffield: Sheffield Hallam University, Centre for Regional Economic and Social Research.

Children's Society (2012) *Holes in the Safety Net: The Impact of Universal Credit on Disabled People*. London: The Children's Society, Disability Rights UK and Citizens Advice.

Department of Work and Pensions (DWP) (2012a) *Housing Benefit: Size Criteria for People Renting in the Social Rented Sector: Equality Impact Assessment*. London: DWP.

Department of Work and Pensions (DWP) (2012b) 'Incapacity benefits reassessments: outcomes of work capability assessments', *Great Britain DWP: Quarterly Official Statistics Bulletin*, 6, November. London: DWP.

Disability Rights UK (2012) *Impact Assessing the Abolition of Working Age DLA*. London: Disability Rights UK.

Edwards, C. (2012) *The Austerity War and the Impoverishment of Disabled People*. Norwich: University of East Anglia.

Oliver, M. and Barnes, C. (1998) *Disabled People and Social Policy: From Exclusion to Inclusion*. Harlow: Longman.

Roulstone, A. and Prideaux, S. (2012) *Understanding Disability Policy*. Policy Press.

United Kingdom Disabled People's Council (UK DPC) (2013) *Disabled Victims of Bedroom Tax Granted Urgent Judicial Review*, www.ukdpc.net/site/news-archive/199-disabled-victims-of-bedroom-tax-granted-urgent-judicial-review-posted-4-april-2013, accessed 2 May 2013.

Wood, C. (2012) *Destination Unknown: Summer 2012*. London: Demos and Scope.

Wood, C. and Grant, E. (2010) *Destination Unknown*. London: Demos.

Index